The Lines of Life

So should the lines of life that life repaire
Which this (Times pensel or my pupill pen)
Neither in inward worth nor outward faire
Can make you live your selfe in eies of men.

—Shakespeare

Life doth her great actions spell,
By what was done and wrought
In season, and so brought
To light: her measures are, how well
Each syllab'e answer'd, and was form'd, how faire;
These make the lines of life, and that's her ayre.

—Jonson

The Lines of Life

Theories of Biography, 1880–1970

David Novarr

Purdue University Press
West Lafayette, Indiana

Book designed by Marlene Kennedy

Published 1986

Library of Congress Cataloging-in-Publication Data

Novarr, David.
    The lines of life.

    Includes index.
    1. Biography (as a literary form) I. Title.
CT21.N68   1986   808'.06692   85-24562
ISBN 0-911198-79-2
Printed in the United States of America

For
My Mother and Father

Contents

Preface

      The origins of this book go back forty years to my own search for criteria by which to measure Izaak Walton's achievement as a biographer. I had set out to write a critical study in biographic technique, based largely on a structural analysis of each of the *Lives*, on Walton's use of his sources, and on his revisions. I meant by structural analysis something different from what a reader in the 1980s might expect: I was interested in the architectonics of a life, in the relation of the parts to the whole, in Walton's use of proportion and emphasis, not in the degree to which he approved of or conformed to a cultural or mythological or ideal pattern (though it was clear to me that the *Life of Donne* increasingly veered toward hagiography in its revisions, and that Walton had other patterns in mind when he wrote the other lives). As I proceeded I found that I had to discuss, too, Walton's purposes; his assumptions, predilections, and principles; his own emotional and intellectual range. I was aware that Walton had been less than candid in projecting an image of himself as a simple, moderate, and artless man. Before I wrote my last chapter, one of summary and assessment, I knew that I would call it, despite Walton's own disclaimers, "The Artist as Biographer," and I knew, too, what issues I wanted to discuss, but I needed some assurance that I had not ignored others which were conventionally considered to be important. I read and re-read what was at hand—Carlyle, Strachey, Maurois, Virginia Woolf—but it was a struggle even to put together a bibliography of the theory and criticism of biography. I looked in vain for a systematic study that would give me easy access to the field, and I wrote my chapter without any certainty that I had covered all the main topics. I promised myself that I would, some day, write something that would help fill that gap for others interested in writing, reading, reviewing, and theorizing about biography.

In the 1940s and 1950s, practitioners of literary theory and literary criticism concentrated on what René Wellek and Austin Warren called "the chief literary kinds—drama, the novel, poetry."[1] In their *Theory of Literature*, Wellek and Warren did not mention biography in a chapter on "Literary Genres," though they said elsewhere that "biography is an ancient literary genre" with its own intrinsic interest, an interest in human personality. They considered biography as part of historiography: "the problems of a biographer are simply those of a historian," problems of interpretation of evidence, of chronological presentation, of selection, of discretion or frankness, and these, they said, are "in no way specifically literary" (pp. 67–68). Since their primary concern was with literary scholarship, they examined biography only in a section devoted to the extrinsic approach to the study of literature, and even here they thought it dangerous to ascribe to biography "any real critical importance" (p. 74).

Northrop Frye's *Anatomy of Criticism* (1957) broadened the vistas of literature, but he conceived of biography as a verbal structure in which the literary or hypothetical intention was not the primary one; it belonged with "assertive, descriptive, or factual writing,"[2] not with "imaginative" writing. He, too, placed the biographer with the historian: "the historian selects his facts, but to suggest that he had manipulated them to produce a more symmetrical structure would be grounds for libel" (p. 75). Autobiography fell within Frye's scheme of genres; he assimilated it into fiction through his category of the "confession" (pp. 307–8). He made no room, however, for biography. To be sure, Frye granted that whether a thing is a work of art or not is determined by "convention, social acceptance, and the work of criticism in the broadest sense" (p. 345), and he granted that "all structures in words are partly rhetorical, and hence literary" (p. 350). Still, in his discussion of the Bible as literature, he accounted for the presence of historical fact in the Bible on the basis of its being "mythically significant" and he minimized the importance of the "descriptive" aspect of the gospels by suggesting that "the basis of their form is something other than biography" (p. 325). The *Anatomy of Criticism* provided literary accommodation for *Gulliver's Travels, The Anatomy of Melancholy, Sartor Resartus, Religio*

Medici, and *Grace Abounding*; it did not mention the *Life of Johnson*.

In the '40s and '50s, biography received very slight consideration in critical discourse. Robert Stallman pointed out in his preface to *Critiques and Essays in Criticism 1920–1948* that fiction was neglected by modern critics, but he made no comment about the complete lack of concern for biography in his collection.[3] The editors of another widely used anthology of literary criticism, *Criticism: The Foundations of Modern Literary Judgment*, said that they had made the range of their collection as great as possible.[4] They included some biographical criticism (Samuel Johnson and Edmund Wilson are here), but the discussion of biography itself was limited to a paragraph in Virginia Woolf's "Mr. Bennett and Mrs. Brown." Nor did biography fare much better in a general survey such as David Daiches's *The Present Age in British Literature*. The chapter on poetry extended over some sixty pages; history and biography (the conjunction is, of course, significant) got three. In the single paragraph devoted exclusively to biography, Daiches wrote, "That biography *is* an art, and not merely a matter of grubbing up the facts or even of constructing a series of plausible psychological explanations, is a belief held in Britain today by a wide number of practitioners."[5] The view of these practitioners did not seem to be shared by a wide number of literary critics.

As I read more widely, I learned that I was hardly alone in my feeling that biographical theory and the study of biography were neglected. From the turn of the century, others had pointed out this neglect and had, with more or less urgency, wished for an Aristotle. In *The Nation* for 1901, the author of an article on "Aspects of Biography," disturbed by biographers who hoped that paste and boards would "do the part of constructive vision" and sophisticated enough to see that the "indiscretion of unfriendliness" was as bad as the "indiscretion of friendliness," wrote that "most literary forms have their laws, by obeying which the most inexpert may be spared the worst indiscretions. Biography, on the other hand, remains an unscheduled realm of the writer's art."[6] "Biography," wrote Carl Van Doren in 1915, "remains a field almost wholly unmapped by criticism," but he was distrustful of reductive criticism which would stringently define subject, scope, arrangement, and style. His attitude was perhaps ambivalent when he wrote, "It is a pity that biography should go unstudied while other forms of literature have specialists in dozens"; it was heavily ironic when he suggested that the pioneer in this field would "become the founder of a new science": "First, he will find in the latest biographical fashion the perfected norm of the art, and second, he will show what symptoms in the earlier practice point forward to it." Pleased though he was that fortune had left biography "still free to be a candid and flexible record of life," Van Doren said that "the laws of method and effect" of biography were not well understood, and he tempted the critics by suggesting that "nowhere else, unless perhaps in the lyric, can one study more simply the great problem of all literary technique, the process by which life passes, through impression, conception, language, symbol into the literature which reproduces it." He felt that the great strength of biography lay in a misconception: it was generally thought to be a means of literary study rather than an end in itself; but at the same time he cautiously encouraged perceptive criticism of "an art not held an art, . . . the only form of literature which life still wears with the natural ease with which, some insist, life wore all forms of art in the beginning."[7] In 1916, Waldo H. Dunn suggested in his pioneering *English Biography* that, despite some fine criticism of biography in nineteenth-century reviews, prefaces, and introductions, biography had proceeded without formal study.[8] In 1927, Charles K. Trueblood welcomed the publication of Alan Valentine's slight *Biography* because it represented "what may be the beginning of formal and specific criticism of the various kinds of effort in the field";[9] and in the same year James C. Johnston prefaced his *Biography: The Literature of Personality* with comments about the "general lack of standards": "The vagueness in the minds of even some of the best qualified critics as to such fundamental matters as definition and classification necessitates the acceptance of the standards furnished by other better organized departments, such as history, drama, or fiction."[10]

In 1957, Leon Edel referred in the preface to his *Literary Biography* to the paucity of published work about the theory of biography "save for certain historical works and occasional essays, largely in learned journals." Biography, he said, "tends to be a subject discussed only by specialists: it is taken for granted, in contrast to the way in which theories of fiction and of poetry are the subject of constant examination and re-examination."[11] In 1962, James L. Clifford introduced the selections in his anthology *Biography as an Art* with the statement, "Unlike poetry, fiction, and the drama, biography has never been the subject of intense critical study,"[12] but Clifford's statement was both historical and comparative. Clifford knew English and American criticism of biography from its beginnings, and he was aware both that a mass of modern commentary was available and that this mass was yet slight compared to what was available for other genres. Some of the best of this criticism from 1560 on Clifford excerpted and reprinted in his useful collection. Shortly after the journal *biography* began publication in 1978, its editors, obviously sensitive to the biographical atmosphere, announced that they would from time to time review books "of pervasive importance to the craft" that had been written earlier; they published a short assessment of Edel's *Literary Biography* and of Clifford's *From Puzzles to Portraits*,[13] but they seem to have abandoned their plan. The first bibliographer of *biography* listed some sixty books and articles about biography, autobiography, and related aspects of life-writing in British and American publications, mainly in 1977; his preface restated the old call: "There is need for the development of a really penetrating, lucid theory of the biographical genre."[14]

When, in January 1981, Leon Edel gave the keynote address at an international symposium sponsored by the Biographical Research Center at the University of Hawaii, he reiterated the sentiment that biography had suffered, "through three centuries, from a lack of definition, a laxity of method," and he said, somewhat too rashly, that "there exists . . . no criticism of biography worthy of the name." He declared, "We have reached a moment in literary history when time and circumstances summon biography to declare itself and its principles," and he set forth what he himself called "fragmentary notes" for his own proposed *Principia Biographica*, though he also said that "every life takes its own form and a biographer must find the ideal and unique literary form that will express it." Edel entitled his address "Biography and the Science of Man"; he announced that "the new 'science of man' offers biography a new role in literature and in history," and that biography "has for too long grasped the 'empirical' and smothered itself too much in externals." He had in mind "the science of anthropology, the observations of the social sciences, above all the explorations of the individual psyche opened up by Freud," explorations of behavior and motivation that permit the drawing of "larger conclusions about an inner life, of which the 'outer' life is constant expression."[15] Edel's pronouncements are a ringing preamble to a volume called *New Directions in Biography*. But the same bells had chimed before; Edel rang a few changes on tunes introduced by Virginia Woolf many years ago.

Despite the neglect of biography by the critics who at midcentury professed interest in all literature; despite, too, the frequent complaint that biographical theory and the critical study of biography have been neglected, biography has been subjected to a great deal of attention in the last century. Proper consideration of biography has been impeded, however, in two ways. First, most of the work has been informal, discursive, and journalistic, causerie rather than treatise, and much of it has been infinitely less sophisticated than critical discussion about other genres. Second, much of the work exists in isolation and seclusion; if the critics know each other, they merely play ring-around-the-rosies; they rarely wrestle or stand on each other's shoulders. Prospective biographers, reviewers of biography, and students interested in biography are not much better off than I was forty years ago when I wanted a guide to important concepts and developments.

My purpose here is to fill, at least in part, a gap in the history of ideas through a descriptive and analytic review, mainly chronological, of the *general* theory and criticism of biography in England and in the United States from about 1880 to about 1970. I summarize and analyze fifty or sixty books and articles— some of them representative and others eccentric, some influential and others almost unknown—most of them entitled, with some slight variation, "Biography," because I think a writer whose subject is unrestricted and unspecialized tends to reveal what he considers the main concerns and questions to be. These frequently arise, of course, from the relations between biography and another discipline which had a dominating effect on biography at a particular time: ethics, history, psychology and psychoanalysis, autobiography, literary criticism, or fiction. I hope to show what these concerns are, the degree to which some of them have been dominant, and when they have been dominant, and thus to re-create the movement of the ideas—their flow and ebb, their shifts, their recurrence—that precede the most recent discussions of theory. At the least there will emerge what the critics have thought it important and profitable to talk about; at most, perhaps, some profitable doctrine and some indication of directions that might profitably be followed.

I am aware, as my readers will be, that I have told only part of a story. The conclusions I reached many years ago about Walton are now, inevitably, part of the history of the ideas I deal with, but they are only implicit here. Many books and articles that I have studied or scanned do not get so much as a footnote—biographies themselves; specialized studies of specific technical problems; general studies in historiography and personality; scholarly accounts of the biographical writing in a particular period, of individual biographers, and of the various biographies about a particular subject, which slowly prepare the way for solidly based theory; Dutch, Spanish, and Polish critiques, which have had little effect on what has happened in the English-speaking world. I am aware, too, that literary theorists tend to depend on practices they think to be exemplary or on their own ideal paradigms, and that the urge for a universal law is nowhere more precarious than it is for biography, which celebrates what is different, unusual, unrepresentative, idiosyncratic. I am even in some degree sympathetic to the formulation that theory and criticism are about as important to writers of biography as the study of ornithology is to birds. I have aimed, however, to map out a main road, whatever fascinating paths may lie beside and beyond it, so that my readers can get quickly to some of the most interesting work of almost a century.

I have stopped short of a full century because, during the last decade or more, the theory of literature, dismissive of biography for so long, has extended its reach so far that it now includes biography and many other areas, and because recent theorists of biography itself, more attuned to modern literary technology than to the history of biographic theory, have shifted synchronically to new roads under construction. To be sure, Wellek and Warren and Frye saw that all language was rhetorical, but they assumed that writing could be usefully divided into what was primarily aesthetic and what was primarily referential. For generations, literature has been equated with invention, feigning, and shaping, with writing that is primarily imaginative, expressive, and connotative; its domain excluded work that is "literally true" or devoid of "fictionality." More recently, semioticians have questioned the nature of the relation of language to reality and experience; some of them would tell us that we do not live in a real world but in an artificial network plantation of metonymy, synecdoche, irony, and metaphor, in a universe of *verba* that only vaguely shadow *res*. Under such circumstances, the boundaries between fiction, history, and biography are largely effaced.

Post-structuralists, too, have endeavored to deconstruct what were customarily considered distinctions between discursive modes, and they are not alone. The modality of biography, long subject to debate, is implicated in the widely quoted statement of a novelist who works with history: E. L. Doctorow maintains that "a visitor from another planet could not by study of the techniques of discourse distinguish composed fiction from composed history," and he proposes that "there is no fiction or nonfiction as we commonly understand the distinction: there is only narrative."[16] For many years, consideration of the mode of biography focused on the writing, not the reading of biography— on the biographer's angle of vision, his subjectivity or detachment; his selection of material and his shaping of it; his use of background and historical context; his use of analysis to explain motive and cause; his means of getting at the internal life; his attempts at reconstruction; his style. To be sure, more than half a century ago Virginia Woolf raised the question of reader-response when she said that the introduction of fictitious materials into biography cast suspicion on the truth that was based on fact, but today the question of how we read biography is enmeshed in the more general question of how we read. Do we respond differently or similarly to a "literary" text and to a "documentary" text? Are our expectations the same for history and epic, for the novel and for biography? However we read, we do not read as Martians. Whatever cultural or social or political reasons lie behind the belief that the date of a person's birth is of special importance, the significance of that date is apparent in its customary documentation, and a biographer's citation of the date is usually verifiable. When Strachey tells us that Henry Edward Manning "was born in 1807" and others specifically state that he was born on July 15, 1808, most of us tend to worry about Strachey's reliability.[17] Why we respond one way to a date on a birth certificate or on a church register and why, despite *Tristram Shandy* and ardent right-to-lifers, we respond another way to the date and circumstances of a baby's conception are important for biography, and not for biography alone. That the newer theoretical approaches of the '70s and '80s are affecting the theory and criticism of biography is evident in the interesting work of William H. Epstein and Ira B. Nadel, but I leave the telling of the newly enfolding story to them and to others.

This essay is dedicated to my parents, whose own lives have endowed the words of Shakespeare and Jonson in my title with a living force that makes me realize how greatly I have wrenched them. Had I not recognized the differences, even the contradictions, in hostages to fortune, worldly achievements, and literary history, I should surely have had them pointed out by my wife, whose measures of their relative importance are different from mine, and probably wiser. I owe much, and so does Time's pencil, to her indulgence and help. I owe almost as much to my grandparents, my children and their spouses, and my grandchildren, all of whom have made me more aware of my involvement in generations than even Erik Erikson's work has.

Professor William H. Epstein has been a caring and wise godfather to my manuscript; his encouragement and suggestions have been invaluable. I am indebted, also, to Verna Emery and Darle Griffith of the Purdue University Press for their advice and help in getting the manuscript into print.

To 1920

LESLIE STEPHEN

Two of the three events of 1882 crucial to the history of biography are obvious: in this year the first two volumes of Froude's *Life of Carlyle* were published and Adeline Virginia Stephen (Woolf) was born. In this year, too, there appeared a short public announcement which affected every biographer and every reader of biography in England. In the *Athenaeum* for December 23, 1882, Leslie Stephen wrote, "I have undertaken the responsible task of editing a new 'Biographia Britannica.' "[1] Very succinctly he dictated his policy, a policy which could be predicted in the main by any reader of the *Dictionary of National Biography*. He wanted "the greatest possible amount of information in a thoroughly business-like form"; he wanted abundant and precise dates and facts; he wanted clear reference to primary sources. "Elaborate analysis of character or exposition of critical theories is irrelevant; but a reader may fairly ask to have characteristic anecdotes in their most authentic form, and a clear statement of the view taken by a statesman of political controversies or of the position in the history of literature of a remarkable poem." A writer in a dictionary, he said, must be "historical, not controversial or discursive . . . he must put what he has to say in a pithy and condensed form; he must, as a rule, say nothing which would be equally appropriate under several other names; and, in short, he must be strictly biographical." To be "strictly biographical" was, then, to be factual, business-like, historical. It was, however, to be something more. Stephen had been asked whether "anything in the way of 'literary style' " was allowable. He answered that there was no room for style that was merely superfluous ornament, but, he said, "style, and even high literary ability, is required for lucid and condensed narrative, and of such style I shall be anxious to get as much as I can. A biography written with a single eye to giving all the information presumably desirable by an intelligent reader may be not only useful, but intensely interesting, and even a model of literary art."

In a later article, Stephen spoke of the "humble merits attainable" in articles intended for a biographical dictionary,[2] but he spoke as a man of letters who had written, prior to his editing of the *DNB*, the lives of Johnson, Pope, and Swift for the English Men of Letters series and who knew modern British history, his biographer says, "from Milton and Hobbes to Tennyson and Carlyle, rather than from Charles II. to Victoria."[3] Both by his announcement of policy and by his example, for he himself wrote 378 articles for the *DNB*,[4] Stephen enforced the idea that biography was to be not only condensed, accurate, and historical (rather than elaborately psychological and critical) but also "a model of literary art." That idea, or ideal, must have been in the minds of the 653 contributors who wrote 29,120 articles for the original 63 volumes of the *DNB* which appeared between 1885 and 1900. It was the foundation of the influential system articulated by Sidney Lee, but before we examine Lee's work, we should see what other ideas were in the air during the years when the *DNB* was appearing.

EDWARD EDWARDS

In 1885, Edward Edwards and Charles Hole published *A Handbook to the Literature of General Biography*, the first of eight pamphlets which were to survey the "Literature of Collective Biography." The little volume probably influenced no one; it was published in Ventnor on the Isle of Wight in an edition of 250 copies, and since Edwards, who wrote the text, died in 1886, the other seven projected parts (one of which was to be about national biography) never appeared. It is interesting, then, only in that it reflects Edwards's ideas, but Edwards was a practicing biographer who had thought sufficiently about biography so that his *Life of Sir Walter Ralegh* (1868) was followed by a separate volume of Ralegh's letters in accordance with his view that "a Correspondence worth preserving should be preserved apart."[5]

Edwards starts provocatively by suggesting that biography has more in common with drama than it has with history: "Part of the enduring charm of Biographical Literature seems to be close akin to the charms of Dramatic Art. . . . A good Biography has a dramatic interest (though not a dramatic completeness) about it, to which the best History of a Nation can never attain" (p. 14). His distinction between history and biography is, however, a gross one. History relates the "outward story" of a nation and its "collective life" or "continuity of spirit"; biography relates the sayings and doings of a man to illuminate the growth of his intellect and "the life of his soul" (p. 15). His juxtaposition of biography and drama is misleading. When he says that "in the well-told story of any energetic and individual life there is always an undercurrent of tragedy, so to speak" (p. 14), he means that a man's life is tragic because a man falls short of his aspirations. Edwards is not interested in the relations between tragedy and biography; he is interested in biography because it reflects on the vanity of human wishes. The good biographer is one who tells "what it really was that the man he writes about gathered out of this life, to carry with him into the next"; he makes his reader "feel that our human life is always a probation, as well as a combat" (pp. 16–17). For Edwards, then, biography is a handmaid of religion. More original is his view of the relation between biography and autobiography. "Whatever the admixture of fallacy, and alike whether the fallacy arise from deceit or from self-illusion," he says, "an Autobiography cannot but be, *in its measure*, a true revelation of the man that composed it. . . . The mental measure of the Biographer would seem to lie in the degree in which he is able to read between the lines of each Autobiographic material" (p. 18). Edwards moves from conscious self-records to "unconscious" ones which are even more "pregnant." Obviously in the back of his mind is the old question of whether Shakespeare unlocked his heart in his works. "The patient annalist," he says—and his spelling is more interesting than his idea—, "can elicit conclusive proof of character" even from writings which "seem to mirror humanity in all its phases without distortion or preference" (p. 24).[6] He provides no methodology, but runs for shelter to what he thinks is safer ground: "But even the SHAKESPEARES are wont to leave us Sonnets."

ELIZABETH PORTER GOULD

The burden of Elizabeth Porter Gould's "The Biography of the Future," which edified Bostonians in 1885, was that current biography focused on "unworthy subjects" and had become "more or less diluted with egoistic puerilities, insipid sentimentalities, and not-to-be-exposed privacies."[7] Her reading of J. W. Cross's *George Eliot's Life* provoked her to say that the book told too much about "the physical and religious weaknesses of Marion Evans the woman," whom she compared with such sterling people as Florence Nightingale, Elizabeth Fry, Mary Lyon, and Frances Willard. She admitted that George Eliot's books were worth reading, though they communicated the existing philosophy of the time instead of "the ever fresh, hopeful, revivifying life of immortal love." She felt, however, that "the leading public of the future" would not care to know more about the lives of "mere artists" than their own books suggest and the "general laws and facts of their development." It would demand full biographies of "those genuine, self-sacrificing heroes whose noble lives are their impossible-to-be-written books." For Elizabeth Porter Gould and, we may assume, for many proper Bostonians, the true and legitimate end of biography was to reveal "the universal and necessary truths of human nature as they have manifested themselves in those worthy of imitation."

PHILLIPS BROOKS

In a lecture on "Biography" delivered to the boys at Phillips Exeter on March 4, 1886,[8] Phillips Brooks, wearing lightly the D.D. recently conferred on him by Oxford, affirmed just such a purpose for biography, but he thought it one of several purposes which biography served. His esteem for biography was so high that he reached toward the illogical to describe its place:

> Biography is, in its very name, the literature of life. It is especially the literature of the individual human life. . . . And since the noblest life on earth is always human life, the literature which deals with human life must always be the noblest literature. And since the individual human life must always have a distinctness and interest which cannot belong to any of the groups of human lives, biography must always have a charm which no other kind of history can rival. (P. 179)

There is no need to comment on Brooks's general assumptions here; he considered biography a branch of history and, we shall see, he viewed literature as written words. Brooks dealt in turn with the subjects, writers, and readers of biography, and his list of proper subjects indicates the various uses he found for biography. His para-phrase of Johnson's words in Number 60 of *The Rambler* shows his belief that "there is not one of us living to-day so simple and monotonous a life that, if he be true and natural, his life faithfully written would not be worthy of men's eyes and hold men's hearts" (p. 183), but he specifically advocated the reading of lives—like those of Johnson and Scott—which have value for their broad humanity, and those which illuminate a period of the world's his-tory, a critical event, an occupation or profession, or various types of characters. The lives of the poets he would not bother with: the "more profoundly and spiritually" a man is a poet, "the more impossible a biography of him becomes. . . . If you have read everything which he has written, you know him" (p. 192). Brooks was more interested in keeping the lives of the poets out of the hands of the boys than he was in encouraging them to read their works. He was not concerned that men no longer read Johnson's books; it was important that they never ceased to care about his broad human qualities: "The unfading interest in Dr. Johnson is one of the good signs of English character" (p. 186). Indeed, for Brooks, the biographer "must only be the friend" who brings reader and subject together. A biography should be read "with as little of the literary sense as possible"; Brooks advocated that his readers turn first to the middle of a biography to see what a man did, and then that they go back to the beginning to pick up details (pp. 202–3). If biography was "the literature of life," it was important to divorce the life from the literature. The object of reading biography was not merely imitation, but inspi-ration. The best biography, like the New Testament, was of value because it was both exceptional and representative; it provided "light and intensity," "sympathy and breadth," and its "su-preme blessing" was in its always "bathing the special in the universal, and so renewing its vitality and freshness" (pp. 201, 206). Biography, then, was not so much literature or history as it was baptism for the good and eternal life.

GEORGE SAINTSBURY

George Saintsbury's "Some Great Biographies" (1892)[9] contains no explicit discussion of the relation of biography to ethics or history or literature. As his title suggests, his approach is pragmatic, not theoretical, and such generalizations as he makes are based on the literary analysis of specific books. His as-sumption is that biography is a literary genre, and unlike critics who find in biography a vehicle of moral and religious instruction, he is as interested in the biographer as in the subject. "A real biography," he says, "ought to be something more than the presentation of mere materials, however excellently calendared, something more than memoirs, letters, diary and so forth. The whole ought to be passed through the mind of a competent and intelligent artist, and to be presented to us, not indeed in such a way that we are bound to take his word for the details, but in such a way that we see a finished picture, a composition, not merely a mass of details and *data*" (p. 107). Saintsbury distinguishes two kinds of biography. "Biography pure and simple" is that in which "the whole of the materials is passed through the alembic of the biographer." This kind of biography in which the materials are altered and digested (exemplified in Tacitus's *Agricola* and Southey's *Nelson*) is "artistically the most perfect kind" (p. 97). Saintsbury's immediate interest is, however, in what he calls "applied" or "mixed" biography, wherein letters, anecdotes, and the like are connected and unified by an author's or editor's narrative and comment; its popularity and its appearance of easy accomplishment prompt his discussion of Boswell's *Johnson*, Moore's *Byron*, Lockhart's *Scott*, Carlyle's *Sterling*, and Trevelyan's *Macaulay* (p. 97).

For Saintsbury, the greatest of these is the *Scott*, and he reveals some of his criteria when he enumerates Lockhart's advantages: ample material and complete knowledge of it, real affection for the subject, nothing which had to be concealed, and general interest by the public in the hero. He focuses mainly on Lockhart's skill—"the presentation is continuous, uniform, uninterrupted. . . . it has the uniform grasp, the sustained and absorbing attraction, of the best works of narrative and dramatic art"—and this skill is related to the degree of intrusion of the biographer into the life. The *Scott* is an "unmatched combination of excellence in the selection and editing with excellence in the connecting narrative," and Lockhart's distinguishing grace is in never obtruding himself but never obtrusively effacing himself. "He is often actually on the scene: he is constantly speaking in his own person; and yet we never think of him as the man with the pointing-stick at the panorama, as the beadle at the function, as the ringmaster of the show. He seems to stand rather in the relation of the epic poet to his characters, narrating, omnipresent, but never in the way" (pp. 101–3).

Moore, Saintsbury says, is sometimes too reticent and sometimes too loquacious and preachy, but he was a man of "thorough literary faculty" and had the good sense to know that since so much had been said about Byron, it was important to let him speak for himself (pp. 100–101). Boswell's method is apparently desultory, but his attention never wandered from the character of Johnson, and every touch delineated his character (p. 99). Boswell becomes a bore, however, whenever he becomes at all original; he "plays monkey to his master's bear in a very diverting and effective manner" and the contrast is effective, "but almost too violent for the best art" (p. 103). Carlyle's subject is "a sorry sight," "an affluent consumptive dawdler," "the father of all the melancholy brood that includes the Arthur Cloughs of real life and the Robert Elsmeres of fiction—the conductor and coryphaeus of the caitiff choir who sing undogmatic anthems to a Nehushtan of negation." Since there is not enough "substance" in Sterling as subject for a fine biography, the *Life* is a great book, but not a great biography; its merits are the "merits not of biography,—that is to say the presentation of a man as he is—but of romance, or the presentation of something as it is not." Carlyle manages to effect the virtual vanishment of Sterling while he presents "an extraordinarily interesting history of the places that he [Sterling] lived in, the men he knew, the events which he shared or did not share, and the personality of his redoubtable and admirable friend and biographer, all thrown up on a background of the shortcomings of the Church and State of England in the nineteenth century" (pp. 104–5).

Saintsbury, then, envisions some harmony of spirit and stature between subject and biographer as providing the sustained tone and finished composition of biography at its best. His constant interest is in the relation between the subject and the writer, in the reaction between the revelation of the subject and the self-revelation of the writer. His focus is enforced in part by the fact that he deals exclusively with "applied" or "mixed" biography, and, moreover, with "mixed" biography in which both subjects and authors are literary men. Essentially he is concerned with artistic construction and his specific analyses are more helpful than his final generalization: "a good life of a man will be found to have been well done itself, and done probably in a rather different way from any other" (p. 106).

MARCEL SCHWOB

Biography for art's sake, the doctrine which underlaid such a work as Walter Pater's *Imaginary Portraits* (1887), received theoretical justification not in England but in France. There Marcel Schwob published, prefatory to his *Vies imaginaires* in 1896, an essay which he called "L'art de la biographie" when it was reproduced in his *Spicilège* in the same year.[10] For Schwob, history is a science which leaves us uncertain about individuals; art, on the other hand, "describes individuals, desires only the unique. It does not classify, it unclassifies" (pp. 7–8). The value of the unique, the idiosyncratic detail, leads Schwob to a paean of praise for John Aubrey's work which pre-empts the largest part of his essay, and this part was later quoted by André Maurois and by Frank Harris.[11] One limitation he finds in Aubrey (in addition to his style): "He never knew how to fix an individual forever in our minds by giving us his special traits against a background of resemblances to the average or the ideal. He put life in the eye, the nose, the leg or the pout of his models; he could not animate the face" (p. 19). It is in the animation, the creation of the artist, that Schwob's main interest lies. Since biographers have, unfortunately, considered themselves historians, he says, they have concentrated on the lives of great men. "Art is a stranger to such considerations. To the eyes of a painter a portrait of an unknown man, by Cranach, is as valuable as a portrait of the great Erasmus. For the name, Erasmus, cannot make a picture inimitable." Truth need not be the preoccupation of the biographer. The biographer, "like some inferior deity, . . . should select unique individuals from the realm of human material available. . . . art must choose what it needs to compose a form that will be like no other form. It matters not if this form resemble something formerly created by a superior god, so long as it is unique and a genuine creation" (pp. 20–21).

Real men are important, then, only in that they furnish a fund of material, provide models or inspirations for the creation of characters by an artist. The subject of a biography is supremely the creation of the artist and differs from a fictive character, we may assume, only in that he bears the name of someone who once breathed earthy air. The biographer may, if he wishes, rearrange life to say, as Schwob does, that Gabriel Spencer played the role of Ophelia before he was killed by Ben Jonson in 1598 and that "Cyril Tourneur was born out of the union of an unknown god with a prostitute" (pp. 176, 193). Schwob does not name the prostitute, but here and elsewhere in his work her name is Clio.

SIDNEY LEE

During the next two decades and more, the dominant figures in the criticism of biography were Sidney Lee and Edmund Gosse in England and William Roscoe Thayer in the United States. When Frederick S. Boas spoke in 1929 of Lee's "sober-suited conception of the biographer's art," he had in mind Lee's subordination of "artistic portraiture and literary style" to truth and utility;[12] perhaps he was thinking also of the bare, judicial, and dogmatic tone of Lee's essays about biography as it contrasts with the passion and the flair of his Shakespearean essays; he certainly did not mean to denigrate the most fully articulated conception of biography before Maurois's. It was a conception formed in the image of Leslie Stephen's, and both Lee's connection with the *DNB* and his stature as a man of letters assured its influence. Stephen had selected Lee as his assistant editor in March 1883, and until the end of 1889, Lee helped Stephen with the publication of the first twenty-one volumes of the *DNB*. The next four volumes were edited jointly, and from the spring of 1891 Lee was the chief editor of the remaining two-thirds of the volumes. He himself wrote 820 articles for the *DNB*, more than any other contributor, amounting to about three full volumes and including the longest article, that on Shakespeare.[13] He wrote the article on Queen Victoria for the first Supplement of the *DNB* (1901) and the one on Edward VII for the Supplement of 1912. Expansions of the Shakespeare, Victoria, and Edward VII, published separately, enhanced his reputation as a biographer. Lee acted as chairman of the first general meeting of the English Association (1907) and was the first president of the Modern Language Research Association; Boas says rightly that before his death in 1926 he was considered the leading Shakespearean authority by the general reading public and that in America and on the continent he was considered the *doyen* of English scholars.[14]

Lee's influence on the criticism of biography starts with his lecture on "National Biography" at the Royal Institution on January 31, 1896;[15] it extends beyond 1929, when his two major essays on biography were reprinted in a commemorative volume. A large part of the lecture on "National Biography" is a justification of the principles of inclusion and of allocation of space in the *DNB*, but the third section contrasts national biography with individual biography and Lee often broadens the scope of his subject. The cast of his opinions here underwent only slight modification in his later essays. Biography stems, he suggests, from the "instinctive desire to do honour to the memories of those who, by character and exploits, have distinguished themselves from the mass of their countrymen"; it deals with "the nature of the achievements or characteristics" that are thought worthy of commemoration (p. 3). Despite his initial stress on both accomplishment and character, Lee makes his preference plain: "no man's life should be admitted to a collection of national biography that does not present at least one action that is 'serious, complete, and of a certain magnitude.' I believe that the individual biographer might not unprofitably note the practical uses of this definition" (p. 14). When he states the differences between national and individual biography, he clearly implies that individual biography may find practical uses for the doctrines of national biography. He contrasts, for instance, the "superior conciseness of statement" of national biography to the "two, or even three, generous volumes" written not by a man of literary capacity but by a near kinsman or a personal friend of surviving relatives. He speaks of the need of the national biographer to focus on "the distinctive aspects of men's lives" and says that it is supererogatory for him to specify that a man has the everyday domestic virtues. He thinks that the national biographer has to cultivate the judicial temper far more assiduously than the individual biographer; he must frankly describe notorious or chronic lapses from public or private duty, but he must give them no more space than their effect on achievement justifies. Since the national biographer engages in a comparative study, is not merely recording reputations but adjusting them, he must constantly exercise tolerance, fairness, proportion, judgment. Lee grants the superiority of individual biography on one score only: "the best specimens of national biography are inferior in artistic value to competent specimens of individual biography," though national biography "may embody some features of literary art" (pp. 11–13). Lee does not elaborate the relations of biography and literary art, but not because he would identify biography and history. He has no use for Carlyle's dictum that the history of mankind is the history of its great men; history describes "the aggregate movement of men" and the manner in which this movement molds events and institutions. "The historian," he says in a sentence which he used more than once and which was frequently cited by others, "looks at mankind through a field-glass: the biographer puts individual men under a magnifying glass" (pp. 5–6).

Lee's *Principles of Biography* (1911) demonstrates that he felt that the dicta of "National Biography" were almost entirely applicable to all biography. This essay, his Leslie Stephen Lecture,[16] is in the main a fleshing out of his earlier opinions. The purpose of biography remains the same: "Biography exists to satisfy a natural instinct in man—the commemorative instinct" (p. 7). When Lee says here that it satisfies this instinct "by exercise of its power to transmit personality" (he says elsewhere in the essay that the aim of biography is "the truthful transmission of personality"), he is not introducing a new idea but clarifying his earlier preference for "action" over "character" (pp. 8, 26).

"Character and exploits are for biographical purposes inseparable," he says, but, he continues, "Character which does not translate itself into exploit is for the biographer a mere phantom." It follows, then, that though Lee says that successful biography depends "on the two elements of fit matter and fit manner, of fit theme and fit treatment," he still holds to his Aristotelian definition of the proper subject of biography, and he insists that "the life of a nonentity or a mediocrity, however skilfully contrived, conflicts with primary biographic principles" (pp. 9–10).

In the fourth section of his essay, Lee refers to two matters he had discussed in "National Biography" and introduces a third: "Biography," he says, "must resolutely preserve its independence of three imposing themes of study, which are often seen to compete for its control. True biography is no handmaid of ethical instruction. Its purpose is not that of history. It does not exist to serve biological or anthropological science" (p. 18). In dealing with ethics, Lee moves beyond his earlier remarks and he censures the "ethical fallacy" which sanctions suppression and extenuation. He insists that candor is a cardinal biographical principle, differentiates hostility and scurrility from candor, emphasizes the importance of proportion and sympathy in handling moral lapses, and warns that lack of sympathy can produce a caricature instead of a portrait (pp. 20–23). His remarks on history contain nothing new except a condemnation of the *life and times* fashion of writing biography (p. 29), but he opens a fresh subject when he speaks of the peril of relating science and biography. He says that Sir Francis Galton and others urged on him as editor of the *DNB* the advantage of adapting the method of the *Dictionary* to the needs of the scientific investigation of heredity and eugenics. Biography, they argued, should collect details of genealogy, habit, and physiological characteristics which would help genetics "to determine human types, to diagnose 'variations from type,' to distinguish acquired from inherited characteristics, and to arrive by such roads at a finite conception of human individuality." Lee believes that such aid must be indirect. He sees dangers for biography if it focuses on the "distant ramifications of every great man's pedigree"; he does not discuss at all the implications which new scientific knowledge may have for the biographer himself (pp. 30–31).

Instead, he dwells on the faults of panegyric and on one of his favorite subjects, the matter of length. Both "National Biography" and the *Principles of Biography* refer to Shakespeare's dramatic production as an action of the first magnitude and to

Wellington's victory at Waterloo as a great but lesser achievement (p. 14), and it is no mere coincidence that the two longest articles in the *DNB* are those on Shakespeare (49 pp.) and Wellington (34 pp.). Lee holds that length ought to be determined by the importance of a man's career, the gross amount of available material, and the intrinsic value or biographic pertinence of the surviving records (p. 39). For him, "a discriminating brevity is a law of the right biographic method" (p. 42). Still, he sees that this law has been broken by what he thinks to be the two best biographies in English—Boswell's *Johnson* and Lockhart's *Scott*—and he puts himself in the position of calling the *Johnson* a "sport" (p. 44). He praises Boswell for always transmitting personality, for his candor, for his industry in collecting material, for the place he gave himself: "It was not in Boswell's nature to efface himself," but he did not bring himself on the stage at Johnson's expense (pp. 46–47). Again, Lee ends his essay by stating that "where the theme is fit, the independent biographer has scope for the exercise of almost every literary gift" (p. 53), but he never specifies nor does he mention Boswell's literary gifts.

Not until his 1918 lecture on *The Perspective of Biography*[17] did Lee make more precise what he meant by the biographer's having scope for the exercise of almost every literary gift, but his statement here provided the framework for many discussions, including those of Harold Nicolson and Virginia Woolf, of the question, Is biography an art or a craft? Since art implied for Lee something essentially creative in its dependence on invention and originality, he viewed biography as a craft. "In the categories of creative art," he says, "biography can claim no foremost place." The biographer needs, he thinks, a "touch" of the portrait painter's creative insight, but "the density of the raw material in which the biographer works hampers the exercise of the creative faculty in a degree unknown to other branches of art, literary, pictorial, or plastic." The biographer's first duty is to sift and to interpret his materials. "Only when that process is accomplished can he hope to give his findings essential form. Unity of spirit, cohesion of tone, perspective, these are the things which a due measure of the creative faculty will alone guarantee. Otherwise, the delineation will lack the semblance of life and reality." Fundamentally, then, a biography is for Lee "a compilation, an industriously elaborated composition, a mosaic"; the biographer differs from the novelist and the playwright in that he cannot invent incident and his "creation" is limited to giving "animation to the dead bones." The compilation of detail and fact is so important to Lee, the freedom of the biographer so restricted that a "character" is for him a "nebulous impressionist study" which has small value or none for a life (pp. 8–9).

Lee's conception of biography as a "craft" dictates in large measure his view of the role of the biographer, and in this essay his main concern is the propriety of the biographer's point of view, his attitude or "perspective." That is why he starts his essay by differentiating the attitude of the biographer from that of the autobiographer, though his remarks seem merely a courteous reference to an essay by his successor as president of the English Association, Herbert Asquith.[18] "The autobiographer," he says, "works from within outwards, while the biographer at least proposes to himself to work from without inward. . . . The autobiographer fixes his gaze mainly on himself. He is before all things an egoist. His success is proportioned to his self-absorption. His biographical kinsman is an altruist. His success is proportioned to his self-suppression. The general distinction is of the kind which separates the lyric poet from the dramatist" (p. 6).

When Lee had referred in *Principles of Biography* to Boswell's lack of self-effacement, he had in mind Boswell's strutting on the stage in the *Life of Johnson*, his personal presence as a character in the *Life*. When he talks of the biographer's "self-suppression" here, he has in mind not physical presence, but the presence of an overriding point of view which vitiates what he had elsewhere called "honest independence of judgment," the "mood of detachment" which makes it possible for "detached and unfettered thought" to weigh ascertainable facts.[19] The heart of Lee's essay is in a single paragraph:

> It is the biographer's indulgence in the partial view, the giving an unchecked rein to his idiosyncrasies, which accounts for most of the wreckage in the biographic ocean. The biographer too often fails to see his facts steadily or to see them whole. His angle of observation excludes from his view much that is relevant, because it does not square with his personal predilection: his drawing is often out of perspective, not merely because he lacks the architectonic capacity of unifying or fusing detail, but because he suffers his private sympathies or antipathies to exclude much that is essential to completeness. Again, the writer's partialities will render his lights too brilliant and his shadows either too dark, or, as is a common experience, not dark enough. Right perspective both in a mechanical and moral sense is a primary condition of satisfactory performance. (Pp. 9–10)

Lee says that neglect of mechanical perspective or coherent arrangement is disastrous,[20] but his main interest here is in the
even more disastrous bias which distorts the biographer's "angle
of moral or spiritual or intellectual observation" (p.11).

The remainder of his essay defines five main kinds of bias,
all of which Lee had warned against in his earlier essays: the family
bias, which fashions a wooden idol for domestic worship; the official
bias, which pays undue respect to the conventional formulas of
public or social life; the ethical bias, which makes biography serve
the irrelevant purpose of moral edification; the bias of hero-worship, which moves beyond sympathy and admiration to obsequious
adulation; the historical bias, which represses unduly the element
of personality. Lee does not mention the scientific bias which
turns biography into case-history, though he had referred to it in
1911. He ends his essay with the subject that had preoccupied him
in "At a Journey's End" (1912) in a justification of the writing
of a biography directly after the death of a man. He sees that the
accuracy of a biographer's angle of observation is substantially
influenced by the time which intervenes between a death and a
biography, that prompt writing exposes the biographer to some of
the biases he has listed, but he thinks the risks are necessary
because "first-hand reminiscence of living contemporaries is the
least dispensable ingredient" (p. 22).

Lee's criticism of biography covers more than twenty years.
Over the years he defined the purpose of biography, its proper
subject, the role of the biographer, his perspective, and the relation of biography to other disciplines. Despite the breadth of
his concerns,[21] his conception of biography was a fairly narrow one.
For all that he says about biography as the truthful transmission
of personality and the necessity of focusing on the distinctive
aspects of a man, he was always more interested in achievement
than in character. For all of his consideration of the pitfalls which
lie in the way of the biographer, he conceived of the ideal biographer as a judicial and candid compiler. His system has the virtues
of neatness and consistency, but it was, in fact, consistent with
the system announced for the *DNB* by Stephen in 1882, and it
was the massive shadow of the *DNB* which filled the room in which
Lee lectured on May 10, 1918. In a book published just the day
before, an author seemed to be precisely of Lee's mind as he wrote
about bad biographies with "their ill-digested masses of material,
their slipshod style, their tone of tedious panegyric, their la-
mentable lack of selection, of detachment, of design" and as he
insisted that the biographer preserve a becoming brevity.
Strangely enough, the book was not an appendix to the *DNB*,

but *Eminent Victorians.* Lytton Strachey had let "art" rather than Aristotle determine his choice of subjects, and he had taken seriously, perhaps too seriously, Lee's words that the biographer has scope for the exercise of almost every literary gift.

EDMUND GOSSE

Strachey censured "those two fat volumes, with which it is our custom to commemorate the dead. . . . They are as familiar as the *cortège* of the undertaker, and wear the same air of slow, funereal barbarism." In 1919, Edmund Gosse wrote, "It is impossible not to agree with this pungent criticism."[22] The reason for Gosse's agreement is not far to seek. Almost two decades earlier he had published an article called "The Custom of Biography"[23] in which he had said, "We in England bury our dead under the monstrous catafalque of two volumes (crown octavo). . . . The custom has now grown into an institution. . . . There must be a pall, two volumes of biography, and a few wreaths of elegant white flowers" (p. 195). Gosse's primary target is the bulky compilation with its "astounding indifference to form, purpose, and proportion" (p. 196). He cites Conyers Middleton's *Life of Cicero* (1741) as the earliest specimen of the life-and-times species which gave modern biography its conventional shape, and he dates the modern custom from about 1830, with the publication of Sir Walter Scott's *Life of Napoleon Buonaparte* in nine volumes. At the same time, he points out the social importance of Middleton's work: in its appeal to educated readers rather than to the Grub Street public, "it first made biography a respectable independent branch of the literary profession." The eighteenth-century notion that biography was work fit only for a drudge lingered on, however, in Macaulay's prejudiced outlook and has impeded Boswell's coming into his rightful intellectual estate (pp. 201–4).

Gosse's essay is more than an excursion into some matters of taste. He suggests that a young man of ambition and energy might do worse than devote himself to the virgin theme of the history of biography in England, and he proceeds to do some of the young man's work. He not only sketches in the canon of English biography, but in assessing particular works he uses criteria which have general relevance. When, for instance, he praises Cavendish's *Wolsey* as a clear-colored portrait of a man set against the dim background of his age, he refers to such a focus as "the real essence of the art of biography" and says that it should be the biographer's sole aim (p. 197). Here, in his distinction between biography and history, his doctrine is precisely Sidney Lee's. Elsewhere, in his discussions of Greville's too exclusive concentration on a thesis and of Walton's aim for edification, he uses criteria which Lee may have borrowed. When, however, he speaks of Greville's ideas as "driving mere homely human features out into the cold" (p. 199) and of "the biographical purity of a Boswell, who faithfully records every manifestation of the character of his subject, believing that character, in its nudity, to be a perfectly worthy theme for our respectful attention" (p. 200), his stress on character moves far beyond Lee's. When he says that Elizabethan miscellanies of discovery and navigation were in no sense biographies because the object of the writers "was not the psychology of the individual navigator, but where he went, what he saw, and what additions he made to general information" (p. 198), he introduces in "psychology" a term which Lee never used in his essays about biography, and the term is symptomatic of the way in which his outlook mainly differs from Lee's.

Gosse ends his essay with a consideration of the main abuses of biography, and here he differs from Lee only in the vividness of his prose. For him, as for Lee, biography is not to be entrusted to hacks, and the worst of all writers is the Widow, who thinks of biography as an annex to Madame Tussaud's gallery.[24] He echoes Lee when he says that the proper subject of a biography should have "possessed qualities, moved in conditions, assumed characteristics, so unlike those of other men as to justify his being raised from their ranks" and when he holds that there should be "a certain proportion" between the size of a biography and the effect which its subject produced in public life. His attitude toward the representation of a subject's faults and flaws is exactly Lee's, but he insists even more than Lee does that the cultivation of decency and reticence, an exaggerated respect for convention and for the feelings of survivors, is a constant cause of biographical failure (pp. 205–7).[25] Here and elsewhere it is primarily Gosse's interest in intimate detail and in character which sets him apart from Lee and which leads him to conceive of biography as a "branch of literature" with a conviction that Lee never felt when he wrote of the literary gifts one might expend on biography.

Even before Gosse made his own major efforts in this branch of literature, he had contributed biographical articles to the ninth edition of the *Encyclopaedia Britannica*. He was the chief literary adviser in the preparation of the tenth (1902–3) and eleventh (1910–11) editions of the *Britannica*, and was himself responsible for the articles on "Criticism" and "Biography" which first appeared in 1910. "The finest criticism," he says, "should take every circumstance of the case into consideration, and hold it necessary, if possible, to know the author as well as the book," but this is his only reference to biography in the article on criticism, though he mentions the supreme importance of Sainte-Beuve in French criticism of the nineteenth century.

When, in the first sentence of his article on biography, he calls biography "that form of history which is applied, not to races or masses of men, but to an individual," he seems to use a Baconian approach, but it is soon clear that his opening definition is historical and that his allegiance is, rather, to the modification of Bacon's (and Dryden's) definition which the *Oxford English Dictionary* had set forth in 1887—"the history of the lives of individual men, as a branch of literature." Among the writers of antiquity, he says, not even Plutarch "clearly perceived its possible existence as an independent branch of literature," and the modern concept of biography dates from the seventeenth century. The modern concept, the "true conception," he calls it, he redefines as "the faithful portrait of a soul in its adventures through life." The key words in this definition Gosse clarifies only by indirection when he tries to differentiate biography "in its pure sense"[26] or "legitimate biography" from the older biography. He insists that biography is not a philosophical treatise, a polemical pamphlet, or a portion of a chronicle, and that early biography went astray in treating a man from a philosophical (by which he means "moral" or "religious") or a historical point of view. Plutarch's moral purpose, he says, blunted his emphasis on "the individual characteristics" of a man; whenever a moral purpose intrudes, "we have to piece together unconsidered incidents and the accidental record of features in order to obtain an approximate estimate," for "frailties or obscure irregularities" will be glossed over.

Gosse never defines "the primitive instinct of sympathy" which he says was responsible for modern biography when it "began to have free play" in the seventeenth century, and he never defines the "peculiar curiosity" which modern biography satisfies. Still, his emphasis on "individual characteristics," "features," "frailties," "irregularities," these observed by eyes "not unduly clouded by moral passion or prejudice," indicates that he would stress the essential man-ness of a man as it is seen by a humane observer with a healthy awareness of the human condition. Gosse is interested, however, in more than objective physical observation of a man. He is concerned with "a soul in its adventures," not with a man in his activities. Biography is, then, not to be primarily a description of a man's accomplishments and actions. Gosse's use of "soul" is not scholastic or even Carlylean, though it is closer to Carlyle's if it is possible to retain his idea of the essence of a man without its transcendental implications. "Soul" is probably to be equated with Gosse's earlier phrases, "character, in its nudity" and "the psychology of the individual."

Gosse's critical remarks are contained in his two opening paragraphs; the rest of his *Britannica* article is a brief historical survey of biography, individual and collective. There is really nothing in these paragraphs which had not already been put more clearly in "The Custom of Biography," but they were provocative in their discrimination between old and modern biography and, moreover, they were widely read. They provided, for example, the basis for a large part of the critical system used by Harold Nicolson in *The Development of English Biography* (1927).

WILLIAM ROSCOE THAYER

A few years after the publication of Lee's and Gosse's first critical work about biography in England, there appeared in the United States a remarkable article on "Biography";[27] the author, William Roscoe Thayer, had directed his literary aspirations toward the writing of history, and it is no surprise that in the first sentence of his article he announces that biography is a branch of history, though, he says, the least successfully cultivated branch. Thayer believes in the Great Man theory of history; he is convinced that "Destiny shapes the course of human affairs" by operating through the will of a few men of genius in each epoch and he has no sympathy for the "fatalists" who think that the man of genius is merely the product of his time (pp. 268–69). He is willing to grant that a period of time may have certain distinguishing features, but he feels that no formula can account for the few conspicuous exceptions who have genius. Moreover, the spirit of the time is not so single as some would like to think, and supporters of the *Zeitgeist* theory are forced to create a more or less imaginary time which assumes the conditions needed to "explain" a genius (pp. 276–77). Thayer relates the contemporary historians' preoccupation with the collective rather than with the special to nineteenth-century scientific accomplishments: ". . . we have been absorbed in watching the formulation of the doctrine of evolution, the capital achievement of the century— the doctrine in which, when first posed, the individual seemed to wither and the world grew more and more. . . . Not the man, but his pedigree; not the specimen, but its series; not the idiosyncrasy, but the likeness, were all in all" (p. 262). Historians interested in discovering general principles and in tracing a continuity rightly disregarded exceptions, but Thayer points out that such abstraction tends to be impatient of the intrusion of individuals just as "the scientific study of the individual, if pushed too far, results in the creation of a fictitious Normal Man" (p. 273).

As an advocate of the Great Man theory, Thayer overrules the objection that the biographic treatment of history results in a false focus: ". . . history, told through the career of a great man—Cromwell, Washington, Cavour—gains in clearness and human interest far more than it can lose through the tendency of a biographer to exaggerate the personal influence of his hero" (p. 267). For him, the biographer's hero-worship provides better insight than theories about life, scientific formulas, or an attitude of disparagement. "Time," he says, "will correct the enthusiast's magnification; but the belittler's underestimate merely measures himself. When a critic writes, 'Emerson is not always as shallow as he seems,' we suspect that Emerson's shallows will be deep enough for his critic to drown in" (p. 273). Thayer, however, has no praise for mere eulogy and panegyric; he is willing to pardon even excessive intimate personal detail, for above all else biography must have "the human touch—truth to nature." So firmly persuaded is he of the importance of "the human touch" that he says its presence redeems a biography, however humble its subject may be (p. 266).

This seems, perhaps, a strange opinion from a proponent of the Great Man theory, but Thayer has unqualified respect, too, for the artist's insight. He thinks that the personalities of real men—at least of great men—have an advantage over fictional creations in their ability to elude final definition, but, he says, "biographers have not kept pace with novelists in skill to reproduce the actual man; they still work too much from the outside; they should live in the heart and brain of their hero and let us see the very springs of action: for the demand for veracity, stimulated by science and by fiction, has grown so keen that readers will no longer tolerate the old school of biographers, who thought it indecorous to show their subjects in anything less dignified than full dress" (p. 266).

Thayer's essay is interesting because he does not feel it necessary to defend his statement that the biographer can learn something about "veracity" from the novelist. It is interesting, too, because he does examine, with some skepticism, the contributions which physiology and psychology may make to biography. Thayer does not underestimate the importance of knowing a man's physiology, but "unfortunately, our records are very meagre,

and furthermore medical science has not yet reached that state
of precision where it can assert positively that a fatal chain of
cause and effect connected given pathological symptoms and established deeds" (p. 270). He praises the work of Lombroso and
others, but questions the rigidity of their conclusions. He mentions
such investigations as those very recently described by Dr. George
M. Gould in his *Biographic Clinics* on the ill health of DeQuincey,
Carlyle, Darwin, and others, but he warns against the error of those
who accept Lombroso's conclusions too strictly: "Any process
which tends to regard genius and insanity as synonymous has itself
an insane taint" (p. 271). Psychology may have a splendid future,
but it is still in its infancy and it cannot penetrate to the causes
of personality. Thayer is alive to the new instruments which may
measure human beings more accurately, but he feels a little imposed upon as he considers the "so-called discoveries of the psychologist": "Next to a religious revival, nothing is more likely
to promise what it cannot fulfil than a scientific theory just
broached. You think you have in it a key to the universe; you
discover at last that it simply fits a new-fangled lock to your old
front door" (p. 272). Despite his awareness of the recent research
in science and his desire to remain open-minded about its contributions to the study of an individual, Thayer believes that it
is the art of fiction which "has been teaching us to distinguish
the nicest variations of character, and to trace the rack-and-
pinion interaction of cause and effect" (p. 277).

When he wrote his article on biography in 1905, Thayer's
reputation, such as it was, was based largely on his two-volume
Dawn of Italian Independence (1893). When he delivered at the University of Virginia his three lectures published as *The Art of Biography* in 1920,[28] he was the distinguished biographer of Cavour,
John Hay, and Theodore Roosevelt, and he was the past president
of the American Historical Association. The structure of his book
is confusing, for he did not maintain his focus on the art of biography as it developed historically but, rather, wrote a short
history of biography in which some critical comment disrupts his
discussion of ancient biography in the first lecture and spills over
into the next two. In his perceptive article of 1905 Thayer had
said that an adequate survey of biography had not yet been written,
and this disappointing little book is an attempt to fill that gap.
Thayer does not seem to have known Waldo H. Dunn's fine survey
in *English Biography* (1916); he makes no mention of Strachey or
Gamaliel Bradford; his last extended critical examination is largely
a castigation of Froude's *Carlyle*. Unlike the article, the book

does not have the crackling excitement of contemporary ideas about it, and it is mainly interesting in the modifications it makes of ideas in the article. No longer does Thayer find it necessary to defend biography as a branch of history, and there is little here on the relation between biography and history; biography is considered independently. Thayer's attitude toward science has hardened a good deal: he does not mention physiology and he speaks less tentatively about psychology. His attitude toward the importance of literature in general for biography remains unchanged, but he adds some comments about the biographer's revelation of himself.

The thesis of Thayer's first lecture, developed at the expense of a detailed summary of ancient biography, is that "the constant direction in the evolution of Biography has been from the outward to the inward," from the description of the visible acts of a man of rank or position to preoccupation with intrinsically interesting persons. Writers started to perceive that "the motive behind the deed was the really essential thing to study and, if possible, to explain or at least to interpret" (pp. 34–35). With this drift Thayer is sympathetic, but he is not pleased with the effect psychology has had on it. He accepts the findings of psychology: "Recent psychologists tell us that nobody is made all of one piece—all good or all bad; but that the state of consciousness in which each of us lives is based on subconsciousness, a compound of physical instincts and desires, of intuitions and inherited tendencies" (p. 25). He admits that the "psychological aspect of personality" never concerned Plutarch or the ancients, that they looked on men and their deeds as uncomplex, but he confesses his sympathy for their "calming simplicity." He prefers the imagination of the poet to the analysis of the psychologist: "Thanks to the divine faculty of the Imagination, Homer and Sophocles penetrated to the bottom of the human heart, so that, although they had no knowledge of double and triple personality or of the Freudian Wish, or of inhibitions and hysteria, they were able to create figures which have never lost their hold on posterity." The reason for his preference lies in the difference which he finds in the point of view of the poet and the psychologist. The ancients, he says, felt the mystery of the will which guides conduct and action, but they kept "a certain spontaneity, a freshness of outlook, and a sense of undulled wonder toward life. . . . In reading their works we are spared the feeling that the author is leading us through the solution of a series of problems." Thayer holds the psychologist responsible for the attitude which "darkens almost every intellectual product of the last half-century" (pp. 26–27). He stresses, as he did earlier, the lessons in insightful penetration into character which biographers learned from novelists, poets, and autobiographers (pp. 36–38), and, despite his awareness of the modern tendency toward "inward" biography, toward explanation and interpretation of motive, his emphasis is still on narrative.

The first aim of biography (and history) is to tell a story "as nearly as possible as the actors or hero underwent it"; the difficulty is "to find means through the art of literature to produce an adequate simulation of lifelikeness" (pp. 46, 51). The best biographies written since 1870 are much closer to life, Thayer says, than those written earlier in the century, and he admits that scientific method, which led to the dispassionate study of men as well as of animals and chemical elements, influenced biography directly and also, by its effect on realism in the novel, indirectly (pp. 102–3). "In the end," he says, however, "the scientific method, applied to the arts, defeated its purpose by substituting material and mechanical standards for spiritual. Science can vivisect bodies, but up to the present the soul of man eludes the microscope and the scalpel" (p. 120). Like Gosse, then, whom he had probably read though he never mentions him, Thayer believes that "the essential subject of the biographer is the soul of man." He moves beyond Gosse in his attempt to determine how this "soul" may be comprehended and represented. When he speaks of Carlyle's ability to flash into the very heart and soul of men and women (p. 128), he reveals not only that his definition of soul is perhaps more transcendent than Gosse's but also that for him the techniques of psychology are no adequate substitute for bardic insight.

This is the heart of Thayer's argument. He comments in passing on the "widow," on the "custom" and the necessity of selection, and on the need for sympathy to provide proper perspective (pp. 111, 114–18, 144–45). He has only one other recurrent concern: the ability of the biographer and his role in a life. Four-fifths of a biography depends on the biographer, not the subject, and the biographer must be an artist (pp. 139, 117). It would seem that Thayer's artist need not necessarily be both prophet and master in the art of expression, for he says that "divination" (sensitivity to the qualities of a subject) may compensate for lack of verbal ability (p. 70). When he praises Boswell's "transparency" (p. 97), however, his not projecting himself between the reader and the text, he is not referring to Boswell's personality or his opinions or his intrusion on the stage of his book but to his style. When he tells us to imagine a life of Johnson written by Walter Pater, it is apparent that expression is as important to him as divination. Indeed, the ideal biographer is so important in Thayer's scheme of things that though he is aware that "fashion in modern biography does not approve the too frequent intrusion of the biographer himself, or his opinions" and though he thinks himself that "strictly speaking . . . we ought to have as little as possible of the personality of the biographer intruded into his work," he not only tolerates but enjoys the intrusion of the biographer so long as it does not wrong the truth (pp. 63, 76).

EDWARD COOK

The role of the biographer is one of the chief concerns of Sir Edward Cook's discursive essay, "The Art of Biography." Cook had published a two-volume life of Ruskin in 1911; his two-volume life of Florence Nightingale (1913) had been praised by Strachey in an extraordinary note after the preface of *Eminent Victorians* as "an honourable exception to the current commodity"; his essay, however, is a sociable excursion, read to the New College Essay Society at Oxford in March 1914, and printed a month later in the *National Review*.[29] Cook insists that biography is an art, but he leans heavily on Sir Sidney Lee. He asks what the conditions and laws of biography are, and he arranges his answers under the catagories of length, relevance of material, selection, arrangement, the attitude of the biographer, and the proper subject. In the main, his comments are predictable in the light of Lee's principles.

"Length or shortness in biography must obviously be relative," depending on the importance of the subject, the quantity of appropriate material, and the design of the book as a work of art (p. 270). Cook has little use for life-and-times or somebody-and-his-circle biography. He praises Lee for rejecting the undue emphasis on ancestry advocated by students of heredity and genetics, and he says that it is the essential duty of the biographer to focus on his subject. "Undue reticence" is as bad as "inconsiderate babbling." The biographer must be honest and generally sympathetic. "The first qualifications of a good subject are that the life of the man or woman should be really memorable, that there should be a marked personality behind the actions, that the character should be distinctive and interesting" (p.

278); here, Cook departs from Lee's preoccupation with subjects of magnitude to express his affection for some of the minor lives in the *DNB* and to approve Ruskin's sentiment (in his preface to Francesca Alexander's *The Story of Ida* [1883]) that there may be great value in the lives of people to whom the world has given little thought. "A second element in the goodness of biographical subject is the existence of material of self-expression clothed in attractive and intelligible language" (p. 279); Cook admits that there is merit in the rule that a biographer should not interpose between the reader and the subject, but he admits, too, that some of the best biographers have intruded freely and that subjects differ in their gifts of self-expression and in their candor. One senses that he is not entirely happy with Lee's idea that the biographer is an artful compiler, but his most interesting comments are almost buried in his bows to orthodoxy. Like Lee, he talks about "architectonic art" and the necessity for "proportion, order, convenience, lucidity and all the other branches of arrangement." He manages, however, to move far beyond Lee. He mentions the importance of a biographer's producing an ordered and coherent impression, and he would allow the biographer very considerable license: "In the case of a full and varied life, the severely chronological method, consistently applied throughout, is almost certainly the worst" (p. 276). Moreover, where a life has already been written, where most of the relevant facts are already known, he thinks that the grace and lucidity of the French "study" are to be preferred to another full-length life (p. 270).

WALDO H. DUNN

In 1916, there appeared a volume entitled *English Biography*;[30] the preface justly stated that "this is the first book in the English language devoted to a careful and somewhat exhaustive study of the subject." The author of this pioneering book, to which so many have owed so much, frequently without proper acknowledgment of their debt, was Waldo H. Dunn, a young professor of English language and literature at the College of Wooster, who did his research mainly at the University of Glasgow. Dunn was thoroughly aware of the roots and development of English biography; he had carefully studied the work of Stephen and Lee, but his sympathies were with Saintsbury and Gosse. His volume was one in the series called "The Channels of English Literature," and the channels were wide enough to hold not only biography but even history and philosophy. Its primary contribution is in its clear delineation of the major canon of English biography in the work of Walton, Johnson, Goldsmith, Boswell, Lockhart, Carlyle, and Froude. The rise and development of English autobiography are treated in separate chapters, and another chapter compares English biography (individual and collective works) and autobiography with the traditions in foreign literatures.

Dunn's history has an important place in the criticism of biography if only because it is a storehouse of opinions which have become commonplaces. He cites Bacon's words on the paucity and utility of biography (pp. 67–68), Sprat's strictures on the publication of private letters (p. 76), and Mason's decision to let Gray become his own biographer (pp. 108–10). He quotes Dryden's description of biography's descent into minute circumstances and trivial passages as Dryden points to Plutarch's defense of the value of the single word or the casual jest (pp. 77–79). He reproduces Addison's attack on Grub Street biographers (pp. 83–84) and Fielding's on writers of panegyric (pp. 100–102). Here is Johnson on the advantages of autobiography (pp. 154–55) and on the merit of a faithful narrative of the life of almost any man (p. 104), a sentiment echoed by Goldsmith (p. 106) and Carlyle (pp. 192, 226). Here is Boswell on the value of chronology, of conversation, of familiar anecdote, of accuracy of fact (pp. 115–17, 123), and Carlyle on the difference between composition and compilation (p. 163). In addition, Dunn cites less well-known opinions which put doctrine memorably: Sir James Stephen on the importance of design and unity of effect (pp. 159–60); Gladstone on the representation of personality, as in a drama, by imparting life and movement to a character (p. 170), and Professor A. E. Hancock on the attainment in biography of "the dramatic vitality of fiction" (p. 194); Leslie Stephen's sentiment that an autobiography "may be more valuable in proportion to the amount of misrepresentation which it contains" (p. 211) and Herbert Spencer's that some misrepresentation is inevitable because a biographer or autobiographer must omit the commonplaces of daily life in order to focus on what is striking and distinctive (p. 225). All these are quoted, but they are assessed by Dunn's own critical standards. When he cites Wordsworth's words that biography, though it differs in some essentials from fiction, is yet an art; that truth in biography is not to be sought without scruple, as in the sciences; that the private lives of men of letters are not to be laid open with the same disregard of reserve as are the lives of men of action (pp. 230–31); Dunn makes it clear that he thinks there is no substitute for truth in biography.

He announces unequivocally the standards by which he judges the products of biography. On three occasions he endorses Gosse's statement that the "true conception of biography" lies in "a faithful portrait of a soul in its adventures through life" (pp. 18, 80, 241–42). For him, a "true" biography is "the narrative, from birth to death, of one man's life in its outward manifestations and inward workings"; "an ideal biography would exhibit the external life of the subject, give a vivid picture of his character, and unfold the growth of his mind" (p. xiv); "pure" biography, in focusing on an individual, subordinates the exposition of general events, references to other persons, and critical discussions of a subject's work. Like Gosse and Lee, Dunn insists on the autonomy of biography from history (and also from ethics and science). He insists, too, that biography differs from autobiography in its "organic and artistic completeness." That is why he introduces separate chapters to show that autobiography moves from the recording of domestic and political events to analysis which is detailed and subjective. And, though he stresses the independence of biography and autobiography as genres, one of his main theses, constantly repeated, is that, after Boswell, biography becomes increasingly autobiographical in method (pp. 130, 156, 158, 233). Since Boswell represents, for Dunn, the supreme accomplishment in biography, since the *Life of Johnson* was in the forefront of his mind when he spoke of "true" and "ideal" and "pure" biography, he approves of the tendency to rely increasingly on the autobiographical method.

Dunn spends an entire chapter on "Problems and Tendencies of the Present," but he disappoints when he merely points out that there is no decline in the volume of biography, that redivival biography continues to flourish, that the line between biography and fiction has become increasingly shadowy, that there is a tendency to avoid panegyric and idealization. Nor is his commentary very telling when he discusses the problems of ordering a life chronologically or topically, of differentiating biography and history, of deciding on the amount of genealogical information and of correspondence, of determining proper length. He reveals, however, that he is infinitely more interested in the role of the biographer than he is in the subject of biography when he says, in delineating the increase of lives of comparatively insignificant and unknown people, that such lives demand the deepest insight and greatest artistic ability. His book abounds in references to artistic construction, style, unity of effect, point of view, and interpretation. If, he says, we think of literature "as necessarily founded upon imagination, as possessing those qualities of beauty of form and expression resulting in the power to inspire and elevate humanity" (p. 264), then biography is firmly within its bounds. When he speaks of the best lives written before Boswell, he says "All of them . . . bear the unmistakable stamp of personality," and he makes it clear that he means "the personality of the writer." "They are great literary productions because their authors possessed great literary ability" (p. 269).

In the last words of his last chapter, "English Biography as Literature," Dunn predicts that biography will be "more unified, more coherent, more selective, exhibiting more completely the qualities of concentration, brevity, and self-effacement; in short, it is destined to be, far more than it has been in the past, a work of art." His intrusion of the criterion of self-effacement here may seem difficult to reconcile with his stress on the role of the biographer and his artistry. His other criteria reinforce his pervasive belief that a biography can present only an aspect of the truth which reflects the particular point of view of the biographer. He had stated, for instance, "It is eternally true that a man is *persona*: he assumes different masks when observed by different people—masks produced, perhaps, by something in the vision of those who do the observing" (p. 176). It is likely that Dunn anticipates greater self-effacement in the biographer of the future because of his awareness that biography has become increasingly autobiographical in method, that the use of materials written by the subject of a biography demands of the biographer "less the skill of unbroken narrative, and more the skill of artistic construction, of selection and rejection, of judgment and taste" (p. 270). The additional self-effacement is, then, related to the kinds of material he expects future biographers to use; it changes the kind of artistry demanded of the biographer, but it does not diminish Dunn's overriding emphasis on his role and his artistry.

LYTTON STRACHEY

When we think of the biographer's role and of his artistry, we think inevitably of Lytton Strachey. The Preface to *Eminent Victorians*, it has often been thought, provided the kind of revolutionary manifesto for biography that Wordsworth's Preface to *Lyrical Ballads* had provided for poetry. But the ideas in Strachey's Preface are neither startling nor new. The impact of *Eminent Victorians* on biography is not in its Preface but in its four short lives. In the first of the two paragraphs in the Preface, Strachey speaks of himself as historian, and his statements are hardly so provocative as those he had made a decade earlier. When he had reviewed Guglielmo Ferrero's *The Greatness and Decline of Rome* for the *Spectator* of January 2, 1909, he proclaimed that "the first duty of a great historian is to be an artist" and that "the function of art in history is something much more profound than mere decoration."[31] He insisted that "uninterpreted truth is as useless as buried gold; and art is the great interpreter." The crowning glory of the greatest history, he said, is that "it brings us into communion with an immense intelligence, and it achieves this result through the power of art": "every history worthy of the name is, in its own way, as personal as poetry, and its value ultimately depends upon the force and the quality of the character behind it." These ideas lie behind what Strachey says of himself as historian in the Preface, but he does not express them with this force: the Preface states that the historian "will shoot a sudden, revealing searchlight into obscure recesses, hitherto undivined"; the review had described him as "lighting up the dark places with the torch of the imagination." If anything in the first paragraph piqued the interest of its readers, it would have been Strachey's cavalier attitude toward logic. He speaks of rowing out over the great ocean of material available to the historian of the Victorian age and of lowering a little bucket here and there to bring up a "characteristic" specimen to be examined with careful curiosity. He equates random selection with what is characteristic rather too facilely, and then he reveals that his choice of subjects was not random but that it was determined haphazardly "by the simple motives of convenience and of art." How seriously could readers take a historian who casually said, "I have sought to examine and elucidate certain fragments of the truth which took my fancy and lay to my hand"?

When, in his second paragraph, Strachey speaks of himself as biographer, there is, again, little revolutionary in his statements that "human beings are too important to be treated as mere symptoms of the past" and that "they have a value which is independent of any temporal process—which is eternal and must be felt for its own sake." To be sure, he calls biography an art, but Stephen, Saintsbury, and Lee had, at the least, made bows in that direction; still, he does express his belief even more firmly than Gosse had: in England "the most delicate and humane of all the branches of the art of writing has been relegated to the journeymen of letters; we do not reflect that it is perhaps as difficult to write a good life as to live one." When Strachey says that the biographer's business is "to lay bare the facts of the case, as he understands them"; when he says, "That is what I have aimed at in this book—to lay bare the facts of some cases, as I understand them, dispassionately, impartially, and without ulterior intentions"; his sentiments are no different from Lee's demands that a biographer exercise "honest independence of judgment" and the kind of perspective that allows "detached and unfettered thought" to weigh ascertainable facts.

There is, then, little in the Preface that prepares readers for the pages that follow. They would merely have nodded in agreement at Strachey's opinion that England had never had "a great biographical tradition": "we have had no Fontenelles and Condorcets, with their incomparable *éloges*, compressing into a few shining pages the manifold existences of men." Strachey may have envisioned himself as emulating Fontenelle and Condorcet even as he may have considered himself dispassionate, impartial, and without ulterior intentions. But in his *Landmarks in French Literature* (1912), he had used only a couple of sentences to mention Fontenelle and Condorcet. He had, however, devoted seven appreciative pages to the Duc de Saint-Simon, and his comments provide a more candid and instructive preface to *Eminent Victorians* than his own Preface. Saint-Simon, he says, had "an incredibly passionate temperament combined with an unparalleled power of observation" (p. 149). Not only did he present the details of his subjects' physical appearance and the "more recondite" effects of their manner and their bearing, but he expended his most lavish care upon "the inward creature," upon "the soul that sits behind the eyelids, upon the purpose and the passion that linger in a gesture or betray themselves in a word" (pp. 150–51). There can be no doubt that "his hatreds exceeded his loves, and that, in his character-drawing, he was, as it were, more at home when he detested. Then the victim is indeed dissected with a loving hand; . . . then disgust, horror, pity, and ridicule finish the work which scorn and indignation had begun." His portraits never sink to the level of caricatures, for "his most malevolent exaggerations are yet so realistic that they carry conviction" (p. 151). He never forgot "to commit the last insult, and to breathe into their nostrils the fatal breath of life" (p. 152). Strachey does not mention Saint-Simon in the Preface to *Eminent Victorians*. When, however, in 1922, in rejecting an invitation from the Royal Society of Literature to become a member of its Academic Committee, he asked Edmund Gosse, himself on the Committee, to express his appreciation of the compliment paid him and to explain why he thought he would feel out of place, it is not surprising that he identified with Saint-Simon: "Perhaps it is regrettable, but the fact remains that, as Saint-Simon said of himself: 'Je ne suis pas un sujet académique.' "[32]

Despite the importance which the focus of the *DNB* attached to the subject of a biography, by 1920 there is very considerable stress on the artistry of the biographer. Stephen and Lee had left some room for it. Although Saintsbury was concerned in his 1892 article with biographies which copiously quoted autobiographic material, his interest was in what the biographer did with his material and, moreover, he stated that biography in which the material had passed through the alembic of the biographer was, artistically, most nearly perfect. Despite Cook's broad reliance on Lee, he seems, finally, interested in the design of a biography as a work of art. Dunn anticipates, to be sure, increasing self-effacement on the part of the biographer when he envisions increasing dependence on autobiographic material, but he constantly emphasizes the primary importance of the biographer's artistry. It is Thayer, not Strachey, who insists that the biographer is four times as important as his subject, but Strachey's achievement in *Eminent Victorians* supports Thayer's assertion.

By 1920, too, there is general exception to Lee's insistence upon the primary importance of a subject's achievement, his opinion that "the life of a nonentity or a mediocrity, however skilfully contrived, conflicts with primary biographic principles," his interest in chronicle rather than in character. The demands of the *DNB* had placed Lee in opposition to Johnson, Goldsmith, Carlyle, Ruskin; biography was, for him, essentially the re-creation of deeds, the animation of dead bones. In 1920, Thayer still insists that the first aim of biography is to tell a story "as nearly as possible as the actors or hero underwent it"; in a memorable sentence, he defines the chore of the biographer as that of finding means "through the art of literature to produce an adequate simulation of lifelikeness." But Thayer also believes that the essential subject of the biographer is "the soul of man." Despite his distrust of Freud, his dislike of the simplifications of clinical psychology, Thayer holds that the evolution of biography has been "from the outward to the inward," toward preoccupation with the motive behind the deed. He may not have cared for Gosse's phrase of 1901 which made "the psychology of the individual" central to biography, but he probably approved of the alternative

Gosse offered in 1910, "the faithful portrait of a soul in its adventures through life." Dunn, too, approves of Gosse's emphasis on character, and his general approbation of the use of autobiographic material stems from its capacity to reveal the inner man. Even Cook emphasizes the importance of "a marked personality behind the actions," and his affection for some of the minor lives in the *DNB*, his feeling that there may be great value in the lives of people to whom the world has given little thought, his advocacy in some circumstances of the French study show that his interest is in the faithful portrait of a soul rather than in action which is serious, complete, and of a certain magnitude. Strachey's Victorians were eminent, and the pragmatism and rationalism suggested by his aim to "lay bare the facts of some cases" does not seem to leave much room for soul. But he is as preoccupied with the souls of his subjects as they themselves were. "In the depths of Gordon's soul," he says, "there were intertwining contradictions," and he sought to explore, not only in General Gordon's soul, but in the souls of Cardinal Manning, Florence Nightingale, and Thomas Arnold, the "intricate recesses where egoism and renunciation melted into one another, where the flesh lost itself in the spirit, and the spirit in the flesh."

II

The Twenties

GAMALIEL BRADFORD

"What I have aimed at in this book is the portrait of a soul." The sentence is a pronouncement of preference for biography which is centered in character rather than in events, which is analytic rather than dramatic. It opens an appendix in which Gamaliel Bradford justifies the method of his *Lee the American* in 1912.[1] Bradford continues, "We live in an age of names and a new name has recently been invented—psychography. This means, I suppose, an art which is not psychology, because it deals with individuals, not general principles, and is not biography, because it swings clear of the formal sequence of chronological detail, and uses only those deeds and words and happenings that are spiritually significant." Still, Bradford proceeds immediately to place himself in a tradition of portrait painters which includes Plutarch, Tacitus, Clarendon, Saint-Simon, and, pre-eminently, Sainte-Beuve. The bulk of his essay considers obstacles to the impartiality of the psychographer: his own political, religious, and social partisanship;[2] the temptation to write for effect rather than for exactitude; his personal affection for his subject; the unreliability of documents and reports; the difficulty of penetrating the motive of action. At the end, Bradford commends "the art of character study" for its utility: "The knowledge of men and women, obscure, imperfect, incomplete as it necessarily is, profits us from cradle to the grave." He defends, moreover, a preoccupation with great men. For one thing, the speech and actions of "the man in the street" are not accessible. For another, the purpose of the examination of the great is not hero-worship but consolation and inspiration: "When it is shown that great personages, who left a name behind them, had only qualities like ours, often defects like ours, and that they made their greatness perhaps by a happy balance of qualities or by an extreme development of some particular quality, perhaps even a little by the kindliness of fortune, it seems to me that we should be led to emphasize rather what we may be than what they were not."

Here and elsewhere Bradford works hard to differentiate psychography and biography. For him, psychography is a separate genre, a more worthy one, rendered distinct by its stress on interiority and spirituality and by its attempt to get at the quintessence of a "soul" as it frees itself from chronology and events. But his aims coincided with what others were demanding above all else in the writing of biography, and they thought his distinction supererogatory. In deference to such critics as Bliss Perry and Thayer, Bradford himself stopped using the word "psychography" for a while.[3] His most specific description of the genre is in an essay entitled "Psychography"; this was the introductory essay in his book *A Naturalist of Souls* (1917),[4] which has an epigraph from Sainte-Beuve: "J'analyse, j'herborise, je suis un naturaliste des esprits." Here Bradford admits that he first used the word "psychography" to attract the attention of the public and he says that he coined it before discovering that Saintsbury had used it a few years earlier.[5] A psychograph differs from a portrait in seeking to extract what is essential, permanent, and vitally characteristic: "The psychographer endeavours to grasp as many particular moments as he can and to give his reader not one but the enduring sum total of them all." Psychography differs from biography in its selectivity and condensation; biography presents an elaborate sequence of dates, events, circumstances, many of which are required merely to make a narrative complete (pp. 3, 5). "Psychography," Bradford says, "is the condensed, essential, artistic presentation of character." He insists that "character" is distinct from "individuality." "Individuality . . . is a vast complex, based primarily upon the body, the material, physical organisation, and consisting of all the past history of that organisation, its name and all its actions and utterances in their sequence and concatenation with other circumstances and events." "Character . . . is the sum of qualities or generalised habits of action" (pp. 6–9). Bradford clarifies the purpose of the psychographer when he praises Sainte-Beuve for his insight into "the deep and hidden motives and passions of the soul," for his power of distinguishing and defining these, for his ability to select the significant and telling words and actions illustrative of his subject. Sainte-Beuve's sole limitation is his adherence to chronology when he might have found idiosyncratic structures, dictated, as it were, by Nature (pp. 16, 18–19).

In 1925, Bradford wrote an article, "The Art of Biography," for the *Saturday Review of Literature*;[6] it purports to be a review of a dozen biographies and autobiographies, but he does not mention most of them. Instead, he writes generally about biography and about the superiority of psychography. But, here, psychography is not so much a separate genre as a sub-genre of biography. Bradford holds that the object of biography is "the portrayal of character, the probing and the revelation of the subtle mystery and secret of personality," and he says that it is sometimes done by "an elaborate process of definite analysis of different qualities" and sometimes by a long series of narrative developments. The pitfalls of biography inhere mainly in its length (the use of insignificant detail, of excessive background, of the various connections and implications of the subject), and length, Bradford insists, is promoted by the use of the chronological method; adherence to chronology leads to amplifications and side issues "which really mean little for spiritual finality but are intimately suggested by the movement of the narrative." Psychography has the advantage of brevity; it cites not whole documents but only their most relevant parts, so that they will be quintessentially significant: "Always, you see, the writer endeavoring to do the reader's work."

In his essay "Psychography," Bradford had sought to show the concern of psychography for character rather than for individuality, and he had managed a kind of distinction between the words. In "The Art of Biography" he says that the sole object of the psychographer is "to present the personality of the character with which he is dealing." If "personality" is an offputting word here, the "which" emphasizes Bradford's conception of the abstraction characteristic of psychography, its business with essence or soul. In the end, however, psychography seems to be one of the two methods (the better one) by which biography attains its object.

Bradford's exploitation of psychography, his interest in souls rather than in people, was in part rationalization for his particular talent. A disappointed novelist, he felt that his novels had failed because of his "lack of contact with the surface of life, which is so necessary to give a novel or play the appearance of veracity."[7] He had qualms, occasionally, about the subjectivity of psychography[8] and about its lack of capacity to represent change or development in character,[9] but he was never so naive as were some of his critics about his method. H. L. Mencken might start a review of one of his books by saying, "This Bradford is the man who invented the formula of Lytton Strachey's 'Queen Victoria,' "[10] and Bradford might even thank him for his "generous" and "intelligent" words,[11] but, privately, he found it difficult to believe that Mencken had read *Queen Victoria*:

> Strachey's work and mine are totally different, so absurdly different that it is hard to see why it ever occurred to anyone to compare them. Doubtless it was because of the grossly superficial resemblance in cleverness and direct vivacity of writing and in the use of the quotations. . . . He employs the old biographical method in its extreme simplicity, tells his story with epic continuity and epic digression and allows his psychological comment to embroider itself upon the narrative where it best may, and almost, as it sometimes seems to me, where it will. My whole conception of psychography is utterly strange to him, the casting loose once and for all from the bonds of chronology and resorting to a method of composition which is purely psychological and aesthetic, with elaborate arrangement of contrast and climax, entirely disregarding the sequence of events.[12]

In over a hundred psychographs, Bradford plied his trade earnestly, soberly, highmindedly, as he probed character. If the critics equated psychography with biography, he himself never made it quite clear whether psychography was a kind like biography or a kind of biography. It was the quintessence of biography in its focus on character. On that Bradford and his critics agreed, and he took his support where he could find it.

JOSEPH COLLINS

One of Bradford's supporters was Joseph Collins, who in 1925 published *The Doctor Looks at Biography*, subtitled *Psychological Studies of Life and Letters*,[13] but Collins is eclectic in his sympathies. His first chapter, called "Biography," contains snippets of theory and history and a good deal of dogmatic comment on recent biographies, haphazardly thrown together. Like Bradford, he says that biographies are written chiefly from a desire to help others live successfully and that they are read for enlightenment about the soul and its motives (pp. 18, 20), but he is aware of other purposes also. Like Bradford, he thinks that biography is "not merely a chronological narrative of happenings. . . . : it is primarily a statement of the subject's thoughts and strifes, ambitions and realisations—and, as thoughts and ambitions condition action, behaviour and achievement, that which we call the 'life' of a man flows from them. Biography presents a picture of a mind, a soul, a heart" (p. 15). Still, the interpretative or subjective element in biography leads him to say that "whereas history is officially admitted to be true, biography, not dealing exclusively with facts, is a stepping stone between fiction and history" (p. 16). He calls Bradford the most prominent representative of the new psychological biography and praises him as a "sane, temperate, laboriously trained writer who has a profound regard for facts" (p. 30), but he considers Geoffrey Scott's *The Portrait of Zélide* both an elaboration of psychography and "the best fictional biography that has been published in English" (pp. 31–32).[14] He believes that "literary qualities" are indispensable in biography (p. 43),[15] but, for him, the greatest modern biographies are Strachey's *Queen Victoria* and Sidney Lee's *Life of Shakespeare*, and he praises Lee for his "tact, insight, erudition, industry and judgment," not his artistry (p. 26).

Although Collins places autobiography within the precincts of biography,[16] he spends a separate chapter on it and uses Lee's distinctions in *The Perspective of Biography* (without giving Lee credit): "the main difference between autobiography and biography . . . is that the former works from within outwards, while the latter works from without inwards; and the autobiographer is successful only in proportion to the self-absorption he reveals; his is a selfish and personal work. The biographer, on the other hand, is successful only in proportion to the self-effacement he shows" (p. 46). Autobiography demands veracity, sincerity, emotional and intellectual self-revelation, not style (pp. 43, 45), but Collins takes a paragraph to mention "that the present generation has produced three extraordinary autobiographies in the guise of fiction" (p. 50).[17] Collins has looked at too much biography and has thought too little about it. His diagnoses are interesting only because they reflect the confusion of the amateur expert of the 1920s as he put a premium on the interiority of biography.

JAMES C. JOHNSTON

The confusion was compounded in 1927 by a volume which aimed at clarification. James C. Johnston's *Biography: The Literature of Personality* is dedicated to Gamaliel Bradford, and Brad-

ford wrote for it an introductory essay in which he praises Professor
Johnston as "a pioneer in the elucidation of an immensely complicated and largely unexplored subject"; in addition, he suggests
that since biography introduces the element of humanity into all
phases of intellectual life, biographical studies may provide a new
core of instruction and inspiration for the old and vanished ideal
of liberal education.[18] Johnston has two main purposes in his book.
First, he wishes to enumerate, describe, and organize the forms
of biographical writing and their development. This he does in
his two longest chapters: one traces historically the development
of biography from *curriculum vitae* and amplified chronology to interpretative biography; another seeks to define and classify the
various genres and sub-genres. His concern with classification determines the organization of an appendix in which he lists by
categories a hundred representative biographical works and it leads
to the inclusion of a glossary of the terms applied to biographical
writing. Second, he wishes to show that biography is fundamentally
the literature of personality. In addition, he wishes to discuss some
aspects of biographical technique,[19] to propose ethical standards
with regard to the biographer's discretion, and to demonstrate
the value of biography for the proper interpretation of literary
works.

    At the heart of Johnston's book is his advocacy of Lee's
dictum that the aim of biography is the truthful transmission of
personality (pp. 18, 106), but it is clear that his sympathies are
with Gosse and, particularly, with Bradford. Like Thayer, he believes that the development of biography has been "from the
outer to the inner, from the acts and achievements to the character and personality of the subject—from what man has done to
what man is" (p. 86). For Johnston, "genuine biography, particularly that which we are sometimes inclined to term 'the new
biography,' " is "not merely the story of a life," but "*life-
writing*"; "the true province of biography, in all its varied
forms" has its center in "temperament, individuality, character, personality" (pp. 18–19). "Deeds spring from character";
"character values deal with those things that exhibit the individual's purpose and action"; "ideals, thoughts, aspirations,
all are but the expression of the spiritual"; the character of a
subject is eternal and inevitable (pp. 18, 95). Johnston refuses to
define *personality* precisely, but "whatever distinguishes a man—
such as his mode of thinking or acting, his habits and manners,
and, indeed, even his language and tastes—contributes to the sum
total of his personality" (p. 105). Personality is "intertwined

with what at times we call temperament, and becomes an expression of . . . character"; it is what a man "really is," not "what he affects to be—not mannerisms, eccentricities, oddities, peculiarities, and the like" (pp. 105–6).[20] "Picturing the souls of men in utter truthfulness," without extenuation and without malice,[21] is the highest aim of the biographer (p. 82). Johnston acknowledges Gamaliel Bradford's hesitancy to identify psychography and biography, but he insists that Bradford exemplifies the highest attainments of biography in the twentieth century in his stress on essential character rather than on mere incidents: "even above Strachey he is the exponent of all that is new in 'the new biography' " (p. 82).

The quintessence of biography for Johnston is, then, the revelation of personality, and this idea governs the inclusiveness of the forms which he discusses. One of the useful things in his book is its all-embracing catalogue of forms which reveal personality, but these, of course, include various kinds of autobiography as well as biographical kinds and everything from table talk to the short lyric. He defines such forms as letters, confessions, memoirs and diaries (memorials, recollections, reminiscences, anecdotes, chronicles, records, memories), biographical essays, literary portraits (sketches, vignettes, psychographs), travels, biographical poetry, but he admits that his species are often not clear-cut. Nor does he attempt a hierarchy of forms; when he finally uses the phrase "minor forms of biography," it is to make room for "personals," obituaries, epitaphs, caricatures, lampoons, and libels.

Johnston's credentials for the job he undertook are impressive: he knows the work of Stephen, Lee, Dunn, and Thayer; of Georg Misch, Hans Glagau, Anna Robeson Burr, and others. He announces that criticism must make a proper appraisal of the biographical product "in matters of ethics and art," not in terms of the intrinsic appeal of the subject of a life (pp. 10–11). But he is far more interested in personality than he is in literature or art. "The crises of life," he says, in a statement which explains the extent of his biographical province and the premium he puts on crude materials, "furnish us with many of the most dynamic literary records—those that represent the urge of genuine experience rather than the desire to hit upon an acceptable art form" (p. 254). The best standard for the appreciation of works of art, he says, and this is the burden of his last chapter, is "*the biographical circumstances out of which they grew, involving always the intent of the author*" (p. 255). To understand works of art, we need to know "the circumstances and conditions that brought the works into being" (p. 265). Johnston's standard is genetic, not aesthetic, and the demand for circumstances and conditions is one which he does not make of all biography, particularly of the inner biography which he prefers. He ends his book with the warning that without knowledge of the facts and conditions in the life of the author that form the background of his work, "reading is likely to be done in terms of art rather than of life" (pp. 265–66). His distrust of artistic criteria is also evident when he speaks of biography itself. He maintains that "the inescapable standard of judgment of a biography as a work of art must be: *Is this the man as he lived among his fellow-beings?* All questions, both ethical and artistic, must be subordinate to this one" (p. 134). A biography is not necessarily, then, a work of art; it may on occasion be judged as a work of art. If it is a kind of literature, it must still be judged by a criterion which is not aesthetic. Despite Johnston's concern for personality, which puts the same umbrella over biography and autobiography, he still pays homage to the "well-recognized canon of biography writing that the more completely the author submerges his own personality the more nearly he reaches the goal of the ideal biography of the objective type" (p. 177); only the writer of a biographical essay may with propriety project his personal views and temperamental outlook. Despite Johnston's stress on interiority and his panegyric for Bradford, he holds that the biographer is "a compiler and critic, and must under no circumstances conceive his office as that of a creator" (p. 223). Where literature is to be interpreted biographically, biography itself must have little taint of art. For all his talk of literature, personality, and soul, Johnston leaves as little room for art as does Sidney Lee.

CHARLES K. TRUEBLOOD

Johnston's book has 300 pages; in the same month that it appeared, *The Dial* published an article called "Biography" by Charles K. Trueblood with precisely Johnston's focus on the centrality of personality for biography, but its nine pages leave far more capacious room for art.[22] Trueblood praises Strachey for "the fine sharp unction of his rhetoric," "his manifest selection and design," "his dexterity in turning to dramatic account the biographic necessity of rendering his subject's world as a world of persons," "his patent zeal for personality," but he questions Strachey's suggestions that the biographer's first business is to preserve a becoming brevity and his second to maintain his own "freedom of spirit" (not to be complimentary, but "to lay bare the facts as he sees them"). These strictures are valuable, True-blood says, but they are hardly relevant for Boswell or for seriously artistic contemporaries like Amy Lowell in her *Keats* and Sandburg in his *Lincoln*. Length should be "appropriate to the complexity and significance of the personality to be depicted, and the variety and number of its contacts to the world." In Strachey's own work, freedom of spirit means an attitude of "mature and delicate malice," and it has enslaved his followers fully as much as uncon-ditional approval has enslaved writers of panegyric. Trueblood thinks that "literalist" biography, "historical, scholarly" bi-ography, which lays bare the facts "with eminently dispassionate thoroughness," more nearly approaches "freedom of spirit," and he praises Sir Leslie Stephen for his insistence on thorough scru-tiny and critical integration of facts and for his stress on historical context. He sees, however, the limitations of the literalist ap-proach: it emphasizes systematic scholarship and conceives of the biographer as "a species of behaviourist who is not to un-dertake the rococo mental interiors that used to be so ravishing in introspective fiction"; it does not go far "in imaginative collaboration with the reader." "A proper art of biography may go further," Trueblood says, and he mentions the nature of the contributions which psychology, criticism, poetry, and fiction bring to biography.

He hits "those Freudian engrossments which would turn biography into a clinic of aberrational psychology," but feels that a psychological approach may implement Plutarch's suggestion that a matter of small moment, an expression or a jest, can reveal character better than the most glorious exploits. He approves the use of psychology which is conscientious and sensible, and com-mends the work of Bradford. Still, Bradford's life of Darwin fails to achieve full interpretation because it neglects Darwin's con-tributions to biological thought. Biography must be an account of mind as well as of character and temperament. Though it is not the equivalent of criticism, it must avail itself of criticism in order to scrutinize the intellectual manifestations of person-ality. Sainte-Beuve is "the model and master-spirit of literary enquiry into mentality." But Trueblood does not think that critical acumen, scholarship, and the gift of style are as funda-mental to the biographer as "the capacity to be impressed by personality," sensitive insight into human beings. Like Thayer, he identifies the biographer with the poet in his dependence on "breadth of accomplishment in sympathy, upon poetic histrio-nism, upon acts of 'studious imagination,' upon conscience[23] and cultivated powers of impression." Biography is, for him, "a serious sort of prose fiction, both in its aspect of interpretation and in its aspect of realization":

> It cannot, more than fiction, grasp the essence of consciousness, the inimitable I of personality. What he ate, and what he did, and whom he saw—these things do not tell the tale. The secret of a man dies with him. Biographic interpretation, like the interpretation of fiction, is neither exhaustive nor exact; it can only speak "with a near aim." The acts and facts of biography are given, not chosen, as is the case with fiction; but this is a difference in the conditions of art, not in the fundamental processes of achievement. Ingenuity in devising plot and character is not the major feature of the novelist's artistic individuality. It is his depth and wealth of impressibility that matter.

Once the biographer has arrived at his interpretation, he must rely on images, realizations, not merely on discussion.[24] Though he may not neglect literalist scholarship, he must not hesitate to take "a reasonable interiority of view" if biography is to be the story of both circumstance and character.

Trueblood has quarrelled with what "freedom of spirit" meant to Strachey because he believes that biography must "find and keep the proper emotional tone": "if it fails in this it may be correct as information, but it is inept as art." Like Bradford, he feels that "nothing could be more characteristic of personality than its feeling-life, its temperament." He views life as the declaration of personality, the assertion of temperament. The biographer must communicate a lifelike sense of his subject's temperament "as the timbre of his thought and deeds." To do this, he must not only utilize the techniques of fiction, but he must also be endowed with bardic insight.

ALAN C. VALENTINE

Like Carl Van Doren,[25] Trueblood does not believe that it is the function of criticism to frame formulas for biography; it is to heighten consciousness of biography as a literary art.[26] He therefore welcomed Alan C. Valentine's recent little pamphlet, *Biography*,[27] though he did not agree with all its ideas.[28] Valentine's purpose is pedagogical: his 50-page handbook is one of the Oxford Reading Courses. He first discusses the nature of biography and then he focuses on fifteen volumes in the World's Classics

series; of these, ten are autobiographies; the biographical volumes
are Walton's *Lives*, Johnson's *Lives of the Poets*, Scott's *Lives of
the Novelists*, Carlyle's *Sterling*, and Mrs. Gaskell's *Life of Charlotte
Brontë* (1857). The requirements of Valentine's chore serve to
produce a curiously contradictory view. His general discussion is a
consensus of orthodox opinions, but the necessity to cope with
volumes which are belletristic and autobiographical pushes him,
almost, into views which conflict with orthodoxy.

Like many critics, Valentine asserts the independence of
biography: "A biography is first and always the story of a man or
woman. It has no secondary motive; its only reason for existence
is its attempt to re-create an individual who once lived. The final
test of any biography is its success in this aim—the vividness and
accuracy of the picture it presents" (p. 7). He echoes Sir Sidney
Lee on the relations of biography with history and science, on the
choice of a proper subject, on the matters of brevity, candor, and
sympathy (pp. 9–12). Like Thayer, he believes that "since the
best biography is the most lifelike one, the artist must, with a
certain studied transparency of style, show the man's will in reaction to events and environment" (p. 10). Like Dunn and
Thayer, he says that the intimate revelations of autobiography
have made biography more intimate and inward (p. 13). Like
Saintsbury, Dunn, and Thayer, he is interested in the relation
between the biographer and his subject, and his position is closest
to that of Thayer: he says of the biographer, "Unless his own
personality is one of rare charm, he must not let it obtrude into
his work, or the hero will be obscured by the shadow of the author"
(p. 12).

Valentine has Saintsbury's interest in practical criticism
and Dunn's literary predispositions, and these are probably responsible for his primary emphasis on the role of the biographer and
his relation to the life he writes. For Valentine, the *Lives of the
Poets* are not great biography: "they serve well as examples of
literary biography" (p. 19). He says that "critical biography at best
has its limitations. It is a hybrid, a compromise between biography
and literary criticism. The most successful biographies are those
in which what a man wrote is brought in only incidentally to throw
light upon his career and his character; the most successful pieces
of literary criticism are found when the writer is looking first at a
piece of literature, and only through that at the man who created
it. Only the most skilled of biographers and critics can score a hard-
won success in the difficult game of combining two arts" (p. 29).
Valentine believes that Johnson failed because his very independence made him full of strong prejudices, but he admits of the

Lives that "in one respect they are of unequalled interest, for they show a first class man of letters, a literary dictator, tracing the lives of leading English men of letters who have preceded him" (p. 19). It is clear that Valentine is more interested in Johnson's relation to the *Lives* than he is in the *Lives* themselves.

Again, he suggests that Scott's *Lives of the Novelists* are valuable for what they tell us of Scott, "for the sword of biography is double-edged, and it sometimes cuts him who wields it as it whirls through the air. Scott's *Lives of the Novelists* offer insight into Scott's own philosophy and theories of art" (p. 27). When he defends Gibbon's *Autobiography* as "substantially truthful" though its vividness is "a little histrionic in manner," his defense is a general one, with radical implications for biography as well as for autobiography: "After all, it is more important to know how life *looks* to a man than how life really *is*, for in so far as human beings are concerned, life *is* what it seems to us to be,—our only world comes to us through the interpretation of mind and senses" (p. 24). He makes the same point about Trelawney's *The Adventures of a Younger Son*, which, he admits, is full of excesses and inaccuracies: "If it is not an authentic history of events, it is an authentic revelation of a man; if it is not a truthful presentation of a series of facts, it is a wholly truthful reflection of a point of view" (p. 32).

Valentine, then, praises the self-revelation of the autobiographers, their *view* of themselves; his interest in the *Lives of the Novelists* is in Scott himself; he does not condone Johnson's "prejudices" because he has qualms about the intrusiveness of the biographer, but his interest in the *Lives* is clearly in what they reveal of Johnson. When he deals with Carlyle's *Sterling*, he says:

> No biographer ever sketched in more skilfully the background of his subject. Sometimes the reader suspects that this background is truer to Carlyle's interpretative eye than as to the accurate existing facts,—that a less interpretative biography would have made us more certain of the bare actualities. But this is straining at a gnat; the value of the work lies in Carlyle's brilliance and artistry of interpretation; the facts as he paints them are in the long run more valuable than the facts uncolored by his creative imagination. . . .
>
> This is another of these biographies written by a great man about one less great, where a part of the interest to the modern reader lies in the light it throws upon the biographer himself. (P. 33)

Despite his strictures about the biographer's not permitting his personality to obtrude, Valentine praises the *Sterling* for what it reveals of Carlyle. His introductory precepts about biography in general may have stressed accuracy and certified facts; his discussions of specific works stress not truth but the facts as seen by the biographer, his interpretation, his charm, his prejudices, his personality. Even Saintsbury, in his emphasis on the interplay between biographer and subject, had not gone this far. Despite Valentine's acceptance of Lee's doctrines, he goes almost as far as Thayer and Schwob in countering the canon of the biographer's self-effacement. It is almost as though the nature and the quality of the texts he had to consider moved him to a position far different from the one he was prepared to advocate.

HAROLD NICOLSON

Valentine had started with Lee's principles and perspectives, and, at the end, had found his main interest in the self-revelation of the biographer and in his point of view. In 1927, the year in which Valentine's pamphlet appeared and the year after Lee's death, Harold Nicolson denounced as nineteenth-century superstitions Lee's canons that the purpose of biography was commemorative, that its subject must be one of magnitude, and that character which does not translate itself into actions is mere phantasm for the biographer.[29] In Nicolson, Gosse finally found a not so young man of ambition and energy to deal with the history of biography in England. To be sure, Dunn would seem to have accomplished the job in 1916, but Dunn's book, for all its fine scholarship, was the work of a young and relatively unknown American professor; it has not, to my knowledge, ever been reprinted.[30] When Nicolson wrote in 1927, he could be sure of respectful and attentive readers: he had already written lives of Verlaine and Tennyson, *Byron: The Last Journey*, and a life of Swinburne for the English Men of Letters series. Earlier in 1927, what may be his best book, *Some People*, had been published, projecting him among the first rank of avant-garde biographers. He himself had prefaced the book with the note, "Many of the following sketches are purely imaginary. Such truths as they may contain are only half-truths"; the reviewer for the *Times Literary Supplement* shrewdly saw that the volume was "part fiction, part biography, but most of all, autobiography."[31] *The New York Herald Tribune Books* commissioned a front-page review by Virginia Woolf.[32] Nicolson had, to be sure, indicated in *The Development of English Biography* his indebt-

edness to Dunn, but he had covered his subject in 150 short pages
compared to Dunn's 300 longer ones. He had, moreover, written
the book for the Hogarth Lectures on Literature Series, and it
has the charm and liveliness of the spoken word. It was published
in the United States in 1928 and was reprinted by the Hogarth
Press in 1933, 1947, and 1959.

In Nicolson, Gosse found more than the historian he
sought for; he found a disciple. If Nicolson had only scorn for some
of Lee's principles of 1911, he had nothing but admiration for
Gosse's *Father and Son* (1907)[33] and for his article "Biography"
in the *Encyclopaedia Britannica* of 1910. Nicolson's story of the
development of English biography is, far more than Dunn's, history
with a thesis; he is much more interested in his thesis than he is
in his history, and his thesis is an elaboration and extension of
Gosse's. Like Gosse, he accepts the *Oxford English Dictionary* definition of biography as "the history of the lives of individual
men, as a branch of literature"; biography, then, must be "a
truthful record of an individual and composed as a work of art"
(p. 8). From Gosse, too, he takes the term "pure" biography,
and, like Gosse, he says that "impure" biography is caused by
the desire to compose a life to illustrate an extraneous theory or
conception. A second cause of impure biography is the desire to
celebrate the dead. A third is the "undue subjectivity" of the
writer. Nicolson admits that "to a certain extent a subjective
attitude is desirable and inevitable"; he admits that the best
English biography inevitably contains or conveys a sketch of the
biographer subsidiary to the central portrait; but he insists that
undue intrusion of the biographer's personality and predilections
leads to impurity (pp. 9–10). Nicolson does not go so far as Lee,
who had thought that the biographer's success was proportioned
to his self-suppression, but he has very much taken to heart what
Lee had to say about the biographer's indulgence in "personal
predilection," in giving "unchecked rein to his idiosyncrasies."
When Nicolson defines the essentials of "pure" biography, he is,
again, very close to Lee's doctrine. The primary essential is that
of historical truth, not merely the avoidance of misstatements,
not the suppression or evasion of "absolute truth," but "the
wider veracity of complete and accurate portraiture" (pp. 10–11).
The second essential is that a life shall be well constructed. Like
Lee, Nicolson primarily emphasizes the biographer's selection of
materials and the interpretation which he communicates by his
power to organize his materials. But, for Lee, the purpose of such
an "industriously elaborated composition" was to produce the
semblance of life and reality. For Nicolson, the ends of selection

and organization are more ambitious: not only do they produce in the reader the conviction that a creative mind has selected and composed facts in such a way as to give to them a convincing interpretation, but they will move beyond the arousing and allaying of curiosity and psychological interest to stimulate sympathy and pity, to evoke associations, to provide experience and an altered attitude of mind (pp. 12–13).

For Nicolson as for Gosse and Lee, the quintessence of biography is "a record of personality" (p. 12). Despite his constant reference to the "art" of biography, he approaches biography with an extraordinary faith in the value of scientific analysis. He assumes that the truths of psychology are as clearly codified and identifiable as the facts of physiology. "Were biography generally accepted as an important branch of psychology," he says, "the high standards inherent in that science would impose their own discipline and sanctions" (p. 12). Such standards would make clear the difference between biography and autobiography, memoirs, diaries, and confessions. To be sure, an autobiographer may have the intelligence to diagnose his own temperament with detachment, but biography necessitates "a scientific autopsy," "the sense of a rigorous post-mortem" (p. 15). If Nicolson's ideal biography seems to come close to case history, it is because he himself intrudes images like "the clinical arc-lamp" (p. 17).

Understandably, psychology replaces God in Nicolson's scheme of things, for "the less people believe in theology the more do they believe in human experience" (pp. 141–42): "In periods when the reading public believe in God and in the life after death, their interest centres on what they would call the eternal verities, their interest in mundane verities declines. At such periods biography becomes deductive, ethical, didactic, or merely superficial. In periods, however, of speculation, doubt, or scepticism the reading public becomes predominantly interested in human behaviour, and biography, in order to meet this interest, becomes inductive, critical, detached, and realistic" (pp. 138–39). The religious impulse is the archenemy of biography, for "a deep belief in a personal deity destroys all deep belief in the unconquerable personality of man." Nicolson insists that to draw a line between the material and the spiritual, between body and soul, is bad for biography: "there is no such dualism in man; there is personality, and that is all" (p. 111).

These criteria—the centrality of psychology, the bias against religion, the necessity of historical truth, the importance of facts ordered and shaped without undue authorial intrusion—dictate some, but not all, of Nicolson's assessments. He agrees with Gosse that Plutarch's ethical bias makes his interest in personality secondary and that Plutarch exercised an immense and fatal influence on English biography of the seventeenth century (pp. 28, 39). He calls Johnson the real founder of pure biography: not only did he first proclaim that biography was a distinct branch of creative literature, but he insisted on truth, on the minute details of daily life, on psychological insight, on composition that creates a sense of actuality (pp. 79, 81, 86). Johnson's religious convictions pose no problem to Nicolson; he insists that Johnson "laboured in doubt. His terror of death, his basic incredulity about life after death, gave him a deeply personal interest in mundane life, induced him to interest himself in the personal and the humane with an almost terrified intensity" (p. 80). For Nicolson, Boswell's great achievement lies in his perfecting the annotative and the analytical methods of biography and in his combining them by his great constructive force: he produced "a biographical formula in which the narrative could be fused with the pictorial, in which the pictorial in its turn could be rendered in a series of photographs so vividly, and above all so rapidly, projected as to convey an impression of continuity, of progression—in a word, of life" (pp. 87, 107). Still, Nicolson thinks that two-thirds of the effect of the *Life of Johnson* is due to "accidental circumstances" (p. 98). The first of these is what readers mistakenly consider Boswell's "charm"; Nicolson holds that Boswell was so acutely conscious of his faults that he deliberately set out to forestall criticism by lying down softly of his own accord; "his constant self-abasement flatters our self-esteem" (pp. 89, 91). The second is that he was fortunate in his choice of subject; Nicolson argues that several people wrote entertaining books about Johnson, and that Boswell did not write "entertainingly" about anything else (p. 98). The other third of the effect he is willing to attribute to the quality of Boswell's intelligence and to his literary gifts, but even here his praise of Boswell is undercut by his theoretical considerations. Boswell, he says, "possessed great mental vivacity, he possessed a remarkably independent intellect; he was above all passionately interested in life." He was neither fool nor genius, but, Nicolson says, "biography—and this is the important point—does not require genius; it requires only a peculiar form of talent," and Boswell had such a talent (p. 99). Nicolson spends several pages on Boswell's literary abilities, his pleasant style, his flair for dramatization, his remarkable talent for construction, his great literary tact, but at the same time he states that such literary gifts are only "secondary qualities" for a biographer (pp. 100–105).[34]

Nicolson is really far more comfortable with Lockhart than he is with Boswell. The criteria of constructive talent, dramatic instinct, and power of selection more readily explain Lockhart's achievement than Boswell's, and it is not surprising that Nicolson admits that he is sometimes inclined to consider Lockhart the greatest rather than the second greatest of all British biographers (pp. 117–24). Froude, too, ranks high among Nicolson's heroes, for his truthful representation of Carlyle, for the impression he gives of "absolute and convincing actuality"; he was, moreover, the first to introduce into English biography the element of satire, "the peculiar brand of sceptical detachment which we realise to be the main element in twentieth-century biography." Still, he must admit that Froude "was not an accurate writer," and he must justify Froude's truthfulness by arguing that "his inaccuracy, unlike the inaccuracy of Mrs Gaskell, is not essential" (pp. 129, 131, 134–35).

For Nicolson, the high points of twentieth-century biography are Gosse's *Father and Son* and Strachey's *Queen Victoria*. He praises Gosse's courage in recording the death struggle of Puritanism in its battle with science as a conflict of the utmost intensity between his own temperament and that of his father; he praises Gosse's originality in focusing on a slice of life, in producing "a clinical examination of states of mind over a detached and limited period"; and he praises Gosse's conscious artistry in writing with detachment and economy (pp. 145–47). Nicolson calls *Queen Victoria* an achievement which required the very highest gifts of intellect and imagination. He finds impressive Strachey's powers of selection and compression, his subordination of public events to the elucidation of personality, his ability to convey a convincing sense of scientific reality, his detachment, his poise, his apparent effortlessness (p. 149). But, he says, though Gosse and Strachey succeeded in producing first-class literature, they did not succeed in producing "pure" biography (p. 154). Each was faced with a body of material too enormous to be rendered as a whole; each had to rely on "some external aids to synthesis," some point of view rather than "ordinary arrangement." Gosse's biography is "impure" because he did not write a full-scale life but focused in detail on the segment important to him. Strachey's biography is "impure" because he limited himself to one aspect of the facts, which he proceeded to examine from the psychological point of view.

In his last chapter, Nicolson grapples with the relation of biography to science on the one hand and to literature on the other. The modern intelligent reader's interest is now, he says, only superficially scientific: he insists on nothing but the truth; before long he will insist on all the truth, on a vast amount of authentic material. He also insists on literary form, on a synthesis which is possible only when the biographer has a thesis, a motive, or a point of view (pp. 141–42). Nicolson believes that scientific interest in biography is hostile to literary interest and will in the long run destroy it (p. 154). When scientific interest insists on all the facts, no synthetic power, no genius for representation, will be able to keep pace. He thinks that scientific biography will become technical and specialized, and he envisions intricate studies grounded in medicine, heredity, sociology, economics, aesthetics, and philosophy (p. 155). When truth and individuality "reach their zenith and combine in the form of scientific psychology," he predicts, they put an end to "pure" biography as a branch of literature (pp. 157–58). The literary element will persist in biographies of satire, of hate, of sentiment, but, in general, literary biography will "wander off into the imaginative, leaving the strident streets of science for the open fields of fiction" (p. 155).

Nicolson says, quite rightly, that Gosse had in his *Encyclopaedia Britannica* article laid no stress on the literary element in biography. Though he is aware that Gosse called biography a branch of literature, though he considers *Father and Son* a work of "consummate literary art," "the most 'literary' biography in the English language," he would attribute to Gosse his own contention "that the essential element in biography is actuality, individuality; that the form of a biography is less important than its content" (pp. 143–44). In the last sentence of his book, Nicolson says that of the three elements in "pure" biography— truth, individuality, art—the literary element was always the least important. Still, he thinks there is a future for "impure" biography, and that "literature, by devoting itself to 'impure' or applied biography, may well discover a new scope, an unexplored method of conveying human experience" (p. 158).

In his review of Nicolson's book, Bonamy Dobrée stated that if we accept the premises, the argument is impeccable.[35] But, he pointed out, Nicolson begins with rather too rigid a definition of pure biography and tackles it from rather too sectarian a point of view. The fact is that in building on Gosse's pronouncements, Nicolson polarized "literature" and "psychology" as Gosse had never done. By instinct a man of letters, Nicolson compensated by imputing to science the omniscience, power, and disinterestedness he denied not only to God but to literary men. When selectivity and point of view are considered "impurities," we may, of course, question the purity even of Boswell and Lockhart. It seems never to have occurred to Nicolson that a medical case-history is selective and has a point of view, that, in his own terms, it is an "impure" approach toward a human being. His espousal and purification of Gosse's interests, his disavowal of Lee's doctrines that biography is commemorative, that it should be reserved for important people who have translated character into action, led him to minimize what he owed to Lee: the emphasis on historical truth, on constructive force, on the unobtrusiveness of the biographer. Still, it was these principles, coupled with a more intense interest in personality for its own sake than Lee had, which led him to the idealism of his own critical system. That system, finally, denigrates the role of literary art in biography in a way which Gosse never intended. Fortunately, in the assessments of particular biographies, Nicolson's taste and tact as a man of letters undercut the literal and rigorous application of his critical precepts.

VIRGINIA WOOLF

Nicolson's use of the future when he wrote that "literary biography will . . . wander off into the imaginative, leaving the strident streets of science for the open fields of fiction" and that "literature, by devoting itself to 'impure' or applied biography, may well discover a new scope, an unexplored method of conveying human experience" was in part modesty and in part irony. Almost certainly he thought that he had already pointed the way in *Some People*. It was this book, not *The Development of English Biography*, which was the subject of Virginia Woolf's review-essay, "The New Biography."[36]

Mrs. Woolf had finished rewriting *To the Lighthouse* in January 1927, and she was casting about for her next subject: "I keep opening the lid and looking into my mind to see whether some slow fish isn't rising there—some new book. No: nothing at the moment."[37] The fish that finally emerged was the result of her preoccupation with the theory, practice, and criticism of fiction and biography, and her awareness of what her friends were writing in 1927. Even as she was projecting a book about fiction,[38] she knew that E. M. Forster was that spring to deliver the Clark lectures at Cambridge on aspects of the novel. She was present when, in June, her intimate friend Victoria Sackville-West received the Hawthornden Prize for her poem *The Land*,[39] and she was constantly in touch with her and her husband, Harold Nicolson.[40] On September 3, she wrote Lytton Strachey, who was work-

ing at *Elizabeth and Essex*, that Forster was to visit her the following week, and she complained, as she had before, "If only every
good spectacled Don and schoolgirl did not think themselves Lytton Strachey and proceed to put it into practice! . . . For God's
sake, come out with Betsy and make them all skip. It's better in
French: I have just read Disraeli by Maurois."[41] In a letter of
October 9 to Victoria Sackville-West, she referred to a statement
she had made earlier, "it sprung upon me how I could revolutionise
biography in a night," and she described, too, what she had done
the day before: "Fiction, or some title to that effect. I couldn't
screw a word from me; and at last dropped my head in my hands:
dipped my pen in the ink, and wrote these words, as if automatically, on a clean sheet: *Orlando: A Biography*. No sooner had I done
this than my body was flooded with rapture and my brain with
ideas."[42]

     Just a few days before, she had finished the last of four
reviews which were published in October as front-page articles in
the *New York Herald Tribune Books*. The second, "Is Fiction an
Art?" was on Forster's *Aspects of the Novel*;[43] the last on *Some
People*. Both are genial reviews of friends' books, but she makes
clear her reservations about both. She castigates Forster and
other critics for too narrow and restrictive a view of the novel,
and she thinks that Nicolson has endangered the values of biography by taking too much freedom. Forster had paid her the
compliment, at the beginning of his book, of considering her in
the company of Richardson and Henry James, Dickens and Wells,
but he had placed her with Sterne among the "fantasists";
"They start with a little object, take a flutter from it, and settle
on it again. They combine a humorous appreciation of the muddle
of life with a keen sense of its beauty. There is even the same
tone in their voices—a rather deliberate bewilderment, an announcement to all and sundry that they do not know where they
are going."[44] In return, she puts Forster among the critics of
the novel who tie it too closely to something they call "life"
instead of taking an aesthetic view of fiction. She censures Forster for saying almost nothing about the medium in which a novelist works, for not concerning himself with words, pattern, beauty.
But she is equally censorious of his view of life with its emphasis
on simplistic vitality, reality, "humanity"; for her, his definition
of life is too arbitrary and it requires expansion. Forster had said
in his introductory chapter that no English novelist had given
so complete a picture of man's life, both its domestic and heroic
side, as Tolstoi; none had explored man's soul so deeply as Dostoevski; none had analyzed the modern consciousness so success-

fully as Proust (p. 16). Mrs. Woolf agrees, but blames the critics in part: "If the English critic were less domestic, less assiduous to protect the rights of what it pleases him to call life, the novelist might be bolder too. He might cut adrift from the eternal tea-table and the plausible and preposterous formulas which are supposed to represent the whole of our human adventure.[45] But then the story might wobble; the plot might crumble; ruin might seize upon the characters. The novel, in short, might become a work of art."

Though Mrs. Woolf felt that the art of the novel had been impeded because novelists stuck too closely to "what Morgan calls 'life,' "[46] she thought that biography since Boswell had broadened its conception of life. Her concern in "The New Biography" is to describe biography's increasing intrusion into the inner life that she considers to be the province of the novel and to draw some lines between the two genres. She starts by citing Lee's dictum that the aim of biography is "the truthful transmission of personality" and says that it neatly splits the whole problem of biography today into two parts: "On the one hand there is truth; on the other there is personality. And if we think of truth as something of granite-like solidity and of personality as something of rainbow-like intangibility and reflect that the aim of biography is to weld these two into one seamless whole, we shall admit that the problem is a stiff one." The truth which biography demands is, she says, "truth in its hardest, most obdurate form; it is truth as truth is to be found in the British Museum; it is truth out of which all vapor of falsehood has been pressed by the weight of research." The value of truth of this kind is, for her, unsurpassed: "there is a virtue in truth; it has an almost mystic power. Like radium, it seems able to give off forever and ever grains of energy, atoms of light. It stimulates the mind as no fiction, however artful or highly colored, can stimulate it."[47]

Still, Mrs. Woolf finds Lee's *Shakespeare* dull and his *Edward VII* unreadable despite his research, for he failed to choose those truths which transmit personality. For personality to shine through, she says, "facts must be manipulated; some must be brightened; others shaded; yet, in the process, they must never lose their integrity." The older biographer obeyed these precepts by assuming that the true life of a subject "shows itself in action which is evident rather than in that inner life of thought and emotion which meanders darkly and obscurely through the hidden channels of the soul." After Boswell, it was impossible to maintain that life consists only in actions or in works; "it consists in personality." The Victorians sought to express both the active outer life and the inner life of thought and emotion, but their "idea of goodness" distorted personality and their undiscriminating use of innumerable words and documents served only to bury it. In the twentieth century, biographers like Strachey and Maurois altered not only the size of biographies, but, more important, they changed, too, the point of view of the biographer, his relation to his subject. The biographer is no longer "the serious and sympathetic companion." He is an equal who "preserves his freedom and his right to independent judgment": "He chooses; he synthesizes; in short, he has ceased to be the chronicler; he has become an artist."

Some People becomes an illustration of the new attitude toward biography, and Mrs. Woolf holds that Nicolson moves beyond Strachey in devising "a method of writing about people and about himself as though they were at once real and imaginary. He has succeeded remarkably, if not entirely, in making the best of both worlds. 'Some People' is not fiction because it has the substance, the reality of truth. It is not biography because it has the freedom, the artistry of fiction." She praises Nicolson for his point of view, his refusal to accept pat philosophic or moral standards, and for the brevity that he achieves by his conviction "that the man himself, the pith and essence of his character, shows itself to the observant eye in the tone of a voice, the turn of a head, some little phrase or anecdote." There are times, she says, when Nicolson "does not cumber himself with a single fact" about his subjects: "He waits till they have said or done something characteristic, and then he pounces on it with glee." When she asks what territory Nicolson has won for the art of biography, she says that he has proved "that one can use many of the devices of fiction in dealing with real life. He has shown that a little fiction mixed with fact can be made to transmit personality very effectively."

Mrs. Woolf concludes, however, by insisting that "truth of fact and truth of fiction are incompatible." Still, the new biographer is tempted to combine them, "for it would seem that the life which is increasingly real to us is the fictitious life; it dwells in the personality rather than in the act. . . . Thus, the biographer's imagination is always being stimulated to use the novelist's art of arrangement, suggestion, dramatic effect to expound the private life. Yet if he carries the use of fiction too far, so that he disregards the truth, or can only introduce it with incongruity, he loses both worlds; he has neither the freedom of fiction nor the substance of fact." She appeals to the reader to consider a few years of his own life, how Morley would have expounded them and Lee documented them, "how strangely all that has been most real in them would have slipped through their fingers." No biographer has yet been subtle and bold enough "to present that queer amalgamation of dream and reality, that perpetual marriage of granite and rainbow." But Nicolson has hit upon a possible direction.

Mrs. Woolf obviously admires Nicolson's use of the *devices* of fiction to illuminate personality; she obviously thinks, too, that the introduction of fictitious *materials* into biography can only be destructive of the truth which is based on fact. She says of *Some People*, "when we find people whom we know to be real like Lord Oxford or Lady Colefax, mingling with Miss Plimsoll and Marstock, whose reality we doubt, the one casts suspicion upon the other." Despite the efficacy and supremacy of truth based on fact, despite the hardness and obduracy of truth founded on re-search, she still maintains, then, that the granite-like quality of such truth can be made suspect. Nor do the facts speak for them-selves: they must be manipulated to reveal personality, and though manipulation may falsify them, it need not do so. Still, for her, personality is not best revealed in actions based on fact but in the inner life of thought and emotion. Though Mrs. Woolf suggests that the inner life is reconstructed from "countless documents," she feels that the biographer of the inner life is not working in the same realm of fact as the biographer who describes a subject's actions. So convinced is she that the proper repre-sentation of the inner life is essentially work for a novelist that at one point she calls this kind of life "the fictitious life."

This inner life does not have the solidity, the concrete-ness, of the life which is expressed in action; Mrs. Woolf stresses its intangibility, its rainbow-like quality. In doing so, she wants principally to indicate that it is harder for a writer to get at. But when she pits truth against personality, granite against rainbow, she *seems* to say that rainbow is not based on fact, that it is not true. And when she equates rainbow with "dream" and granite with "reality," she comes perilously close to saying that the inner life is not "real." Her own fiction and her disapproval of what Forster calls "life" make it clear that the inner life of thought and emotion is for her as real, as important, as vital a part of life as is "the world of brick and pavement; of birth, marriage, and death," and even as she thinks that this is the proper territory for a novelist to exploit, so she thinks a good biographer must exploit it. She knew, too, that the critics of fiction believed that "life" and "reality" resided in the works of Dickens and of Wells, not in hers, and she was aware that the risks and dangers for the biographer—who had to rely on fact at the same time that he wished to reveal the inner life—were, if anything, greater than they were for the novelist.[48]

ANDRÉ MAUROIS

Mrs. Woolf's "The New Biography," Forster's *Aspects of the Novel*, and Nicolson's *The Development of English Biography* provided the springboard for André Maurois's *Aspects of Biography*. Invited to give the Clark lectures at Trinity College, Cambridge, in May 1928, the author of *Ariel* (1923) and *Disraeli* (1927) felt liberated from the stipulation that he concern himself with a period or with periods of English literature by Forster's decision the year before to focus on aspects and by the appearance of Nicolson's history. He could, then, indulge his propensity to see biography not merely as a historical problem but as "an ethical problem and an aesthetic problem." In doing so, he followed his own advice to a young Frenchman leaving for England—"When you want to convince them, don't reason too clearly. . . . they rather distrust an argument that is too well reasoned"[49]—and the lectures, full of sparkling quotations and of personal confidences, are charming and deferential, if not too well reasoned. They were first published in France, and then in England and in the United States in 1929.[50]

Maurois is familiar with the work of Lee, Gosse, Schwob, Dunn, Thayer, Trueblood, and others, but most of the questions he is mainly interested in had recently been considered by Mrs. Woolf and Nicolson. Like them, he finds modern biography characterized by what he calls "the courageous search for truth" (p. 24), by free inquiry, not by deliberately imposed moral restraint and by preconceived ideas (pp. 12–13). Like them, he finds in modern biography an awareness of the complexity and mobility of human beings (p. 24).[51] Like Nicolson, he feels that modern man seeks to find in biography "brothers who share his troubles" (p. 31), that he "is grateful to those more human biographies for showing him that even the hero is a divided being," and he quotes with approval Nicolson's statement that "biography is the preoccupation and solace not of certainty, but of doubt." His main question is also that of Nicolson and Mrs. Woolf: "the search for historical truth is the work of the scholar; the search for the expression of a personality is rather the work of the artist; can the two things be done together?" (p. 32). He cites Nicolson's opinion that they cannot, that in the struggle between content and form, form will have to go, and he indicates Mrs. Woolf's

qualms by quoting the first paragraph and a half of her essay. It is
his own hope to show that art and science can be reconciled: "A
scientific book, perfectly constructed, is a work of art. A beautiful
portrait is at once a portrait resembling its subject and an artistic
transference of reality. It is perfectly accurate to say that truth
has the solidity of stone and that personality has the lightness
of a rainbow; but Rodin and Greek sculptors before him have at
times been able to infuse into marble the elusive curves and the
changing lights of human flesh" (p. 34).

In his second chapter, "Biography as a Work of Art,"
Maurois sets forth a theory of art and undertakes to show that
biography may adhere to his criteria for art. He says that the two
qualities essential for all aesthetic activity are "an ethical neutrality and a reconstruction of nature by man" (p. 39). For him,
the primary requisite for art is detachment, contemplation un-
colored by emotion. Building, perhaps, on Nicolson's statement
that the art of biography is intellectual and not emotional, that
biography is doomed with the intrusion of "any emotion (such as
reverence, affection, ethical desires, religious belief)," Maurois
insists that "at the moment at which we ourselves display emotion, we are incapable of observation. Our emotions are too strong
and leave no faculty of aesthetic criticism at our disposal" (p.
36). The second requisite is that art order and simplify life, that
it replace "a divine and inexhaustible multiplicity" with "a
measurable and human simplicity" (p. 39). Biography, Maurois contends, may meet these requisites. Real characters and known
events have, after all, been the subjects of Greek and Shakespearean tragedy, and, indeed, known events and dénouements
induce that "peace of mind" which is favorable to the proper
aesthetic attitude (p. 41). Moreover, when the biographer selects
the essential qualities in his subject he is very precisely performing
the artist's function. To be sure, the choice of a proper subject
is important, as it is in all art: some lives have a "natural
beauty" or a "mysterious symmetry" (p. 45). Lee's dictum that
the subject should be of a certain magnitude is advantageous not
only because such a subject generally insures the availability of
information but also because a man who has played an important
part in history or in art finds himself modeled by the function he
has to perform and his personality acquires a unity which is not
wholly artificial (pp. 48–49).

Maurois proceeds to set down a few of the rules by which a
biographer can "get somewhere near the art of the novelist"
and at the same time maintain a scrupulous respect for scientific
truth (p. 50). He advocates the use of chronological order, since it

best demonstrates a subject's development and change; he prefers
to see everything through the eyes of his hero; he argues at great
length for selection, and with liberal citation of Schwob and Johnson, for the use of revealing details. Only then does he manage,
rather awkwardly, to return to his aesthetic assumptions. He hits
Johnson's explicit moral judgments of Milton; insists that, like
the novelist, the biographer must "expose" and not "impose"
(p. 63); and announces once more that "objectivity and detachment are the supreme aesthetic virtues." And, in a huddled and
simplistic fashion, he would show that biography can have a "poetic" value, that it can transmute nature into some beautiful
form by the biographer's representation of the essential "mo-
tifs" of a life.

  Maurois's assumptions about the nature of art and the
place of biography within the realm of art as he defines it are not
wholly persuasive. His argument that biography is not a science is
far more telling, for the pragmatic biographer replaces the theo-
retician. He chooses Nicolson as his antagonist, and his argument
is a refutation of Nicolson's thesis that the future of biography
lies in its increasing reliance on scientific truth, but he also has
in mind Virginia Woolf's idea about truth as it is to be found in
the British Museum. He allies himself with Froude, who approved
Tallyrand's dictum that "there is nothing which can so easily
be arranged as facts" (p. 68), and he examines in detail the kinds
of material available for the discovery of truth. He emphasizes
the difficulty of properly interpreting personal documents, such as
letters and diaries, says that they are valuable "only in so far as
they are put face to face with each other and with the complete
picture of the man's personality," and insists that this process
is "the work of the artist rather than of the scholar" (p. 77),
that it "depends upon a sense of artistic perception much more
than upon scientific method" (p. 75). He considers at some length
the problems involved in interpreting fiction autobiographically,
in reading a man out of his works. Not only does he say that a
character in a novel may reflect only a very tiny fragment of the
author's ego (or his observation of others than himself), but also
that the mere description of an emotion in a character may be
enough to prevent the author from feeling it again. Very tentatively, then, Maurois puts forward an expressive, a therapeutic
function of art rather different from his assumptions to this time,
and he speculates that it may be true to say that "Meredith
pilloried the egoist because he was himself an egoist, and Meredith
ceased to be an egoist because he had written *The Egoist*" (p. 80).
He suggests that an author's work may be an attempt to gain for

himself in an imagined world what life has denied him, says that public pressure may force an author into the mold of a character he has created, and feels that the identification of an author with his work is more likely to be valid when each of his works contains the same character under a different name or when the author is a young man (pp. 82-83). He considers, finally, the utility of the memoirs of contemporaries of a subject, and he says, "finding no one of the elements of a biographical truth to be strictly scientific, we are compelled to have recourse to a kind of psychological imaginativeness, and, in many instances, the truth about a particular event is impossible to determine" (p. 85). Biography, he insists, moreover, cannot be treated like physics or chemistry, for it deals with the individual and the instantaneous and they with experience which can be controlled, observed, repeated (p. 86). Even if scientific documentation of the sort Nicolson envisions were available, Maurois says, it would not contain "the truth about a man" (pp. 90–91).[52] He thinks, then, that it is dangerous and absurd to try to establish too close a parallel between "the exact sciences and the historical sciences": the truth about a life is totally different from that pursued by the chemist or the physicist (p. 92).[53] "It is a confused medley of actions, thoughts, and feelings, very often contradictory, yet possessing a certain unity which is, as it were, a sort of musical tone" (p. 91).[54] In order to produce "the sound of that individual and authentic note," a biographer must not only exercise care for the truths of fact as far as he can attain them but also for "that profounder truth which is poetic truth" (p. 92).

Thus far in his discussion of art and of biography as an art, Maurois's key terms have been ethical neutrality, detachment, objectivity, contemplation, intellect rather than feeling. He had casually introduced into his third chapter the notion of an expressive or therapeutic function of art, and this idea, "the most important aspect of the question" (p. 102), is the subject of his fourth and central chapter. "For the artist," he says, "the work of art is, before everything else, a deliverance." His accumulated emotions "swell within him and fill his soul almost to bursting-point; it is when he feels the urgent need of freeing himself that the work gushes out of him with an almost spontaneous force. Art is for him a means of expression" (p. 102).

Maurois argues "in passing" that "this subjectivity of emotion in no way hinders the work of art from being objective" (p. 103). By this he means that writers express their own feelings through the medium of their works without necessarily recording their own histories, that there is sometimes a wide gulf between

the fictitious subject and the real subject. He insists that biography, like other arts, can be a means of expression, that it can
have the benefit of passion within it. In the same way that a
novelist can attain self-expression "by quite indirect means and
through the medium of characters very far removed by circumstances from himself," so a biographer can attain the same power
of expression "through the medium of characters in actual life"
and still not endanger truth (pp. 104–5). Maurois's evidence is
personal, and he recounts the "secret need" in his own nature
which led to his "passionate" interest in Shelley[55] and in Disraeli. Such biography, he says, will be written "with more natural
emotion than other kinds . . . ; to a certain extent it will be
autobiography disguised as biography" (p. 111). He is aware that
since the life, emotions, and attitudes of the biographer and his
subject rarely coincide,[56] the biographer risks defacing historical
truth and opens himself to Nicolson's charge of "undue subjectivity" (p. 114). He maintains that history must be respected,
that the biographer has no right to invent or omit in order to
construct a hero according to his own needs and desires, even that
perfect congruence of author and hero occurs rarely,[57] but he maintains, too, that "in certain rare cases . . . the biographer may be
able to express some of his own feelings without misrepresenting
those of his hero" (p. 117) and that only by "the recollection
of our own passions" (p. 112) can we understand the feelings of
others. He states flatly that in every psychological truth there has
to be "an element of divination," that critical reasoning alone
will not lead to understanding. The method of self-identification
is dangerous, but "there is no other method": "We can understand
a fact of science by analysis and synthesis; we cannot understand
a human being by an exhaustive compilation of detail. . . . We get
our understanding by a coup d'état" (pp. 118–19).

Maurois then suggests that the reader of biography, like
the writer, seeks a means of expression. He says that "every work
of art, in so far as it arouses the emotions and thereby the desire
to act, touches upon morality" and that the moral influence of
biography (a morality which is individualistic, not social) is particularly strong because the reader believes in the truth of the
narrative and in the reality of the characters (p. 121). Still, he
says, the writer may only hint at moral judgment, for "as soon as
it is formulated, the reader is recalled to the sphere of ethics and
the sphere of aesthetics is lost to him" (p. 127).

Maurois's examination of biography as art, as science, and
as a means of expression has led him to a lively skepticism of the

possibility that one can know the truth about a man, if not to a positive denial, and in his last two chapters he asks whether this truth exists in autobiography or in the novel. He does not find it in autobiography, which is inaccurate or false for several reasons. The autobiographer is subject to normal loss of memory, particularly about his childhood and his dreams. If he is a gifted writer, he deliberately omits and selects in order to shape the story of his life into a work of art. Truth is defaced by the natural censorship which the mind exercises upon whatever is disagreeable and by the censorship provoked by a sense of shame, especially in sexual matters. It is impeded by the tendency of man's memory toward rationalization so that life may be organized into a coherent system and by his desire to protect others who have acted with him. Maurois concludes that authentic autobiography cannot be written; he cannot envision an autobiographer who can combine the analytic genius and perceptions of Proust with proper impartiality, objectivity, and detachment toward his own life. Truth is to be found only in some of the autobiography which focuses on intellectual development, for men are not afraid to recount their fumblings where ideas are concerned, and, even here, the isolation of intellectual development from the whole life is artificial. For Maurois, then, the more personal involvement which is intrinsic to autobiography endangers its truth. Though his concept of biography as self-expression makes biography a kind of disguised autobiography, his juxtaposition of the chapter on autobiography with that on biography as a means of expression clarifies in some measure his argument that biography, even if it is in part subjective, may still be detached and objective, at least relative to autobiography.

Truth is to be found in the novel. Maurois declares, finally, that where the biographer's knowledge is confined to an action, "it is almost impossible to interpret it," and that even when he seems to have some clues about a man's inner life in letters and in diaries, he cannot grasp "the continuous flow of thoughts, the secret images passing through the mind, the chain of resolutions and regrets" (pp. 162–63). On the other hand, the novelist has the advantage of omniscience; he can describe an action as it appears to spectators, tell at the same time what a character thinks and feels as he performs the action, and show the relation between the points of view. If Virginia Woolf had doubts about the biographer's ability to harmonize granite and rainbow, Maurois is even more pessimistic: "It is in this impossibility of attaining to a synthesis of the inner life and the outward that the inferiority of the biographer to the novelist lies" (p. 167).[58] Still, he thinks that the biographer can learn from the novelist and, even, that he has certain advantages which the novelist lacks.

Maurois demonstrates these by applying to biography some of the topics Forster had treated from the novelist's point of view. The novelist is, to be sure, free to create his own pattern, but complete freedom of form may lead to an excess of construction, to an arrangement which is too nearly perfect, too clever. Maurois thinks that "a series of events . . . borrowed from actual life and then transmuted by the novelist's art will always ring truer than entirely imaginary events. The absurdity of truth is magnificent and well-nigh inimitable and a man must have a genius to be as flagrantly absurd as God" (p. 176).[59] The biographer, he says, has an advantage in being forced to take over a shapeless mass of unequal fragments; the restraints imposed on him, the resistance of the material he inherits may force him to invent a felicitous form in keeping with his matter. When Maurois considers Forster's topic "the story," he merely says that the story of a biography may be as interesting as that of a novel. When he takes up the subject of "characters," he compares *Homo Biographicus* to Forster's *Homo Fictus* and *Homo Sapiens* and finds that he is much more in action than either and that he talks and meditates far less than *Homo Fictus*. Still, he thinks the good biographer may endow him with the inner life which characterizes *Homo Fictus* without injury to truth. He concludes by saying that if biography is a difficult form of art because "we demand of it the scrupulosity of science and the enchantments of art, the perceptible truth of the novel and the learned falsehoods of history," it is also the most convincing of art forms.

Maurois's book remains the most ambitious attempt to justify biography as a form of art. As a work of aesthetic philosophy, it is, of course, flawed; Maurois never convincingly reconciles or synthesizes the objectivity he feels necessary for art with his belief in an expressive function for art. His presentation of an expressive theory complicates and comes close to denying his earlier point of view. It sanctions in some degree a moral point of view rather than ethical neutrality, involvement rather than detachment, feeling rather than intellect, the personal rather than the objective. Other inconsistencies mar the book. Though one of Maurois's basic conceptions is that the writing of history is an art, he also maintains that the historian is something other than an artist when he says that the search for historical truth is the work of the scholar and the search for the expression of personality the work of the artist. He only confuses his reader when he says it is

dangerous and absurd to try to establish too close a parallel between the exact sciences and the historical *sciences* (p. 92). On the
one hand, he wants the biographer to approximate the art of the
novelist while he maintains "a scrupulous respect for scientific
truth" (p. 50); on the other hand, he feels that the process of
interpreting documents of a personal sort depends more on artistic
perception than on scientific method (p. 75). If he hoped at the
beginning of his lectures to show that art and science could be
reconciled, that a scientific book, perfectly constructed, could be
a work of art, he never proves these points logically.

At the heart of the trouble with some of his argument is
his seeming agreement with Nicolson on some questionable matters. In his second chapter, he takes over Nicolson's idea that
biography is good when it is not disturbed by emotion, that the
art of biography is intellectual, not emotional. The process by
which the Anglo-Saxon biographer best builds up and interprets
facts is one which Nicolson describes as intellectual, though it depends not on any consecutive process of reason but on "sweeping
lighthouse flashes of intuition and imagination." Like Nicolson, Maurois, too, thinks that the biographer arrives at understanding by a *coup d'état*, but for him this depends on processes of
identification and divination which can hardly be called intellectual. Moreover, though Nicolson plays down the value of the
consecutive process of reason, he argues generally that psychological truth is most accurately reached by scientific analysis. Maurois feels that the psychological truth about an individual cannot
be attained by scientific analysis or by critical reasoning. Again,
when Nicolson says that readers of biography will increasingly want
all the truth, he defines what he means by "a vast amount of
authentic material." Maurois wants the truths of fact so far as
the biographer can attain them, but he wants also "that profounder truth which is poetic truth."

Maurois's emphasis on poetic truth reveals his fundamental difference from Nicolson, a difference his uncontentious and
gentlemanly argument does not emphasize sufficiently. Nicolson
had insisted that of the three elements in "pure" biography—
truth, individuality, art—the literary element is always the least
important. For him, truth and individuality reach their zenith
when they combine in the form of scientific psychology. For him,
too, the art of the biographer is largely architectonic, a matter
of form based on the biographer's powers of construction and organization. Art is a kind of skill which he is content to describe
as "the literary element" in a work. Maurois's conception of
the biographer as artist goes far beyond a preoccupation with form,

much as he emphasizes that aspect of art. The artist is not merely a craftsman but a man endowed with bardic insight, and it is only insofar as the biographer is an artist that he can represent individuality and arrive at the truth. It is no mere accident or coincidence that Maurois views the biographer within an aesthetic context which is essentially Wordsworthian. For all the logical inconsistencies in his book, no one has made a more persuasive case for the imaginative involvement of the biographer with his subject, for the ways in which the biographer functions like a novelist. Although, not surprisingly, Maurois himself contradicts the idea in several places, his book emphasizes the primacy of the biographer, and his description of the role of the biographer is the culmination of ideas suggested by Saintsbury and Thayer and leads to later expressions about the symbiotic nature of the relation between biographer and subject.

III

The Thirties

OSBERT BURDETT

Maurois's championing of the truth available to the biographer who works like a novelist and his emphasis on the centrality of the biographer were challenged within a year by Osbert Burdett in a lecture called "Experiment in Biography."[1] Like so many other critics, Burdett holds that "human character . . . should be the biographer's quarry. What a man was is infinitely more important to us than anything which he did, or than the success which attended him." "No one," he states, "complains that Pepys left out of his diary his useful work for the Navy. On the contrary, he is cherished and honoured because he confined himself to personal revelations of his tastes, indulgences, and whims" (p. 167). He finds even Strachey deficient as a biographer, for, he says, the real subject of his books is the earnest Victorian ideal which he ridicules and his primary end is to attack "the heresy of whitewash"; he is not interested in portraiture for its own sake, and "it is useless to look in his works for a gallery of portraits" (pp. 169–70).

When Burdett speaks of the experimenters who are writing biographical novels or romances, he does not fault their focus on portraiture, but he disputes their claim that the distinction between biography and fiction is false, their avowal that the novelist is the true biographer. Much as he welcomes the experimenters in romance with a biographical root, he stresses the distinction between the biographical romancer, who uses the convention of omniscience in order to entertain, and the biographer, who must confess his ignorance when he is ignorant because his object is to be reliable and true (pp. 172–73). He praises Maurois for his care in calling *Ariel "a Shelley romance,"* not a life,[2] but he attacks his implication in the *Aspects* "that there is no real difference between biography and fiction": "he would have us believe that intuition is infallible, a theory natural to a novelist but one that no biographer would admit" (pp. 173–74). Burdett warns that the theory is dangerous for biography because it makes the author more important than the subject, because the author who relies on intuition "will necessarily dominate the page, whereas in a good biography the subject will fill it and make us feel that we are face to face with him." Intuition, he grants, has its place in biography, "but we require also fairness, not to the subject only, but to the materials, gaps and all" (pp. 174–75).

In his lecture, Burdett deals not only with Strachey and with Maurois and biographical romance, but also with an experimental approach which, he says, has scarcely yet been tried: "During the past fifty years a new science, still in its infancy, has appeared under the forbidding name of analytic psychology. The term is most convenient when not too narrowly defined, for the definitions differ. For our purpose it may be termed the analysis of human motives, the dissection of human personality, of the way our minds work, of the nature of our impulses, of the manner in which human beings react to their interior stresses and to external circumstances, of the evidence provided by our dreams" (p. 176). Burdett thinks that since the method of analytic psychology is highly technical, it has not yet led to any full-scale biography, but he expects to find psychoanalysts among the biographers of the future. He mentions "the purely medical method" among the number of approaches which advancing specialization in other fields of knowledge offers to biographers, but, unlike Nicolson, he holds that such experiments "enrich our means, but they do not replace our primary conception, that biography is the history of an individual as a branch of humane letters." They provide new aspects for study, but they will not absorb biography itself (pp. 177–78).[3]

HESKETH PEARSON

Burdett's representation of Maurois's position in the *Aspects* is at least a touch inaccurate. Maurois had tried with some care to distinguish biography from the novel, though he thought it inevitable and advantageous that the biographer function like a novelist. It was only to be expected, however, that emphasis on personality, interiority, quintessential and "poetic" truth would lead to positions more extreme than his. In 1930, there appeared Hesketh Pearson's *Ventilations: Being Biographical Asides*,[4] a book which discursively treated various aspects of biography at the same time that it characterized the principal Edwardian writers in brilliant anecdote, much of it invented. Pearson did not know Maurois's *Aspects*; he had written his book while he was on tour as an actor in 1928,[5] and he approaches biography not as a novelist or a biographer but with an actor's propensity for impersonation and mimicry. The premium Pearson placed on artistry, invention, intuition, and self-expression is an extension of Maurois's principles, and Burdett's remarks about Maurois are more fittingly critical of Pearson's doctrine than of Maurois's.

On his first page, Pearson insists that there is no such thing as truth. "In biography," he says, "this question of truth is always cropping up. A short while ago Mr. Harold Nicolson wrote a book in which he declared that truth is the primary requisite of what he calls 'pure' biography. But the very finest biographer can only tell the truth as he sees it, and the probability is that it will not be the truth as other people see it. 'Pure' biography is therefore a chimera, a dream." He believes that "every literary portrait of value is and must be an imaginative portrait. That is to say, it is written from a certain angle—the angle of the author— and its subject can only be seen from his peculiar point of view" (pp. 85–86). Still, he thinks that the attempt to arrive at truth is likely to be warped unduly in two ways. First, nothing is so dangerous to truth as intimate knowledge; personal contact blurs the vision, and the tradition that only a disciple can be trusted to write a life has ruined biography (pp. 52–53). Insofar as a "personal" biography contains anecdotes revealing character, its value to the impartial biographer may be great, but "the more intimately we know a man the less completely do we know him. Just as a natural object can only be seen in its true proportion from a distance, so a man's character can only be seen in its true proportion from outside his immediate circle of friends" (p. 55). Second, Pearson goes beyond Nicolson, whom he quotes on the fatal influence of any emotion (especially religious earnestness) on biography, to say that "any form of moral earnestness, any ethical standpoint whatever, is fatal to the art of biography" (p. 103). He feels that some of Nicolson's own work has been disabled by a tendency to moralize, and that morality, religion, high ideals, didacticism, and partisanship have had dismal effects on biography (pp. 103, 167). Like Maurois, he is aware that criticism of action may be implied in the bare relation of action, and he does not object to this since he thinks that indirect criticism or criticism by implication can always be taken in two or more ways. But, again, like Maurois, he says that the biographer who delivers himself of a definite moral judgment commits an unforgivable sin against his art (p. 105).

Pearson defines the ideal biographer as "the detached artist-biographer, the synthetic portrait-painter, the imaginative yet scientific writer" (p. 66). For him, Boswell does not measure up to the ideal, though he is "the most trustworthy writer of 'personal' biography in the language": we believe in his fundamental honesty because he exposes himself as clearly as he exposes his subjects (p. 187). But Pearson finds signs of Boswell's partiality in his unsympathetic portrayal of Goldsmith and in his suppression and evasion of evidence (pp. 11–12, 37–48), and, for him, it is Strachey who, temperamentally and imaginatively, approximates the ideal biographer most closely. Strachey, he says, "has mastered the most difficult part of the biographer's art: fusion"; since he "has unified a hundred or more (sometimes conflicting) glimpses of character supplied by others," his portraits are "rounded, coherent, convincing," and he has got as close as possible to "the ideal of absolute detachment and impartiality" (pp. 168–69). Pearson's circle of ideal biographers includes, in addition, only Johnson and Maurois, though he finds in Arnold Bennett many affinities with the ideal biographer: he has no political axe to grind, no belief in Utopia or in God, no panacea for cosmic diseases; he observes men keenly, has a detached view of people and things, loves human eccentricity, subscribes to no "ism," delights in remaining neutral, and has a curiously objective attitude toward life (pp. 73–75). Pearson has reservations about Lockhart. For him, the *Scott* is the best example of "unimaginative biography," "a most satisfying piece of biographical photography" (p. 133), and his ideal biographer must be an imaginative and creative artist.

Although he says that the extent of imaginative work permissible in biography can never be determined, Pearson places no restrictions on imagination so long as its use convinces and satisfies readers (p. 134). He cites Dumas's statement that historical novels are "more interesting than history, and more accurate," and suggests that "if historians drew on their imaginations a little more than they do, their work would be more truthful than it is." "We all," he says, "instinctively question the truth of facts; we all instinctively accept the truth behind legends" (p. 131). Since it is the duty of the historian or the biographer to get at "the essential truth," he must be an artist (p. 132). For Pearson, to be an artist is to work imaginatively, and he does not boggle at the biographer who invents anecdotes and alters occurrences (p. 133). To be an artist is also to express one's self in one's work. No man, except perhaps Plato, he says, has ever "definitely used biography as a medium for self-expression," and, since he thinks that "purely creative biography is the expression of one man's personality through that of another," he cites only Plato's portrait of Socrates, the Evangelists' portraits of Christ, and Boswell's Johnson as the classic examples of creative biography (p. 209). Boswell's creative genius lay in his ability "to get inside the mind of another man and reveal it in that man's own arrestingly individual style" (p. 17). Pearson agrees with Shaw that Boswell "created" Johnson much as Shakespeare created Falstaff and Hamlet (p. 14), and he insists that Boswell "improved" on the real Johnson and produced "something more characteristically Johnsonian than Johnson" (pp. 17–18).

On several occasions, Pearson turns to his own work in order to illustrate what he means by the use of imagination or creativity in biography. He reproduces a dialogue between Shaw and Chesterton, originally published in the *Adelphi*, and says, "I will now admit for the first time that it was not true, in the sense that it never happened, but that it was true in the higher sense that it might and certainly ought to have happened" (p. 18). He introduces a sketch of Chesterton by saying, "What follows may not be quite accurate, but it is probably more true to life than what actually took place, because the memory aided by a knowledge of the man is a better guide to truth than the note-book aided by a knowledge of Pitman" (p. 106). He analyzes Sir James Barrie's career and says, "What I have said may or may not be strictly true, but I am positive it is broadly and fundamentally true" (p. 138). He says of his portrait of Sir Herbert Tree, "By using his vocal inflections, I could tell exactly how he would say a thing; and after studying him fairly closely, I knew pretty well what he would say under any given circumstances. All the circumstances were of course given me, and I think I made the most of them. Where my conscious memory failed, my intuitive faculty had little difficulty in bridging the gap. My portrait of him is therefore creative and fundamentally true" (pp. 211–12). He tells three stories about Tree and holds that the one he invented himself is the most characteristic (p. 147).

When Pearson attacks Chesterton's religious bias as a biographer, he refers to Chesterton's suggestion that if Robert Louis Stevenson "had sown his wild oats in a Catholic country instead of a Protestant one, his vices would not have been so vicious," and he says, "Now that may or may not be true. I neither know nor care. What I do know is that it is not biography. What might have happened to someone if only something that did happen to him hadn't happened to him, and how he might have turned out if only circumstances had been different from what they were—such speculations are doubtless both profitable and absorbing, but they have nothing whatever to do with biography, which is a record of what *did* happen" (pp. 113–14). Still, though he holds that anecdotes should not be invented indiscriminately and that imagination should not be allowed to run without restraint, he feels that the biographer should be given free rein "where he can definitely improve on fact," for "by the mere process of selection, arrangement, and presentation, he is constantly improving on fact" (p. 141). "Art," Pearson finally says, "being experimental, is usually fallible on matters of fact. It is not concerned with the outward but with the inward truth of things. The path of art is strewn with unimportant errors." Though he does not prefer inaccuracy to accuracy in biography, he advocates the sacrifice of "the unessential facts" in order to achieve "essential truth" (pp. 182–83).[6]

HOWARD MUMFORD JONES

Several months after Burdett spoke in London about contemporary experiments in biography and their possible contribution to the domain, Howard Mumford Jones read a paper called "Methods in Contemporary American Biography" before the American Literature section of the Modern Language Association meeting in Cleveland,[7] in which he concludes that there is no real need to adopt any particular biographical methodology labeled as "new." Jones is not interested in propounding his own theory of "what biography truly is," and he refers his audience to the discussions by Dunn, Johnston, Lee, Nicolson, Bradford, Strachey, "and others" (pp. 121–22).[8] He is content to state that no type of biography "yet invented has solved the essential conflict between the demands of biography as 'science' and the demands of biography as 'art.' In biography truth lies in a sort of middle between various extremes, and to attempt a logical theory

of a form essentially illogical in its attempted fusion of contradictory elements is usually disastrous." He does think, however,
that the best biographies have been written by men "who knew
their subjects in the flesh" and who followed "the traditional
lines of careful scholarship, sympathetic insight, and mastery of
the materials" (p. 122).

Jones's main concern is to account for the poor quality
which characterizes modern biography despite its extraordinary
popularity. The first half of his lecture deals with the forces which
cause authors and publishers to vulgarize their product, adver-
tising practices which lead to widespread sensationalism and misrepresentation, and commercial competition which leads to haste,
cheapening of style, and shoddiness of investigation. The second
and more interesting half is a consideration of the attitudes and
methods out of which the new biography springs, and Jones comments on eight types of biography. The newness of most of these
he finds to be associated with some particular psychological or
medical presupposition, system, or theory; the others rest on some
historical or literary presupposition (pp. 113, 119). His account is
an almost unmitigated attack.

Jones's statement about the rarity of biographers' com-
petence in both Freudian psychology and in literature is a prelude
to an enumeration of the defects in the Freudian approach to
biographical writing. The biographer of a dead man cannot tell
whether the data he has are significant, for "an essential element
in Freudian psychoanalysis is the uncovering of submerged memories through free association under skilful direction." Because
the symbolic interpretation of an author's literary remains must
rest upon or be referred to data gathered from free association,
there is no way of knowing whether a particular interpretation is
correct. Not only do the selection and interpretation of symbols
vary from biographer to biographer, but the interpretations are
not subject to impartial controls and each psychoanalyst is conveniently free to insist upon the validity of his own interpretation
(p. 114). Jones dismisses "medico-pathological" biography by saying that it descends from naive nineteenth-century views of heredity and materialism and by citing Maurois's objections to it (pp.
114–15). Though he finds the use of Adlerian formulas—inferiority
and superiority complexes, defense mechanisms, frustrations and
compensations—"less eccentric, and more usable," he thinks
they generally lead to oversimplified interpretations (pp. 115–16).
Psychographic biography, which he finds in Suetonius, Plutarch,
and Sainte-Beuve, as well as in Bradford and Strachey, is deficient
insofar as an author chooses facts to suit the "character" he
has pre-determined; it tends to view personality as absolute rather

than as fluid and contradictory; it tends to explain significant action by a psychology which is purely fictional (pp. 117–18). The biographical romance he views as a direct descendant of psychographic biography, and he thinks that candor would label it fiction (pp. 118–19). "Consciously informal biography," which seeks to humanize a subject by emphasizing his informal and ordinary actions, is as incomplete as that in which the biographer stresses merely the deeds of his hero, and it slides easily into "debunking" biography. This type not only depends upon the accumulation of derogatory detail, but it is subject to the subtler fallacy of the "new" history practiced by the school of historians who, like Charles Beard, read the American past in terms of economic and social determinism (pp. 119–20). If "debunking biography" errs in applying contemporary standards of taste or morality to the past, the archaeological biography, which tries with detachment to see its subject wholly in terms of   own era, frequently ends in belittlement because of its emphasis on quaintness (pp. 120–21).

Throughout his examination, Jones feels impelled to say, so exuberant is his desire to deflate modern biographical experiment, that there is nothing new in the new biography, that a number of its resources are ancient. That suggestion, true as it is in some instances, is not necessary to the force of his argument, which, in its business-like tone and in its reliance upon categorization and specific example, serves to undercut experiments dependent on the exploitation of the possibilities offered by psychology and fiction. The main attack on attempts by biographers to get at motive and the inner life in the representation of personality come, however, not so much from literary critics as from the historians, and James Truslow Adams, Bernard De Voto, and Arthur Bryant tried to explode both the practice of contemporary biographers and the theory of Gosse, Nicolson, Woolf, and Maurois which sought to justify it.

JAMES TRUSLOW ADAMS

Adams's "New Modes in Biography"[9] is, in the main, a piece of social criticism directed at the worshippers of science and those who have no belief in the dignity of man. He finds the most powerful cult of the age to be that of science, and he says that "science in the popular mind has made man a mere animal, if not a mere automatic switchboard of incoming and outgoing 'calls'—impressions and reactions." Another chief characteristic of the age stems from the theoretically possible opportunity in a democratic society to attain any social, economic, intellectual, or ethical position, and Adams maintains that this has led to an unconscious sense of inferiority which makes people desire to bolster up their own self-esteem by pulling down all men of all times to their own level. His major assumption is that "the multifold biographical writing of any period is . . . merely a picture of the mind of that period."

Since Adams thinks that psychology and psychoanalysis are "among the least firmly established . . . on a scientific basis, of all our branches of knowledge," he derides biographers who believe that "such facts as can be studied 'scientifically' possess a superior validity."[10] He characterizes as "sheer drivel" the opinion of Harry Elmer Barnes that all biographies written before 1900 are " 'rhetorical goose eggs' " because there was no " 'valid psychology' " before the last generation and Harold Nicolson's prediction that biography will become a branch of science. He connects Strachey with those who interpret their subjects "according to the 'science' of psychology and, more narrowly, psychoanalysis," and, though he calls him "an extremely able interpreter of character," he denies that his subjects have scientific validity once Strachey moves beyond the realm of attested fact and chooses facts to fit a predetermined personal thesis. Freud's pronouncements about Leonardo's psychic development, he says, grow more certain as his study proceeds through "a whole phantasmagoria of incredibly unscientific assumptions," and he has no use for "the half-baked knowledge paraded under the name of science" in psychoanalytic biography. The biographers are, he says, "blind to the fact, first, that they are dealing with mere guesses, and, second, that whatever *influence* certain factors or traits may have had, they cannot explain the *whole*" of a man and his career. Adams is equally contemptuous of debunking biography. In such biography, material is selected "solely with a view to picking the last vestige of greatness off all humanity, past as well as present, when the selection is not simply, though not frankly, pornographic." He concludes by saying, "A period that is interested in ethical values will ask to have those stressed in the lives of the people about whom it reads. A period that is interested in what goes on in the bathroom will find biographers willing to pry there for them." He hopes that in time "the label of science will be better understood, as will also the fact that a man is no more 'human'—perhaps, indeed, essentially less so—when he is saying 'God damn' than when he is saying '*Pater noster*,' even when he is equally sincere in both expressions." Meanwhile, he reserves his praise for books like Beveridge's *Lincoln*, which is based on completely and soundly authenticated fact, on the scholarly presentation of "genuine science, in the sense of exact knowledge" rather than on the "pseudo-scientific balderdash" of most of the psychoanalytic school or on the personal interpretation of states of mind, even when this is done with Strachey's skill and charm.

Adams's essay, "Biography as an Art," which appeared in 1931,[11] starts unpromisingly with a reference to Johnston's *Biography: The Literature of Personality* of 1927 and a magisterial statement that "almost nothing has been written about biography as an art." Despite his title, art pre-empts little of his essay. With one eye focused almost certainly on Gamaliel Bradford,[12] he points out that the danger of the biographical "character" or "appreciation" lies in its distortion or refraction of a subject through the mind of a biographer who has not recorded the ascertainable facts. The result, he says, is a composite portrait of sitter and painter, and though he grants that "a superb biographer may play the artist," he holds that an ordinary craftsman had better be "the photographer of the obvious." As in his earlier piece, he plays the social critic, and pronounces once again that since modern biographers have accepted "the as yet by no means proved theory that man is of no lasting or cosmic importance," they assume that intimacy and human interest consist in watching a man perform "his lowest physical or mental acts" and they tend to think that "there is no difference in value between the operation of the bowels and those of the brain."

Adams does not show the relation between art and the central question he asks in his essay: is the chief purpose of biography to teach by example in presenting "a noble life in its noblest aspects" or is it "as Sir Sidney Lee said, 'to transmit a personality' "? Much as one senses that Adams would prefer the first alternative, he does not overtly do so, but, instead, he complicates the second. Recent biographers, he says, have not decided what personality is or what man is; as a result, they tend to select episodes in which a hero departs from accepted mores. He finds their criterion of selection cheap and absurd, for not only do accepted mores change from time to time, but biographers distort "by dwelling on the points in which their heroes of the *past* departed from the *mores* of *today*." He protects himself from the charge of idealizing hagiography by allowing for the inclusion of "what we might call damning facts" in two instances—when whitewashing a man besmirches his contemporaries and when the facts had a real and lasting influence "on the man himself, his career and personality."Adams insists, finally, that "the competent biographer has got to think out a philosophy of man and nature before he can select his facts." He makes clear his own philosophy when he states that to consider a man from the point of view "of the unconscious, of biological functions, of chemical reactions, or of atomic structure is not biography." He places himself firmly against the advocates of the use of psychology and of other methods of representing the inner life of thought and emotion when he announces dogmatically that "the clearly defined field of biographical treatment" is the "realm of self-conscious life and of observable and recorded acts."

ARTHUR BRYANT

In his article, "The Art of Biography,"[13] Arthur Bryant praises Strachey as a "great and revolutionary artist" who made the past real and says that he would not give up a single sentence Strachey wrote for the sake of more thorough research. But, despite such homage to art, and despite the fact that Bryant never refers to Sidney Lee, his article is a strong call for a return to Lee's principles. Lee had insisted in *The Perspective of Biography* (1918) that the creative artistry of the biographer is limited to giving "animation to the dead bones." Bryant insists that biography is "primarily the art of making the dry bones of a dead man live." There are, he says, "two cardinal offences against the art: that of failing to make the bones live and that of utilizing any other ingredients but bones for the operation. The first was the besetting sin of the Victorian biographers, and the second is that of the modern. The Victorians assembled an imposing heap of bones in two volumes and called it a full-length portrait. The Georgians conjure up a neat phantasy of psychological and ironical conjecture and call it a penetrating study."

Like Adams, then, Bryant would restrict biography to the realm of self-conscious life and of observable and recorded acts, but he puts major emphasis, as Lee had, on the work or achievement of the subject. He goes so far as to say that even if a man's entire private life is unfolded to his biographer, the primary study of the biographer must still be the work of his subject. "We do not need," he says, "the details of Shakespeare's private life to understand what manner of man he was. A Rhodes or a Loyola is our friend or enemy, as we approve or detest the giant structure he raised: we apprehend him, though we know nothing of his loves, his private hopes and fears, his struggles with himself." Unlike Burdett, he holds that Pepys's self-portrait is partial and mis-

leading because it does not record the scope of his work, his
achievement of laying the foundation of British sea power: "to
its making," Bryant says, "went all the best of him and the
enduring part of his heart. And where the heart lies, *ecce homo.*"[14]
His chief point is that the biographer who would truly understand
a man "must comprehend the direction of the man's work, for
it will be along this line in the main that the man's character
will advance; and whether his hero succeeds in keeping to that
path or is driven from it, his desire to follow it will provide the
key to his soul."

Bryant is aware that. though "a great man's work is the
ultimate purpose of his life," it is not the whole of his life, and
he grants the probability of many vital influences and occurrences
which have nothing to do with work, which may, often, be at cross-
currents to it. To arrive at such "essential clues," the biographer must collect every fact he can lay hands on. Bryant cites
the Preface of *Eminent Victorians* to describe Strachey's method
of fishing for facts, says that his pupils tend to assume that any
stray fact is significant, and attacks the psychological biographers
who use facts which are found by casual browsing among previous
biographies of their subject: "Each of these facts, divorced from
its context, from life, even from ordinary probability," he says,
has been made to support some psychological theory "culled from
the text-books of one of the professors of that omniscient science." The biographer, he maintains, is not absolved from the
historian's labor; he must have the historian's grasp of the atmosphere of an age, his knowledge and astuteness in finding evidence and using it with discrimination, his respect for chronology,
and even, ideally, his first-hand experience of the duties of civic
life. When Bryant turns to the "art" of the biographer, he says
only that he must use his knowledge of life to piece together
"some semblance of reality" from the broken fragments of fact
he has. One of his key terms is "proportion" or "scale." "For
the rest," he says, "the art of biography is the art of selection."
Despite the particularity of his definition of the historian, he offers
only a Falstaffian explanation of the art of selection. "No principles can guide the writer here—only instinct."

BERNARD DE VOTO

If Bryant leaves no more room for art in biography than
Sidney Lee does, Bernard De Voto irrevocably divorces art and
biography in a swashbuckling piece of polemic, full of outrage and
contempt, which he calls "The Skeptical Biographer."[15] De

Voto equates truth in biography with fact even more adamantine than that found in the British Museum, and, for him, the findings of literary men and of psychoanalysts are on the other side of a fixed line, along with "guesses, improvisations, fairy stories, and mere lies." Biography, he says, differs from imaginative literature in that readers come to it primarily in search of information; the cardinal sins of the biographer are, then, ignorance, misinformation, omission of evidence, guesswork, and interpretation which masquerade as fact.

"Creative" biography is, for De Voto, merely the distortion of evidence for special effects. He grants Strachey a talent for irony, a prose style of great distinction, an enormous knowledge of history and literature, which was, however, a "reading" knowledge, one which tended toward pedantry and preciosity. He implies that the course of Strachey's career disqualifies him as biographer: "For a while he wrote literary criticism, an activity in which uncontrolled speculation is virtuous and responsibility is almost impossible." A work by Strachey, he says, "is an adult form of art, and anyone who happens to know something about its subject may derive from it an intense aesthetic pleasure. But God help the man who comes to Strachey ignorant and desirous of learning the truth. Mr. Strachey was not in the truth business." His brilliant portraits are studies in deliberate deception. The most brilliant interpretation is wrong if the facts are wrong.

De Voto states bluntly that "literary people should not be permitted to write biography." He contends that the literary mind may be "adequately" described as the mind least adapted to the utilization of fact, for it is too simple, too inaccurate, too naive. Literature works through selection and omission to provide an illusion of the whole; biography cannot simplify and must not omit. Literature relies on intuition, appearance, rumor and conjecture, imagination; the first condition of biography is "absolute, unvarying, unremitted accuracy." The proper medium of literature is fantasy, and the charm of the literary mind lies in its unspoiled freshness, its eager willingness to believe, its awe and wonder, its lack of involvement with the world, its ignorance of the conditions of practical life; biography demands the skepticism and cynicism which are best cultivated in human intercourse.

De Voto next attacks the use of psychoanalysis in biography, where, he says, it has no value whatever as a method of arriving at facts. Interestingly enough, he moves into the subject by describing it as one of the preposterous instruments for the ascertainment of fact which the literary biographer, who is unfitted to understand the nature of fact and who is endowed with credulity, has relied on. His quarrel is not with the professional psychoanalyst, whose aim is therapeutic; it is with the amateur who feels that psychoanalysis is an infallible instrument for biography, who thinks he need not worry about the empirical world of his subject, bestrewn with dark places, bare spots, conflicts of testimony, and sheer chaos, since he assumes that all his subject's mind is of a piece, all his life a unity, and that he can recover anything he wishes from anything else, or, if he finds a conflict of evidence, relies on the principle of ambivalence, which tells him that all evidence means the same thing. Such a biographer uses psychoanalysis as a substitute for research. He does not need to know what happened; he deduces from an *a priori* principle, and he thinks he knows what *must* have happened. The biographer who employs psychoanalysis, De Voto says, "cannot arrive at facts but only at 'interpretations,' which is to say theory, which is to say nonsense."

A biographer's integrity may be estimated most accurately by the force of his refusal to depart from verifiable fact. De Voto does not worry about the biographer who is so flagrantly partisan that he reveals his hand; he despises the biographer who uses the technical devices of fiction in place of factual instruments, who incorporates passages from his subject's written works irresponsibly and without any understanding of context and circumstance, and who thinks he is free to recreate his subject's mind. The interior of that mind, De Voto says, is forbidden the biographer by the nature of reality. The biographer "may tell us what the subject has said or written about his mind, but he may not on his own authority make any statement whatever about the immediate content of that mind. He cannot know what is there, he can only guess." If a guess is not dishonest, it is at least theoretical; if theoretical, then it is "contingent, inexistent, and mystical," and therefore improper to biography. The moral of all this, De Voto says, is "Back to Lockhart, back to Froude, back to Morley. Back, in short, to Victorian biography." He wants to return to the days when biographers had integrity, when they submerged their own personalities because they assumed that a reader's interest was not in them but in their subjects, when biography dealt with fact. This implies, he thinks, the disappearance of the literary from biography, and even though "most historians and most scholars appear to write with something between a bath sponge and an axe," he is willing to sacrifice beautiful writing for an accurate and honest representation of the past. He grants, finally, that "interpretation" has a valid place "as the most intelligent of literary guessing games." He grants, too, that psychography in the hands of someone like Bradford, may be an honest interest and a legitimate field, but he does so because, unlike most of Bradford's critics, he thinks that Bradford differentiated his interest in "soul" from biography. For De Voto, "biography knows nothing about the soul"; the biographer's job is only to discover evidence, to analyze it, and to assess it. Biography aims to recover something trustworthy from the past, and it has no room for the cocksureness of the theorist, the ingenious nonsense of the interpreter, the special pleading of the doctrinaire.

Nicolson had polarized psychology and literature, and Burdett had followed him when he described the biographical romance and the biography dependent upon analytic psychology as experiments of different kinds. The historians saw that reliance on artistic intuition and imagination and the application of psychological and psychoanalytical techniques worked to the same end in biography—toward interiority, toward the representation of the inner life of thought and emotion, toward the roots of motivation. It was easy enough to theorize about two distinct categories so long as one had in mind the wildly imaginative biographical romance on the one hand and the purely technical case history of the psychologist on the other. But Freud's *Leonardo* was as inventive as Elinor Wylie's *Orphan Angel*; in fact, literary biographers interested in interiority were quick to wed the formulas and symbols of psychology and psychoanalysis to their intuition, and the most professional of psychoanalysts had, in biographical work, to rely on imaginative reconstruction of a kind that would not be tolerated in the consulting room. Although Jones, Adams, and Bryant made a bow in the direction of art as it applied to biography, each found fault with a focus on interiority which he thought beyond the possibility of scholarly documentation and each in his way found both "literary" and "psychological" biography deficient. De Voto thought it unnecessary to call down a plague on two houses; to him it was clear that literature and psychology occupied the same place.

The historians' call for biography to avoid imaginative reconstruction of the inner life through the use of intuition or of psychological doctrine, to restrict itself to the realm of self-conscious life and to observable and recorded acts, even to stress, primarily, a man's work, effectively undercut the more ardent advocates of untrammeled freedom. Some of the critics of the 1930s, like Lewis Mumford, David Cecil, and Edgar Johnson thought the historians had gone too far, but most spoke more warily than Maurois and Pearson of the place of art in biography.

LEWIS MUMFORD

Mumford's essay, "The Task of Modern Biography,"[16] quiet and moderate as it is, still makes a charge of timidity against the modern critics who proclaim that the whole duty of the biographer is to verify and set down "the facts." The facts of any life, Mumford says, are "the sum total of its experiences in living; they comprehend all that the subject has ever seen, felt, sensed, touched, heard, remembered, or otherwise encountered." There can be, then, no one-to-one relation between a life and the most exhaustive biography; biography must be selective, based on facts which seem "from one standpoint or another" to be significant. But the biographer must be more than an astute selector of evidence. Since there is no necessary connection between the important elements in a life and the records of that life which have survived, he must be "an anatomist of character" and, like the archaeologist, a master in restoration who can reconstruct parts which are missing. He must also have an eye for the seemingly insignificant datum which is revelatory. Mumford thinks that the perception of "the significance of the insignificant" is one of the distinguishing marks of modern science, that the biographer's awareness of its utility was not so much dependent on the scientist's method as it was parallel to it, and that the biographer's respect for events which do not stand high in the conventional scale of importance was reinforced and amplified by the work of novelists like Virginia Woolf. The biographer, too, must be a social historian, an expert in milieu and environment, so that he can distinguish characteristics in his subject which are specific and distinctive from those which are generic and communal when they are seen in relation to a particular place or tradition. Most important, a biographer must be a student of the unconscious; he must examine and reveal not only "the shell of outward events" but also the "partly independent, partly autonomous, partly unconditioned inner life" of his subject, for the one is not the simple manifestation of the other and the two are only fitfully in harmony.

Mumford has no illusions about the dangers of probes into the inner life. He says, for instance, that interpretations based on a subject's written works are most sound when they can be supported by a body of independent data. He sees that the desire of modern biographers to strip "the moral mask" from their subjects in order to read character clearly has led to the loss of an important clue, for "the mask itself is as important an aspect of a life as the more devious tendencies it conceals"; like the face of a clock, it is the very part of the instrument which records the action of the works. Moreover, the debunking biographer replaces the moral mask with a "negative" one which is more artificial and more arbitrary, for the original mask "was a work of art produced by the subject himself and it bore his own veritable imprint." For all his awareness of the dangers in the task of biography as he sees it, Mumford's answer to De Voto[17] is clear: "It is better to make mistakes in interpreting the inner life than to make the infinitely greater mistake of ignoring its existence and its import."

Mumford's challenge to the annalistic approach of the historians focuses mainly on the utility of psychology for the revelation of the inner life. To be sure, he says that novelists like Meredith had dealt with the phenomena of the inner life long before the biographer dared to handle them, and that novelists like Virginia Woolf had exploited the importance of seemingly unimportant data, but, however much he implies a fundamental reliance on imagination (he refers, rather, to "uncanny perception"), he never refers to the "art" of biography and he never refers overtly to the use of art in biography or to the biographer as artist. Reassertion of the primary role of art in biography came in two very different ways from Lord David Cecil in a brief Introduction to *An Anthology of Modern Biography*[18] and from Edgar Johnson in the last paragraphs of the Epilogue to his book, *One Mighty Torrent*.[19]

DAVID CECIL

Cecil's cool and mild little essay starts with a disarming sentence. When he writes that "Biography is not an important form of literary art," the lack of importance he attributes to biography as a literary art makes his assumption that it is a literary art seem equally unimportant. Indeed, the tone of his essay is such that he seems unaware that his assumption has provoked controversy, and the tactic of his essay is such that his own comments seem uncontroversial. He does not argue; he simply reports what had taken place. He states that modern biography is a new form of literature brought into being by a shift in the intention of the biographer's primary purpose from giving information and telling the truth to producing an artistic impression through the exercise of his creative powers and the expression of his personal vision. Boswell, Carlyle, Macaulay, Belloc may have turned a true story into art because they had literary talent, but the creation of a work of art was not their primary intent. It was, however, Strachey's, and Cecil maintains that Strachey wrote about Queen Victoria not in order to give information about her but because he thought her life "an excellent subject for a work of art." He grouped facts into an order and proportion that would make his picture as vivid and entertaining as possible. He did not write "with the impersonality of the pure historian"; "His whole narrative glows with the colour of his individual vision, sparkles with the light of his individual humour. It is as much an expression of a personality as David Copperfield."

The new medium established by Strachey is, Cecil says, a complex form. Like the novel, it is dramatic and pictorial, but the biographer's creative impulse expresses itself in a different way from that of the novelist. Since his incidents and characters are ready-made, since he must stick to the truth, he cannot invent scenes and characters; his creative artistry lies in interpretation, in his capacity to discover the significance of a given story, in his discerning in his raw materials "that continuous theme which will compose them into a work of art." His art is one of arrangement: his invention is limited to a design into which facts can be fitted and his imagination is limited to the vitalizing of his material. His form is not out of sympathy with the scientific spirit. In fact, it was brought into being because the cool and critical age of science is not favorable to the practice of other literary forms, more enthusiastic in their emotion and more exuberant in their fancy. The new form of biography makes it possible for an artist to convey his personal vision and at the same time to tell the truth with scientific detachment. Indeed, the enormous advance in the study of psychology has made it possible, as it never was before, for the biographer to give a full account of human character.

For Cecil, the new biographer is "under an equal obligation to art and to life, his book must be equally satisfying as picture and as likeness." He does not exploit the implications of this statement for other artists. He merely says that some modern biographers have sacrificed art to life, that more often they have sacrificed life to art. Only when he expresses his admiration for Queen Victoria, when he calls it "a model biography," does he move from description of the new form to evaluation. It is, perhaps, his feeling that biography as he has described it is so new that it has not led to many masterpieces which makes him say that a form of literature which must preserve a delicate balance between life and art is less important than one which is free to leave life behind.

EDGAR JOHNSON

The calmness and detachment of Cecil's exposition contrast sharply with Johnson's impassioned rhetoric. Cecil's essay casually introduces a pleasant group of biographical snippets;[20] Johnson's Epilogue is the culmination of a massive and urgent undertaking, and he does not stand apart from the context of argument he is involved in. He does not, however, write with Adams, Bryant, and De Voto in mind; the historian whose approach he advocates is Preserved Smith, who did not think that the detailed research of the historical specialist was incompatible with the more important work of the synthesizing historians, and he uses Smith's point of view to refute Nicolson's thesis that the bulk and the intellectual difficulty of scientific data will lead to a diminution of the role of art in biography. Like Nicolson, Johnson envisions some biographies based on increased specialization in the sciences and social sciences, but, like Burdett, he thinks that the biographer is capable of absorbing technical studies and approaches into his work. The biographer, he says, must master whatever science can propound about society and psychology. Like the novelist, he need not be daunted by the complexity of his data: "What the mind can discover the mind can organize," and the biographer is at least as capable as any other artist in his ability to synthesize. Despite the fears of Nicolson (and of I. A. Richards), science has not disinherited the artist, and Johnson cites Wordsworth's words, that when " 'what is now called science, thus familiarized to men, shall be ready to put on, as it were, a form of flesh and blood, the Poet will lend his divine spirit to aid the transfiguration, and will welcome the Being thus produced as a dear and genuine inmate of the household of man.' " For Johnson, the biographer is an artist who can bring every scientific test of precision to his task of revealing the richness of human personality. So long as he does not lose sight of his "animating purpose" as an artist, so long as he does not forget that he is giving information as a man, not as a technical specialist, the biographer can absorb the contributions of science into his work, and that work, in which "science passes through the transubstantiation of art," will radiate a new power.

By the mid-thirties, the points of view set forth by Lee and Gosse had not only been examined and amplified but their importance had been freshly reasserted. The forceful restatement

of Lee's doctrines by the historians did not go unchallenged, but
it is fair to say that it tempered the enthusiasm of the more
ardent proponents of the primacy of art and the aesthetic imagination, the centrality of personality in its relation to the inner
life, the fundamental importance of the role of the biographer. If
the critics were not prepared to follow De Voto all the way back
to Lockhart and to Victorian biography, the effect of his views
was reflected in a search for a middle ground, in qualification and
retraction of extreme positions, in a desire to have it both ways.

MARK LONGAKER

In the Foreward to his book, *Contemporary Biography*,[21]
Mark Longaker states that his point of view is "neither strictly
contemporary nor strictly impartial" and he hopes that his studies "may help to bring to the critical standards of biography a
much-needed definiteness." The very organization of the book,
with its chapters on Strachey, Bradford, Maurois, Ludwig, Guedella, Belloc, and some American biographers, would seem to assume a theory of biography which puts its main focus on the role
of the biographer. Longaker's concept of the biographer's role
is tolerant and flexible enough to make for sympathetic and just
descriptions of the methods and careers of the biographers he
studies, but it is precisely this flexibility which undercuts his attempt to bring "definiteness" to critical standards for biography. He believes that "the chief value of any fact lies in its
proper interpretation" (p. 51), but he finds fault with Maurois's
allowing his intuitive concepts of Shelley's character to shape
the design of his portrait and he thinks that Maurois's concept
of insight by *coup d'état* works best when it is coupled with the
method of presenting evidence, weighing its worth, offering a few
deductions, and permitting the reader to draw his own conclusions
(pp. 96–97). He puts a premium on the detachment of the biographer
(p. 51), thinks it makes for clear-sightedness, but sees value in a
biographer's intimacy with his subject, even in his admiration or
hostility (p. 197). He thinks good biography flourishes when loyalty
and prejudice are reduced, but he thinks, too, that some men's
prejudices are worth listening to (p. 52) and even that Bradford's
detachment, impartiality, and aloofness make for a point of view
that lacks the "subjective depth which underlies the penetrating re-creation of character" (p. 77). At the same time he is
generally skeptical of Maurois's theory of self-expression; "by its
very nature," he says, biography cannot be "the satisfying ve-

hicle for self-deliverance that the novel is," for it is "rare" for the biographer to find a subject which will allow for self-deliv erance without the warping of the subject (pp. 94–95, 115). If he feels that Bradford lacks subjective depth, he still praises Gue-della's *Palmerston* and his *Wellington* because the reader is not so conscious of the author's voice here as in his other works, and he thinks that Belloc is temperamentally ill-equipped to write bi-ography because "the ardor with which he defends or attacks men of history is scarcely consonant with dispassionate judgment" (pp. 181, 194).

Longaker holds that biography needs both science and art, and he accuses Maurois and Strachey of placing too much stress on art and Nicolson for stressing science too much (pp. 111–12). Though he somewhat disparages psychoanalysis and feels that psy-chological devices have not yet reached maturity (pp. 13, 19), he says that "every good biographer is a good psychologist, but every good psychologist is not necessarily a good potential biographer" (p. 234). But biography must be more than the study of personality, more than the exposition of character; it must be life-writing as well, a narrative account of a man's life (pp. 44, 114). He recognizes the place of a kind of artistic insight into "the universal and ageless heart of man" (p. 137) and says that the methods of fiction are of value to the biographer (p. 117),[22] but he also asserts the importance of understanding an age, a tradition, an environment, even a specific place (pp. 137, 206). Longaker opts for that kind of biography which embraces historical scholarship, psychology, and literature in a happy union (p. 249), yet he finds good words for works which do not pay homage to each component. His approach does not encourage that "definiteness" in the critical standards of biography which his Foreword advocates, but, rather, an appre-ciation of the possibilities and excellences inherent in a diversity of emphases.

ELIZABETH DREW

Like Longaker, Elizabeth Drew was a teacher of literature, and, since she includes her essay on "Biography" in a book called *The Enjoyment of Literature*,[23] she allows, as does Longaker, rather more room for art than Lee and the historians do, though the weight of their argument has influenced her and leads her almost to self-contradiction. Like Lee, she says that a biographer is helpless unless his subject is "in some way remarkable," and, though she does not explicitly stress the achievement of the subject, she maintains that he must be "an important, or in some way unusual, figure" (p. 84). She agrees in the main with Lee and Nicolson that biography demands talent, not genius, and asserts that the problems of the "honest" biographer are primarily those "of synthesis and analysis, of selection and arrangement," for, she says, "The biographer has no need of the power to create character, since that is already his subject, and the very quality of his material—its almost inevitable limitation to documentary evidence—excludes so much of the emotional possibilities which the novelist or dramatist is free to create as he will" (p. 85). Still, Miss Drew opens the door rather more widely than Lee and the historians when she says that Johnson's *Savage* illustrates the two great essentials of all good biography: "First, it is concerned exclusively with the faithful presentation of a personality; and secondly it is concerned to present that personality in the form of a work of conscious art" (p. 84). Moreover, if she thinks the chief reason for the excellence of Boswell's *Johnson* is that it is about Johnson, she insists, too, that the chief excellence of the *Savage* is that it is by Johnson.

Miss Drew divides biography into precisely the two categories which Saintsbury had used many years before, but the very language in which she describes them tends to minimize the extent of the possibilities for self-expression on the part of the biographer for which Saintsbury had left room. He had described the category of "applied" or "mixed" biography as a method by which documents, anecdotes, and facts were connected and unified by an author's narrative and comment; Miss Drew describes her "impersonal approach" as one dependent on the collection and arrangement of materials, one in which the author views his material from no special "standpoint" and in which the material does not receive the "deliberate coloring of his own personality" (p. 90). "Biography pure and simple" was, for Saintsbury, biography in which the materials had been altered and digested, in which all the materials had "passed through the alembic of the biographer"; Miss Drew's "personal" approach is one in which the biographer aims "to give a definitely personal view of the evidence, to direct the reader's attention toward a certain valuation of the facts" (p. 96).

When Miss Drew puts Boswell's *Johnson* in her "impersonal" category, she explains that the personality of Boswell is an "unconscious element" in the *Life* (p. 90). When she speaks of the way in which the "personal" method works, she says, " . . . in any criticism of personality, there is generally one aspect of the facts, one pose of the sitter, which seems to hold the truest view of the subject. If the biographer can catch this pose, can capture that vision which seems to see most of the facts, and to relate their significance most justly to each other, the result is then an artistic composition which is peculiarly powerful in its effect, because it includes a double rhythm within it, a contra-puntal movement which is peculiarly satisfying. The complete personality which is being presented will be there, vivid, living, unmistakable; and it is exhibited in a searching, clarifying light, whose own quality adds enormously to the quality of the whole" (p. 101). The "double rhythm" and "contrapuntal move-ment" Miss Drew describes do not result from the interplay of the personality of the biographer with that of his subject. The biographer does not pose his subject; he catches a pose of the subject. The "vision" and the "searching, clarifying light" are not so much an active contribution of his aesthetic imagi-nation as something which he is perceptive enough to catch in and from his subject; they are something which "is exhibited" in an artistic composition, not the poetic gleam which results in a work of art.

If it seems a little difficult to see what is essentially personal in Miss Drew's "personal" method, she clarifies what she means when she says that only "the vision of a Shakespeare can perhaps envisage and interpret every kind of human personality" (p. 101). Her "personal" approach is, then, when it is successful, a matter of the biographer's negative capability, his empathy. Though she says that "the personality of the artist must inevitably color his art" (p. 90), she feels that a biographer's personality may limit his achievement "in width" even if it intensifies his success "within those limits" (p. 101). That is why she praises Johnson's *Savage* and Strachey's *Victoria* and *Manning* and why she thinks Johnson's *Milton* and *Swift* and Strachey's *Nightingale* and *Gordon* less successful. She finds "an obvious astigmatism in the vision of Lytton Strachey toward certain types of character very differ-ent from his own"; the light which his own personality sheds on a picture is ever present, "constant in its own quality," but his emphasis is wrong, his manipulation is faulty, his subject is not perfectly posed (pp. 101–2). Miss Drew leaves some room for the intrusion of the biographer's personality; she even leaves the door a little ajar for intuitive and psychological reconstruction of the inner life when she says that biography is "almost" inevitably limited (but not wholly limited) to reliance upon documentary evidence and when she says that it excludes not all but "so much" of the emotional possibilities that the novelist or dram-atist can create. But, for her, though biography is a conscious art, it is an art so considerably more restricted and so considerably farther removed from fiction than Maurois thought it to be that she conducts her discussion of biography with almost no overt mention of its relation to fiction.

VIRGINIA WOOLF

The relation of biography to fiction had, of course, been precisely Virginia Woolf's concern in her 1927 review-essay on "The New Biography." In reading the essay, one senses that it had not been easy for Mrs. Woolf to deal with that subject in the context of a review of Nicolson's *Some People*. There is no question that she welcomed the increasing intrusion of biography into the inner life of thought and emotion in its attempt to delineate personality, that she approved its movement away from the conventional counters of the world of brick and pavement, for these directions reflected the enlightened view of man which she thought to be the proper province of fiction. There is no question, too, that both for intellectual reasons, and personal ones, she wished to say some kind words about the nature of Nicolson's experiment, the "possible direction" he had opened for biography. But, despite her statement that Nicolson had proved the utility of many of the devices of fiction in dealing with real life, that he had demonstrated that "a little fiction" mixed with fact could be made to transmit personality very effectively, one is aware that she is at heart unhappy about what Nicolson did in *Some People*. The tentativeness of her opinion that Nicolson has found a "possible" direction, the bluntness of her statement that "truth of fact and truth of fiction are incompatible" hint, at the least, at the likelihood that the context of her remarks led her to leave rather more room for fiction in biography than she really wished.

Almost a dozen years later, Mrs. Woolf returned to the subject of biography, and this time the occasion was not so restricting. The very title of her essay, "The Art of Biography,"[24] would seem to provide the broadest leeway for her thought. Still, every essay has a context of a kind. Mrs. Woolf had started preliminary work on a life of Roger Fry in October, 1935. She did not, however, turn her main energies to the life until about April 1, 1938. By mid-December, when she completed "The Art of Biography," she had also written two-thirds of the *Fry*.[25] It is the rather conservative approach toward biography which she uses in the *Fry* which is in large measure reflected in the essay.

The little essay has four parts. In the first, Mrs. Woolf

announces that biography is "the most restricted" of all arts. The novelist is free: he creates without any restrictions except those he himself chooses to obey. The stuff of which biography is made is far different, and the biographer is "tied" to and by "the help of friends, of facts." In the past, biographers obeyed "the widow and the friends" who urged him to cover up or omit information, but, since Froude, they have won "a measure of freedom" which is reflected in the work of Gosse and Strachey. In her second part, Mrs. Woolf says that when Strachey came to his *Victoria* and to his *Elizabeth*, he had learned his job, proved his brilliance, and was capable of using all the liberties biography had won; she maintains, therefore, that his books are of such stature that they show what biography can and cannot do, whether it is an art, and, if not, why it fails. She calls the *Victoria* a triumphant success and the *Elizabeth* a failure, and holds that it was not Strachey who failed but "the art of biography." In the *Victoria*, she says, Strachey treated biography as a "craft" and submitted to its limitations. He used to the full the biographer's power of selection and relation, but he adhered strictly to verified statement and authenticated fact. In the *Elizabeth*, he treated biography as an "art" and flouted its limitations. Since little was known of Elizabeth, he was tempted to invent; still, something was known, and his invention was checked. As a result, Elizabeth moves in an ambiguous world, between fact and fiction. Mrs. Woolf concludes, therefore, that biography imposes conditions. It must be based on facts that can be verified by people other than the author. If the biographer invents and tries to combine what he has invented with facts that are authentic and verifiable, his two kinds of material destroy each other. Here, her conclusion is precisely the one she had reached in "The New Biography"—truth of fact and truth of fiction are incompatible.

The third part of the essay maintains that Strachey's experiment has shown biographers the way in which they may proceed. Though the biographer is bound by facts, he has the right to all available facts. These facts, Mrs. Woolf says, are not unchanging once they are discovered but are subject to changes of opinion brought about as "the times" change. She refers particularly to "facts won for us by the psychologists," who have shown that what was once thought to be a sin may be, instead, a misfortune, a curiosity, or a trifling foible; to the changed accent on sex, which has destroyed a good deal of dead matter about men; and (again she reverts to one of the main theses of "The New Biography") to the breaking down of arbitrary and artificial distinctions about the high points of a life. In the light of changed attitudes and new tools, she says, a biographer may now better detect "falsity, unreality, and the presence of obsolete conventions." In addition, "since so much is known that used to be unknown," since information is now available not only about successful men but also about those who have failed, about the humble as well as the illustrious, a biographer has a wider range of subject and he is in a position to "revise our standards of merit and set up new heroes for our admiration." The premise of her fourth part is that the life of biography differs from the life of poetry and fiction, that it deals with "a life lived at a lower degree of tension." She holds that, though "few poets and novelists are capable of that high degree of tension which gives us reality," the imagination of the writer of fiction "at its most intense fires out what is perishable in fact; he builds with what is durable; but the biographer must accept the perishable, build with it, imbed it in the very fabric of his work." She concludes, therefore, that the biographer is "a craftsman, not an artist; and his work is not a work of art, but something betwixt and between." She goes on to say that "we" are not capable of living wholly in the intense world of the imagination and that almost any biographer, by respecting and adhering to "the true facts," "by sifting the little from the big, and shaping the whole so that we perceive the outline," does more to stimulate the imagination than any poet or novelist except the very greatest. He can give us, she says, "the creative fact; the fertile fact; the fact that suggests and engenders."

The essay is attractive in its relaxed simplicity and geniality; it moves with lovely facility from one major idea to another, uncluttered by the shrillness of polemic, the bite of irony, the rigor of argument, the heaviness of documented evidence; it is almost neo-classical in its appeal to the few easy truths which need to be known in order to be saved, and, at the same time it is richly suggestive. It is, also, not free of confusion and ambiguity. The first two paragraphs, for instance, are offputting, as Mrs. Woolf reaches rather too conveniently to justify raising the question of whether biography is an art. She assumes there must be something behind the question merely because it "asks itself so often" and because few biographies survive of the many written; she plays rather naively with the idea of the relative newness of biography ("Interest in our selves and in other people's selves is a late development of the human mind"). She develops her thesis that biography is restricted by focusing, first of all, exclusively on the effect of the help, and interference, of friends; very awkwardly, she tucks in a reference to "the help . . . of facts" which seems a non sequitur until the reader later becomes aware of the way in which biography is restricted by fact and can work out for himself the relation between the restrictions imposed by friends and by facts.

The fact is that Mrs. Woolf's definition of "fact" and her discussion of the role which fact plays in biography are confusing. She starts by saying that biography "must be based upon fact," and, she continues, "by fact in biography we mean facts that can be verified by other people besides the artist." But, she goes on, "these facts are not like the facts of science—once they are discovered, always the same. They are subject to changes of opinion; opinions change as the times change." She implies, then, that all the facts of science are immutable and unalterable and that all biographical fact is subject to re-interpretation. It is difficult, however, to see any difference between "For every action, there is an equal and opposite reaction" and "X was born on January 25, 1882, and died on March 28, 1941." It seems equally true that both these can be variously viewed, depending on their context; science as well as biography knows the condition in which facts will support different hypotheses and interpretations equally well. Moreover, though Mrs. Woolf says that the "facts won for us by the psychologists" open up new opportunities for biographical re-interpretation, those "facts"—since they are, by her definition, scientific, rigorous, immutable—would seem, rather, to limit and restrict opportunities for re-interpretation.

Even more confusing is Mrs. Woolf's method of determining whether biography is an art. I do not have in mind her too easy ploy of using Strachey as a test case but the uncertainty which stems from her indirection in introducing and defining her criteria. In the second part of her essay, she introduces what seems to be the primary criterion for art when she says that Strachey "had wished to write poetry or plays but was doubtful of his creative power" and that "biography seemed to offer a promising alternative." Art is, then, dependent on what an author puts into his work, upon his creative power, his invention, his originality. In thus stressing fictionality and originality, Mrs. Woolf does not take into consideration the point raised by Trueblood and by Maurois that the writer of fiction frequently deals with historical characters and known events, nor does she consider the point, made so well by John Livingston Lowes,[26] that the use of common materials and common language "with a new distinction, a fresh vividness, a more compelling power" offers to originality its richest field. Moreover, in the context of her own statements, it is not clear whether biography is deficient as art because it does not allow sufficient opportunity for creative and inventive power or because the mixture of invention and fact is self-destroying.

Creativity is not, however, Mrs. Woolf's only important criterion for art, though she delays her discussion of a second criterion until the last part of her essay. She had, to be sure, hinted at this criterion in her third part, where she states that the character of fiction "lives in a free world where the facts are verified by one person only—the artist himself. Their authenticity lies in the truth of his own vision." She goes on to say, "The world created by that vision is rarer, intenser, and more wholly of a piece than the world that is largely made of authentic information supplied by other people." It turns out that her criterion for art in her last section is dependent not on what the writer puts into his work but on what he leaves out. When she says that "the artist's imagination at its most intense fires out what is perishable in fact," she does not use "fact" in the sense either of an unalterable scientific truth or of an interpretation of a real event but she refers, rather, to the raw materials of the artist's own imagination and creation. She has in mind something like Forster's dictum that the novel has no necessary relation to chronological life, to the uninteresting flats and routine involvements of life, and she rightly suggests that the biographer, who must represent the normal tenor of a man's life as well as its high points if he is to present an accurate picture, must embed more of the usual or "perishable" into his story than the novelist, who is free to focus on what is special and idiosyncratic. When Mrs. Woolf says that biography differs from poetry and fiction in that it constructs "a life lived at a lower degree of tension," when she says that fiction is capable of "that high degree of tension which gives us reality," she does not explicitly define what she means by "tension"; but, clearly, she is not referring to degrees of pushes and pulls on a life but to the tight control which a writer of fiction exercises on his materials, to his ability to prune away extraneous material which may dilute the kind of world he is constructing and the unique effect he is after, to what, in *Orlando*, she called "the cardinal labour of composition, which is excision." Although she here points to a difference between fiction and biography which is easily recognizable, she does not take the trouble to demonstrate convincingly that the criterion of selection (or simplification, or omission) prevents biography from being an art. She merely announces that "even Dr. Johnson as created by Boswell will not live as long as Falstaff as created by Shakespeare."[27]

"The Art of Biography," Mrs. Woolf entitles her essay, and after reading it carefully we are still uncertain whether or not she considers biography an art. In her second part, she implies that biography is a craft, that it differs from art in that it has limitations which cannot be flouted. In her last part, she concludes that the biographer is a craftsman, not an artist; his work is not a work of art, but something "betwixt and between." Still, she chooses to call her essay "The Art of Biography," not "The Craft of Biography," and it is fair to say that she considers biography an art, though one different from fiction. At least as early as 1909, Mrs. Woolf had come to the conclusion that "the bare statement of facts has an indisputable power, if we have reason to think them true" and that this power is aesthetic; "the aesthetic effect of truth," she said, "is only to be equalled by the imagination of genius."[28] In "The New Biography," she referred to the biographer as an artist because he had to choose and synthesize materials and manipulate facts, and she insisted that truth of fact has the almost mystic power of giving off, infinitely, grains of energy, atoms of light. Her opinion does not change in 1939. There is a "peculiar virtue" in fact; it has its own "suggestive reality, its own proper creativeness." Despite her own explicit announcement that the biographer's work is not a work of art, that he is a craftsman rather than an artist, her equally explicit announcement that the biographer can give us "the creative fact; the fertile fact; the fact that suggests and engenders" indicates that, though she considers biography different from other arts, more limited than fiction, she still conceives of it as a kind of art.

Although Mrs. Woolf makes no reference in her essay to the historians' views of biography, or, for that matter, to anyone else's, its effect was to lend support to their ideas. Here was a writer best known for her bold experiments in fiction, for her desire to extend the possibilities of fiction; a writer equally renowned for the wildest of biographical excursions in *Orlando*; and here she is, maintaining that biography inhabits a special, limited domain, one very much different from that of fiction. What her readers remembered, mainly, about her essay was her stress on fact in biography, her emphasis on its limitations, for the structure of the essay enforces the ideas that her chief concern is to determine whether biography is an art and that her major effort is to discriminate between fiction and biography. Her stress on the value and power of fact and its delimiting the field of biography tend to minimize and hide her unusual definition of biographical fact, the premium she puts on interpretation. Nor does she deal so thoroughly and overtly as she had in "The New Biography" with the necessity of representing personality through the exploration of the inner life of thought and emotion. Though she advocates a revision of "the old chapter headings—life at college, marriage, career" precisely as she had in "The New Biography," though she feels deeply that the biographer's power of interpretation may prove daring and revolutionary in revising standards of merit and in setting up new heroes for admiration, these ideas are buried in a couple of paragraphs at the end of the third part of her essay. Though "The Art of Biography" of 1939 revises only very slightly one of the ideas in "The New Biography" of 1927, their effect on the biographical climate was very much different. The argument of "The New Biography," followed by *Orlando* in 1928, had helped to create an atmosphere of change and excitement for biography, a sense of the opening of vistas. The appearance of "The Art of Biography," followed by the publication of the *Life of Fry* in 1940, gave the impression that Mrs. Woolf was far less adventuresome, far more conservative, the advocate of an age of sobriety in biography.

Despite Mumford's reassertion of the place of psychology and of the centrality of the inner life in biography, despite Edgar Johnson's reassertion of the place of science in biography and his impassioned declaration that biography as an art could profit from and amalgamate learning of all kinds, the criticism of biography in the thirties was largely directed against the intrusion of psychology and fiction. If no one was so ferociously anti-literary as De Voto, if most critics still made some overtures toward biography as an art, the flirtation of biography with the novel had the general effect of making the term "art" suspect in its relation with biography; Mumford avoids it, Miss Drew's discussion is as much guarded as it is discriminating and subtle, Mrs. Woolf's is filled with ambiguity and misleading emphasis. Because recognition of her own powerful allegiance to fiction was widespread, her effort to separate fiction from biography was probably more influential than De Voto's. In the same way, De Voto's blast against psychology and the usual disdain of the historians toward it may not have been so persuasive as other efforts. They are hardly so instructive as Maurois's fable about the dangers of psychoanalysis, *La Machine à Lire les Pensées* (1937), in which he invents a thought-reading machine or "psychograph" that records automatically and without discrimination, in optimal Nicolsonian fashion, a person's daydreams and fugitive thoughts as well as the chosen beliefs which guide and control his conduct, and in which he concludes that the machine presents a view of character which is less true than that derived from the examination of a man's actions.[29]

It is likely, however, that the most telling statements about the relation between psychology and biography are the ones which came from the psychologists themselves. Unlike many other critics, they do not, of course, question the validity of the findings of psychology for biography, but they emphasize the difficulty of communicating these findings effectively and look to the art of the biographer and the novelist for help. Gordon W. Allport had written the first American dissertation on the question of the component traits of personality; this led to a book (written with his brother Floyd), *Personality Traits: Their Classification and Measurement*, published in 1921. His course in personality at Harvard in 1924 was probably the first such course offered in an American university. In 1937, his book *Personality: A Psychological Interpretation* appeared.[30] He was, then, probably the most distinguished psychologist in the field of personality when he wrote, in 1938, "Only a pedant could prefer the dry collections of facts that psychology can offer regarding an individual mental life to the glorious and unforgettable portraits that the gifted novelist, dramatist, or biographer can give."[31] His colleague at Harvard, Henry A. Murray, wrote in the same year, "A psychologist who believes that he can tell the truth without being 'literary' has only to try writing a case history or biography, and then compare what he has done to a character sketch by any novelist of the first order."[32]

The thirties end, then, not only with one of the pre-eminent novelists of the time drawing the lines between biography and fiction, but also with two pre-eminent psychologists lending their voices to the appreciation of the role of art in biography, at least to the extent of stating that the effective representation of the truths of psychology is dependent upon art.

PHILIP GUEDELLA

The dominant movement of the thirties, however, was a return to the principles of Sir Sidney Lee, a reassertion of biography's fundamental link with history. The prevalent point of view is the one expressed by Philip Guedella in his lecture "The Method of Biography" before the Royal Society for the Encouragement of Arts, Manufactures and Commerce on May 24, 1939.[33] Oddly enough, Guedella does not mention Lee. For him, biography is "a simple thing to define," and he plucks from Gosse's article on "Biography" in the *Encyclopaedia Britannica* of 1910 the introductory definition that Gosse had used in a historical sense; biography is "that form of history which is applied, not to races or masses of men, but to an individual." Guedella omits Gosse's further definition of biography as "a branch of literature," and though he says that Gosse's additional attempt at definition— biography is "the faithful portrait of a soul in its adventures through life"—is questionable, there is no question that he does not approve of it. For him, biography and history have "the same mission, the same method, and the same material, which they must judge by the same rules of evidence." The biographer must, then, "run a very straight course," a course which excludes excursions "between two particularly green and tempting fields," psychology and "pure literature."

Although Guedella admits that "a definite enlargement of curiosity" has extended the field of biography beyond a man's public acts, public works, and public achievements into his thoughts, feelings, and motives, and he seems, almost, to approve of this, he still speaks of psychology as "rather squashy ground," as a "specious path," half of which consists of "something we all knew before" and the other half of "something which is not so." Although he admits that there are times when it is possible to obtain evidence about secret thoughts and private motives, he thinks that it is almost impossible, even for a man possessing a historical imagination, to interpret that evidence properly, and he says that the resulting conjecture moves the biographer out of history into fiction. Guedella insists that the biographer ("the historical biographer" is his phrase) must not digress into "pure literature," that it is his "humbler duty" to go only where the historical facts take him, and that, unlike the "pure artist," he has no business making his subject conform to a design of his own making, no right to "curve" his subject "like a vase." He suggests that he is conscious of biography as an art when he refers on one occasion to "the art of biography," but he reduces the biographer's "duty to literature and art" to his writing with a pen rather than with a pick-axe. For him, art in biography means, merely, to take the reader on a trip along historical rails "with as little discomfort as possible."[34]

IV

To the Mid-Fifties

The formulations summarized in Guedella's article persisted for the next decade and a half. They dominated the 1940s almost by default, for publication in the area of the criticism of biography was negligible. When discussion resumed during the first years of the fifties, it was to restate and support the main attitude of the late thirties. Interestingly enough, however, the two relevant articles published in the forties are more hospitable to the art involved in biography than were the historians of the late twenties and of the thirties.[1]

WILLIAM G. WEEDON

The first of these, William G. Weedon's "Concerning Biography" (1941),[2] fascinating as it is, stands outside the critical and theoretical debate. Whatever influence it may have had is unacknowledged; its publication is referred to only twice in the next thirty years in the main line of critical writing.[3] Though Weedon seems aware of prior work in the theory and criticism of biography, his article does not contain a single overt reference to any of it; except for fleeting comments on hagiography and the gospels, the only life he mentions is that of Hiram Maxim by his son. His approach is a technically philosophic one, and he relies on fundamental aspects of aesthetic theory. His aim is to elicit "certain facts concerning the manner, means, and objects of biographic representation which shall enable us to distinguish the art from other allied representative arts" and to estimate the importance of biographic art to intelligent human activity (p. 251).

Weedon starts by declaring that "biography is defined by a certain intersection of history and drama" (p. 247). Like many others, he says that its components involve "a genuine obligation to matter of fact, and a no less genuine structural unity whose tragic and comic elements may mingle in a bewilderingly complex pattern" and that the synthesis of elements is "a problem of delicate adjustment in which the sturdy factual ingredients contend with the more subtle demands of dialectical simplicity." He distinguishes biographic art from graphic art in that it represents not a thing but a life or a "living" (p. 248), an "entity in time" (p. 249), and he says that in order to handle "entities partaking of passage," one must reduce their complexity by using a variety of conventional simplifications. "Biography," he explains, "is a set of symbols, and the art of biography is the technique of employing these symbols in such a way as to represent univocally a unique living" (p. 249). Since "it is impossible to represent any unique living without automatically indicating an ideal pattern" (p. 251), a unique living must be represented "as illustrating, or as falling under, some invariant pattern." Without the pattern, he says, the uniqueness is barren, "for the pattern is the container of alternatives within which the unique is a selection," and without the uniqueness, "the pattern is empty, a mere form, lacking in the determinate specificity which characterizes anything we know as a 'living.'" It is, then, he maintains, the pattern which gives significance, and the unique living to which significance is given, and, he further maintains, "the representation of bare matter of fact (if that is, indeed, quite possible) is not biography, even when of some unique subject" and "the speculative demonstration of some pattern, even though this pattern have a unique exemplar in fact, fails to fulfill the requirements for genuine biography" (p. 250).

Weedon points out that the function of pattern in biography differs from its function in most science and in Aristotelian tragedy. He starts by making a distinction between a particular which *falls under* a given species and an individual which *is seen as associated* with some ideal pattern (p. 259). The theoretical physicist assumes that natural activity is ordered activity, and once he has defined an activity, he assumes that no new values "will be ingredient" to it.[4] The medieval theologian, he says, worked in the same way: he treated human values as the physicist treats

physical values because he chose "to define his entities in advance in respect of the formal properties of the activities dis-
played by these entities." That is why hagiography deals in types
of living rather than in an individual living. But, he says, "biography is essentially a protestant art": "it designates a unique
living because that 'living' is of some special significance and
interest." It aims at "subsuming under a certain set of ideals
which taken together form a pattern, some unique living for the
purpose of forming a judgment." Weedon differentiates two methods or types of biography. In the first, "the activity is given and
the ideal disclosed in the representation." In the second, "the
ideal is given and the representation discloses a unique activity
whose existence has been indicated." The second type shades into
the first, however, when representation forces a reconsideration
and modification of the ideal to produce an emergent ideal (pp.
259–61). In an interesting aside, Weedon says that biographers of
historical figures try to use only a minimum of ideals and "to
suppress, in so far as possible, any pattern which might extend the
significance of the represented 'living' over a considerable area."
They do this, he thinks, in an attempt to avoid the charges of
"preconceived opinions, dogmatism and Hegelianism," and he
thinks, too, that their policy is unfortunate. What is important
here is to recognize that the ideal, the pattern, is used as *hypothesis*: "So far as the pattern is used as hypothesis, it means
merely that the unique living is the subject always for further
investigation, of which the hypothesis will display a certain aspect,
and that its significance will not be regarded as abruptly restricted
to some other limited domain" (p. 262).

Weedon further clarifies the function of pattern in biography when he considers the question of the "completeness" of
any action with respect to biography. All activity, he says, involves
"a welter of relationships"; how, then, "can any action be
complete in itself if relatedness ramifies indefinitely"? He holds
that "completeness" is a formal property, an ideal: "By 'complete,' we mean simply that there is a pattern under which the
'living' is subsumed during the process of representation." In
biography, completeness is, then, "the requirement that a selection occur among a welter of alternatives suggested by the
associated pattern" (pp. 262–64). Biography becomes trivial, he
maintains, when it becomes merely the illustration of an ideal; if
an ideal is strictly adhered to and perfectly illustrated, a life is as
predictable as the trajectory of a bullet in Newtonian mechanics.
A good biography, on the other hand, "should suggest an ex-

trapolation beyond the actual confines of the represented activity to new situations not explicitly in the realm of the actual" (p. 263).

Finally, Weedon shows that the biographer uses pattern differently from the writer of tragedy. In Aristotelian tragedy, he says, a single set of values is invariant throughout the action (though it is strained to its limits) and the notion of character is that of "a moral agent whose nature is single," however rare singleness of moral purpose is in reality. The tragic pattern as defined by Aristotle leads the writer of tragedy to edit the "living" in such a way as to eliminate those elements which are irrelevant for tragic action. A biographer may indicate a tragic pattern along with a "living," but he also has an obligation to matters of fact; he must take the whole of the evidence of the "living" into account, a "living" far more complex than any tragedy suggests.[5] In Aristotle's own terms, Weedon says, "biography is something 'less philosophic' than tragedy." Biography, he continues, is "the technique of representing the mingled reflections of comedy and tragedy in the actual." Since, in comic action, "a certain set of values is disrupted rather than maintained," since laughter breaks up conventional standards, biography moves beyond the pattern of tragedy (pp. 265–66). The importance of biography, Weedon holds, lies in its ability to display new ways of understanding change and motion, to suggest new ways of interpreting ourselves which move beyond the routines which enmesh thought and life. Moreover, in exposing the "bloodless ideals of manhood and manly conduct" present in most ideologies, in representing a man as he is, biography may subvert "the various forms of 'vicious intellectualism' which seek to package the facts too neatly or solve too glibly the problem of the ultimate end of man" and may aid in the discovery of the elements of stability in life (p. 267).

Weedon's article is a kind of sport amongst those we have been examining. Literary critics, historians, and students of biography are not likely to be sympathetic to what they consider to be the vicious intellectualism of philosophy. I have myself omitted a large part of what Weedon has to say about biography as a representational art: he makes fundamental distinctions between biography as "mime" and biography as words, but he dismisses painting and sculpture quickly as "merely 'graphic' " arts which aim "at the representation of some presentationally immediate image or object, or of some eternal object which is in a sense out of time," whereas biographic art "has as its end the representation of some entity in time" (pp. 248–49). He is interested in the concept of imitation, in the problem of representing activity rather than stasis, in the falsification involved in representation, but when he discusses some basic matters of verbal discourse he does not seem to recognize sufficiently that these are not peculiar to biography but common to all verbal art. Moreover, his definition of biography as an intersection of history and drama seems arbitrary and convenient. He does not bother to explain why he opts for the drama rather than the novel, and if he does not himself conceive of tragedy in a narrowly Aristotelian sense, he chooses to treat it in that way, even as he limits himself to a Bergsonian approach in his brief discussion of comedy.

Still, Weedon's assumption that biography is a representational art sheds light on the nature of biography, particularly in his demonstrations that the biographer must avail himself of pattern and that the good biographer will reveal the limitations of formal patterns. Again, though his treatment of pattern or ideal is general (he does not discuss in any detail the differences of theses, stereotypes, unannounced assumptions, points of view toward a subject, broad metaphysical attitudes), he does emphasize the central role of the biographer. He shows more persuasively than anyone before him that if every good biographer must utilize a pattern of his choice, he must also be aware that an individual life is so complex that it will not conform to a pattern. He shows effectively, too, not only that pattern provides a standard for measuring the individuality of a life but also that the individuality of a life helps in the re-examination of an ideal so that it may be qualified or modified. He clarifies how, in Virginia Woolf's terms, biography is in a position "to revise our standards of merit and set up new heroes for our admiration."

JAMES THOMAS FLEXNER

Although James Thomas Flexner's short article, "Biography as a Juggler's Art" (1943),[6] is like Weedon's in that it does not mention prior criticism or specific biographies, its approach is far more traditional. Like many other critics, Flexner conceives of biography as a complicated art which combines things seemingly irreconcilable: "Concerned with the depiction of personality, the biographer must be an imaginative writer; concerned with the resurrection of actual men and events, he must be a meticulous scholar. On one hand, he leans towards the technique of the novelist; on the other, towards the technique of the documentary historian." Flexner's most telling comments are about the biographer-as-documentary-historian who insists that his work is "completely impersonal and nonpartisan, entirely accurate." He says nothing new when he points out that even such a writer is selective, that in dwelling on the documents he considers most significant he depends on his own interpretation of his subject's career, but Flexner does not stop here. "Biographies made up entirely of facts, dates, and quoted source materials," he contends, "are in one way more misleading than those in which the author permits himself some leeway. When a writer draws his conclusions on paper instead of solely in his mind, we may recognize his point of view and take it into consideration as we read. But when an author keeps himself always in the background, we may only discover his prejudices by making a new study of the source material." The value of the "purely factual" biography is that it may serve as a source book for a biographer.

Flexner quickly dismisses the biographer-as-novelist who neglects sound scholarship to produce a dramatic story, full of improvisation and invention. He concerns himself with the limitations of the writer who, though he respects both accuracy and readability, is content to base a new interpretation of his subject on the obvious printed sources, including previously published lives, rather than on a re-examination of the primary sources. Since even the most scholarly study is a selection which reflects a specific point of view, it follows, Flexner says, that the biographer who merely uses several such interpretations can only produce "an interpretation of interpretations." It is the writer who goes to original sources who is likely to find the "evidence that was unimportant from the point of view of his predecessors but which will open up to him new vistas of interpretation."

The mastery of primary sources is just a beginning, Flexner says, and the biographer must make "a synthesis of his material similar to that a novelist makes from the observed facts of life": "Before him lies the tangled record of a personality acting within a fixed period of years. He must weigh evidence and draw conclusions; he must interpret and explain." The phrases "observed facts of life" and "personality acting" introduce limitations; despite his emphasis on personality, Flexner says nothing about the place of interiority, of the inner life of thought and emotion, in biography. Moreover, despite his pronouncements about point of view, he introduces restrictions even where that is concerned. Although the biographer recognizes that "he cannot so far escape the limitations of the human mind as to write pure truth uninfluenced by his own personality and environment," Flexner maintains that he must strive to do so: "The broader his view-point, the closer he comes to a universal approach, the more valuable his book will be." He still, then, equates "complete intellectual honesty" with "impartiality." Again, when he says that impartiality need not imply lack of color, that a good writer can make a life exciting and dramatic, it becomes clear that his concept of the role of art in biography is limited. The writer who "alters" events to create suspense and climax has probably not grasped "the inherent possibilities" of his subject; like Maurois, though in a different context, Flexner says, "Facts are stranger than fiction; the imagination of nature is more audacious than that of man." Only in one matter does he allow the biographer some of the novelist's freedom. Though he feels that chronology is "the only natural thread on which the events of man's life may be strung," he thinks that the biographer, like the novelist, may on occasion anticipate happenings and work back to their explanation and that he may even resort to the "dangerous expedient" of grouping like events together even if they happened in different years.[7]

Flexner's conclusions, then, are essentially conservative and of the sort which the historians of the thirties would have approved. But, even if his view of art is limited, even if his call for impartiality tends to subdue his discussion of the inevitability of point of view and his advocacy of a clearly articulated point of view in biography, some of his statements go farther than his conclusions in providing leeway for the imagination of the biographer.

HAROLD NICOLSON

The fifties start with a cautionary article which must have warmed the hearts of the historians of the thirties. More than two decades had passed since Harold Nicolson had written *Some People*; he was, in 1953, Sir Harold, the author of the recently published official life of George V when his article "The Practice of Biography" appeared in the *Cornhill Magazine*.[8] His old urbanity is still present when he writes about "the young men and maidens who, without possessing any compulsive creative gift, think that it would be nice to write a book" and are attracted to biography "since it provides them with a ready-made plot, need entail no tremendous energy of research, and enables them to relieve their sensibility without placing too taut a strain upon their imagination"; but there is nothing in his article to persuade the young men and maïdens that they are mistaken.

Much of the article is culled from *The Development of English Biography*, but its general tenor is such that the ghost of Sir

Sidney Lee must have smiled approvingly. Nicolson retains his bias against religion, his advocacy of the *Oxford Dictionary*'s definition of biography, and his distinctions between pure and impure biography. His opinions on most subjects are unchanged, but he expresses them somewhat more dogmatically. Whereas in the *Development* biography as a branch of literature meant that it must be "composed as a work of art" (though even here his concept of art is narrow), art now means that a life "must be written in grammatical English and with an adequate feeling for style." When he speaks of the writer's imagination, he defines it as the adding of the colors of fiction or romance to narrative, and he calls for a check upon imagination in biography. In the *Development*, he had spoken of the "undue subjectivity" of the biographer and had insisted that the intrusion of his personality and predilections led to impurity, but he had pointed out that a subjective attitude was in some measure inevitable and desirable and that the best English biography contained or conveyed a sketch of the biographer subsidiary to that of the subject. In "The Practice of Biography," he continues to maintain that "biography is always a collaboration between the author and his subject; always there must be the reflection of one temperament in the mirror of another," but, he continues: "The biographer should thus be careful not to permit his own personality to intrude too markedly upon the personality that he is describing; he should be wary of assigning his own opinions, prejudices or affections to the man or woman whose life he writes; he should take special pains to deal fairly with views which he does not share, or interests that bore him; his egoism should be muzzled and kept on a chain. He should constantly remind himself that it is not an autobiography that he is composing, but the life of someone else; the statue of Modesty should dominate his study, a finger on her lips."

In the *Development*, Nicolson had praised Froude for introducing into biography the element of satire, the kind of skeptical detachment which is the main element in twentieth-century biography. Here, his admiration for Froude is unabated, but he warns that the satirical attitude easily degenerates into "false history and false psychology" and that skepticism turns easily into derision. He disapproves of Strachey's "ironical titters" and says that he enjoyed paradox more than he respected precision, had little sense of history, and exaggerated the lights and shadows of his portraits—and he respects even less what he terms the superciliousness of Strachey's imitators. His reference to "false psychology" is the only one to psychology in the article; it contains none of his old faith in the pre-eminent value of psychology and of scientific analysis for the understanding of personality.

Most of the article is an account of the "extraneous purposes," the "perils and illnesses," "infections," "pests and parasites" that undermine pure biography: "an undue desire to commemorate, a too earnest endeavour to teach or preach, a tendency to portray types rather than individuals, the temptation to enhance self-esteem by indulging in irony, the inability to describe selflessly, and the urge to slide into fiction or to indulge in fine writing." The "positive principles" Nicolson recommends are few—knowledge, sympathy, and tact—and the last of these gets the most discussion. The ideal subject is "one of which the author has direct personal experience and with which he can enter into sympathetic relationship." Nicolson thinks that the advantages of writing about a contemporary far outweigh the problems of discretion; the biographer need only remember that his reader will pay more attention to passages which reveal hitherto concealed defects than to those which praise familiar merits, and he must tactfully indicate the defects and shadows so that they will not assume importance out of proportion to the whole portrait.[9] In concluding, Nicolson, having stated that "without seeking for one moment to preach a lesson, a good biography encourages people to believe that man's mind is in truth unconquerable and that character can triumph over the most hostile circumstances, provided only that it remains true to itself," raises the question of whether what he has said implies a return to hagiography. He holds that it does not, that he means only to point out that the biographer should be as "cautious" in his choice of subject as in his method.

WILMARTH S. LEWIS

Almost the whole of Wilmarth S. Lewis's "The Difficult Art of Biography" (1954)[10] derives from Nicolson's article. Lewis cites with approval and uses as framework for his own article Nicolson's interpretation of the *OED* definition of biography. He is chiefly interested in developing Nicolson's statements about the advantages of dealing with a contemporary subject, and he stresses, as Nicolson had not, the great advantage which a contemporary biographer, completely familiar with the customs, manners, speech, and attitudes of his own time, has over one who must attune himself to the nuances of remote periods. He points out, in addition, that the same advantage accrues to the biographer who is younger by a generation than his subject, with the added one that the younger biographer's slightly different point of view adds another sense of dimension to the life. Only in one matter does Lewis differ somewhat from Nicolson. Nicolson's advocacy of sympathy leads Lewis to maintain that the "chief" danger to the biographer lies in his identifying himself with his subject to such a degree that he becomes an apologist for his subject and himself, and he thinks that the non-contemporary biographer is more vulnerable here than the contemporary who has met his subject and seen and felt his weaknesses. He introduces one matter which Nicolson had not treated—the biographer's ignorance not only of the precise details and circumstances of critical moments in his subject's life but also of his inner life, his moral and spiritual struggles, the regions of his soul "which Plutarch likens to the unknown portions on old maps where 'all beyond is nothing but monsters and tragic fictions.' "[11] In all these matters, Lewis has as little to say about the biographer's imagination as Nicolson does. For him, biography "as a branch of literature" means, as it does for Nicolson, the writing of decent prose, and he announces that the best literary styles in English are based on familiarity with the Greek and Latin classics and with the King James Bible.

HESKETH PEARSON

The most extreme argument for biography as a branch of literature had been made by Hesketh Pearson in 1930. In 1955, Pearson, who had more nearly equated the art of biography with the art of the novel than even Maurois had, gave a lecture, "About Biography," before the Royal Society of Literature.[12] The most interesting thing about it is his preliminary remark that he had reread his *Ventilations* and disagreed with most of what it said. Still, much of what he had said there he repeats here.

In his book, Pearson had stated that any form of moral earnestness, any ethical point of view was fatal to the art of biography, and here, too, he hits biographers who have an axe to grind (p. 61). In *Ventilations*, he had said that personal contact with his subject blurred the biographer's vision; here, though he feels that "the biographer must on the whole like his subject, because truth is revealed to sympathy, concealed from antipathy" (p. 58), he still maintains that personal friendship is not conducive to "the sympathetic detachment so necessary to the biographer" (p. 66). He had said in 1930 that Strachey had got as close as possible to "the ideal of absolute detachment and impartiality"; here, he continues to praise him, and he says that even though "absolute impartiality and passionate disinterest" cannot be attained, they are the qualities which make for good biography and must be strived for (p. 61). In *Ventilations*, his remarks both about moral earnestness and personal contact had indicated his concern for whatever truth was attainable; that concern was expressed, however, within the context of his assertion that there is no such thing as truth, his belief that "unessential" facts may be sacrificed in order to achieve "essential truth," and his refusal to place limits on the biographer's fictional creativity and his freedom of invention. Here, Pearson disparages "the fictionized arty stuff of today" and says that "if a biography is not as true as a writer can make it, it is not only valueless but pernicious" (p. 57). Again, in *Ventilations*, his advocacy of detachment, paradoxical and almost contradictory though it may have appeared, had seemed to indicate not his preference for one point of view rather than for others, but the best way of arriving at a point of view; it did not undercut to any large degree his belief that "pure" biography is a chimera and that the biographer can only tell the truth as he sees it. The discussion of detachment in the lecture omits the primary thesis of the book—that biography is the expression of one man's personality through that of another, that every biography must be written from the angle of the author, from his peculiar point of view, and that to make his point of view effective the biographer may give free rein to his imagination and intuition. Without this thesis, the lecture becomes a retraction, a major retreat which moves toward objectivity of point of view and toward belief in a kind of objective truth.

HUMPHRY HOUSE

Nicolson had minimized the art in biography not by treating its relations with fiction and psychology head on but by diminishing the biographer's opportunities for self-expression in his discussions of undue subjectivity and extraneous purposes. Both he and Lewis had restricted art in biography not by confrontation but by definition, by their narrow interpretation of the relation of biography to literature. Pearson had not directly refuted his earlier views, but had retracted them. In his article, "The Present Art of Biography," published in 1955, Humphry House picks up where Jones, Adams, Bryant, De Voto, and Guedella had left off, and his argument is pointedly directed against interiority, against self-expression, against relating biography to "literature."[13] His thesis that "biography should not properly be spoken of as an art" (p. 267) is all the more persuasive since in the course of making it he shows himself to be a sensitive literary critic, exquisitely attuned to the power and nuances of style.

House maintains, as Guedella had in 1939, that Macaulay had introduced a "healthy" tradition of biography and that in the later part of the nineteenth century the qualities which Strachey demanded of biography—selection, detachment, design, and becoming brevity—were almost the formula of a convention.[14] He maintains, too, that these qualities were "an inadequate manifesto of the revolution" which Strachey sought to bring about (p. 260); the clue to Strachey's revolution lies, he thinks, in his use of the word "art," but since Strachey never fully explained his use of it, House cites Cecil's views of 1936 as a statement of what "the art of biography" has, in the light of Strachey's work, been thought to consist in. He says that in advocating a kind of biography which was a work of art rather than of history, which was primarily literature in its focus on the writer's individual vision and in its concern for the expression of the biographer's creative powers and of his personality, Cecil moved the whole conception of biography some distance from Strachey's own principles. Strachey had, to be sure, said that the biographer should "maintain his own freedom of spirit," but in so saying he was not giving *carte blanche* to the biographer for the uninhibited expression of his own personality but indicating the necessity of his not being hampered by the conventionalities of discretion. Cecil's views are inconsistent with Strachey's emphasis on the detachment of the biographer, though Strachey's own occasional deficiencies here may have led his imitators astray. They were misled into thinking that his veneer of patronizing aloofness, of irony, and of mockery was the essence of his work (pp. 260–61).

Cecil's view, House says, has led to a limitation of the biographer's vision, and he thinks that the limitation has been caused partly by "an imperfect apprehension of the findings and gropings of psychology." "Artistic" biography has, he says, neglected the "superego" in its search for the "ego"; it has emphasized the "private" life at the expense of the "social life"; it has stressed personal relations more than the wider social context; and it has been more concerned with emotional considerations than with intellectual considerations (p. 261). He illustrates what he means in a short analysis of Gerald Bullett's life of George Eliot and in a longer one of Cecil's own essay on Thomas Gray in *Two Quiet Lives*. Bullett's book, he says, has traces of Strachey's aloof and patronizing tone, and he finds it inadequate as a life because Bullett never stresses adequately Eliot's massive learning and her intellectual achievements. These are mentioned chiefly to support a theory that they interfered with her artistic creativity; Bullett does not relate them to her moral and emotional life, and he emphasizes, rather, the emotional needs of her personality and her personal relations. Cecil merely repeats the oft-quoted remark that Gray was one of the most learned men in Europe, but he never allows his reader to appreciate Gray's real place in the development of the studies he pursued; he uses the studies only as the topic of letters between Gray and his friends, and this use not only enforces the impression that Gray's life was a quiet one but makes him appear "altogether a smaller personality than he really was." Moreover, Cecil's "self-conscious," "mannered" style, the "softness and weakness" of his prose, make for a "light, thin, cobweb-like" effect which influences the reader's attitude toward Gray so that he appears to be far more "effete and exquisite" than his own robust, precise, and energetic style in the letters suggests (pp. 262–65). House maintains, then, that the element of selection involves not only the ordering of documents and evidence but also the fair allotment of attention and sympathy to all the voices in which a subject speaks, and he insists that when a biographer has a highly personal style, "a new kind of unconscious and illegitimate selection" occurs which distorts these voices and affects even the context in which they are heard (p. 266).[15]

House feels that the writer of "the first full biography of a dead man"[16] who puts too much emphasis on brevity and design will inevitably oversimplify and empty of some of its richness and vitality the very quality of his subject's consciousness and action. "Biography should not properly be spoken of as an art" because "an artist creates his own limits without the violation of anything except his own larger designs," but "a biographer has to adopt and adjust limitations under the stress of a great many different external influences" (pp. 266–67). For him, then, as for Virginia Woolf, the biographer is not free; he is tied by fact. He goes on to say, moreover, that the last thing the biographer should express is himself; though he cannot be wholly detached, his every sentence should be an exercise in detachment designed to bring forward the whole context of a life, all its circumstances and its social setting.[17] He says that unlike Strachey, who, at his best, knew facts intimately and laid them bare as he understood them, practitioners of the "artistic" convention lack solidity and range in their knowledge and understanding of fact (pp. 267–68). In accusing the biographer who treats biography as an art closely allied to "literature" of inadequate learning, of emphasizing the private and emotional life of his subject at the expense

of his social role and his achievements, of projecting his own personality and indulging in self-expression at the expense of his subject, House moves even beyond De Voto in the deficiencies and
limitations he finds.

J. I. M. STEWART

The mood of the criticism of the early fifties is reflected
in J. I. M. Stewart's essay "Biography," an examination and
assessment of the biography of the last twenty-five or thirty years,
published in 1956 as part of a symposium called *The Craft of Letters
in England*.[18] Something of House's argument, which was perhaps
the last and most cogent expression of the anti-aesthetic point
of view, seems implicit in the assumptions of Stewart's survey,
but his own critical frame is most obviously dependent on Nicolson's "The Practice of Biography." Stewart expands Nicolson's
reference to Strachey's "ironical titters" into a discerning analysis of the irony, and he finds it irresponsible and malicious though
he phrases his objection very generally: "Since few lives are so
much of a piece as not to command at least some ebb and flow
of sympathy, it is to be questioned whether artistic effects depending upon an unflawed texture of irony are apposite in biography" (p. 10). Again, when he calls Strachey a superb story-teller,
he supports Nicolson's strictures about Strachey as historian and
finds it "yet more questionable" whether a story should be made
better by "fudging the facts." Stewart approves of the candor
characteristic of modern biography, even in lives written by relatives and friends; at least he says that "the making of elegant
literary diversion out of one's immediate forebears" has become
"sanctioned" for biographers and that "even malice will pass
when it is at once gentle and well ballasted with humour and
affection" (p. 14). But his paragraphs are hedged with qualifications and he remains basically sympathetic to the old-fashioned
view of the place of decorum and edification in biography (p. 12).
He does not like lives in which "the balance of sympathy is felt
as tilted sharply away from the subject" (p. 14) and, fundamentally,
that is why he condemns Richard Aldington's life of D. H. Lawrence.
He sees that Aldington is intent on "progressively discovering
how he really feels about his subject," but such an aim can only
lead to "impurity" in biography by making it too much "a
vehicle for self-expression" (pp. 15–16). In his emphasis on sympathy and on undue intrusion, Stewart agrees wholly with
Nicolson.

He would appear to depart most widely from Nicolson when he comments at length on psychology and, in doing so, holds that "if biography is to be, above all, a record of personality, it cannot . . . neglect those branches of psychology which seek to trace in the inner development of individuals the working of intelligible laws" (p. 19). Still, his whole approach is cautionary, and he says that psychology has been most useful when it has been "exploited with marked discretion." He uses the lives of Wordsworth by Sir Herbert Read and by F. W. Bateson to show that even when the same basic psychological assumptions are made, the facts prove susceptible of divergent interpretation. He uses Ernest Jones's *Freud* to raise the question of how much of the biographer's equipment must remain "traditional," and he says that the excellence of the book stems from the "literary tact" Jones drew upon in deploying the resources of psychoanalysis, from his ability to express his own technical insight without parading it, from his simultaneous dependence upon all the "prescriptive resources of the orthodox biographer." Although he thinks that Peter Quennell's *Ruskin* is genuinely perceptive, he discerns in it the general tendency to seek biographical material in subjects who lend themselves to a "more or less sensational, 'psychological' approach," and even Quennell neglects Ruskin's work, "that to which, in any reasoned estimate, Ruskin must be judged to owe his fame" (p. 20). He states, parenthetically, that it is tenable to think that a man's creations are "something won from the void and in no essential relationship to his 'life,' " but his own view is, without doubt, the "simple" one that a man's works are an essential part of himself. Still, since he believes, too, that psychological inquiry into motives and purposes is itself motivated by a desire to provide a new key to explain the mystery of a man or his work, he finds in such inquiry an example of Nicolson's impurity caused by dependence on extraneous theory, and he maintains that books like Middleton Murry's *Keats and Shakespeare* (1925), *Blake* (1933), and *Shakespeare* (1954) have broken the boundary between biographical and critical study. There is something of disapproval in his tone as he speaks of the violation of the Johnsonian formula, but he leaves in the air the question of the proper relation between a man and his works, between biography and criticism. He merely points out that now a biographer treats a man's work much as an analyst uses dreams and free associations, in order to explain the man, and, correspondingly, that he carries over his psychological view of the man into the analysis and evaluation of the work.

Stewart loses his tentativeness when he discusses the achievement and influence of scholarship on biography (p. 22), when he praises Roy Harrod's *John Maynard Keynes* as "an admirably objective book" (p. 23), when he commends some biographers for their "positive sympathy" (p. 25). He reveals the reason for his discomfort with Strachey and for his guarded attitude toward psychology when he refers to "the best quality that contemporary biography can show" (p. 23). For him, Sir Sidney Lee had put his finger on "an impulse that is real and valid" when he announced that the aim of biography was commemorative; he castigates Nicolson for insisting that Lee's dictum leads to impure biography, and he says that Nicolson's life of George V is a triumphant success "precisely because 'the instinctive desire to do honour' is present and is rationally directed upon an adequate subject" (p. 24).

Stewart concludes by suggesting that, though nothing is more detestable than fictionalized biography, the "pure" biographer may have learned something from the great novelists of the last hundred years; he says, too, that some of the best modern biographies are the work of distinguished novelists. His conclusion surprises, for it runs counter to the drift of his survey. Early in his essay he had asked what "purely literary equipment" the historian or biographer might "safely" be allowed (p. 11). In fact, he had already implied his answer. He had begun by citing Forster's view that Strachey had revolutionized the art of biography. That is, with one exception,[19] his sole reference to biography as an art. In making it, he says that it is at least true that Strachey made biography vastly more entertaining, but that it is not easy to determine whether the entertainment is altogether legitimate. The rest of the essay, in its assertion of the legitimacy of Lee and Nicolson, clearly provides his answer.

C. V. WEDGWOOD

Stewart's reluctance to consider biography as an art is typical of the criticism of the early fifties. The historians of the thirties had dampened enthusiasm for the conception of biography as an art, and for two decades their ideas that biography was a branch of history and that historical and biographical truth had little to do with art had, in the main, prevailed. But the very collection in which Stewart's essay appeared contains an article which reflects the changing view of historians toward their work. Miss C. V. Wedgwood does not entitle her essay "The Art of History" or "The Craft of History" but "Historical Writing."[20] Her first statement is that "the business of the historian is to communicate intelligible information about the past as clearly and accurately as he can"; her second is that "historical writing therefore allows of less innovation and experiment than the novel, or poetry or drama." Although she insists that "the straightforward task of conveying information" prevents the historian from indulging in "the bolder and more ingenious experiments which constantly revitalize other branches of literature," she still conceives of history as a branch of literature. She makes it clear that something is wanting in "scientific" history and in history which is written co-operatively or collectively and that she prefers history which combines scholarship and literature, books which bear the imprint of a single mind (p. 187). She says, in fact, that the idea that history should have no dealings whatever with literature has almost wholly vanished. To be sure, she focuses chiefly on the value of the study of literature to the historian, on the importance of a clear and disciplined style, but she leaves abundant room for the wholly personal, fierce insight of a Carlyle or an A. L. Rowse and for the history which, like Toynbee's, is based on an idiosyncratic organization and interpretation of historical facts (pp. 188, 197, 201).

Miss Wedgwood's approach is hardly a new one: it echoes Stephen's admiration of Froude in 1902 and Strachey's pronouncements in his 1909 review of Ferrero's *The Greatness and Decline of Rome*. But she obviously thinks it necessary, in 1956, to reassert these ideas, even though she says that they have been generally accepted.

FREDERICK B. TOLLES

In the climate of opinion which Miss Wedgwood describes, it is no great surprise to find a historian who starts an essay called "The Biographer's Craft" with the statement, "Whatever else it is, biography is an art."[21] Frederick B. Tolles says that it is other things, too, an exercise in historical research, but he is concerned with the biographer's problems as a writer, with the art that conceals scholarship, not lack of it (p. 520). His approach is not theoretical, nor does he refer to the main line of criticism; it is pragmatic, based on his own experience in writing *George Logan of Philadelphia* (1953), and his essay is most effective when he relies on that experience. He accepts in principle Bradford Smith's view that the biographer "uses the techniques of the historian to get his man and get him right, yet he must use the art of the novelist to bring him back alive."[22] He maintains that one of the biographer's essential "tools" is "imagination," but he has in mind "a disciplined historical imagination" (p. 509), and his primary concern is to flesh out Lee's dictum that the biographer's creative artistry is limited to the animation of dead bones and Thayer's statement that the biographer must rely on literary resources to produce an adequate simulation of lifelikeness.

Tolles's specific suggestions break no new ground. He shows the artificiality and dullness of biography arranged by topics or categories and prefers that which is narrative and chronological, which unfolds events as they unfolded to the consciousness of the subject (pp. 508–9). The biographer should learn from the novelist and the dramatist how to compose in scenes which reveal the character of his subject; he will not invent them but read his sources with an eye for them. He will ever keep the "spotlight" on his subject, and he will insinuate into his narrative only the minimal historical background necessary to provide an adequate context for his subject. He will reveal the "personality and personal life" of a man, not portray a "public figure" (pp. 512–13). He will rely on his subject's own words, reproduce conversations when they can be reconstructed, and he will not allow his subject's ideas and writings to overwhelm the narrative. Tolles's concern is, then, with lively representation, but even here, for all his advocacy, he categorizes the lives by Strachey, Maurois, Ludwig, Rupert Hughes, and W. E. Woodward as "popular or debunking biographies" apt to be written too glibly and he cites Sir Charles Firth's words that Strachey adopted " 'a very bad style in which to tell the truth' " (p. 519).

He does touch on two other important matters. He raises the question of the biographer's relation to his story, his point of view, and he differentiates three approaches, all of which he considers legitimate: the biographer may be omniscient, "an Olympian who sees all, knows all"; he may be "a Greek chorus, commenting on the action as it unfolds"; he may be "a critical intelligence, interrupting the narrative from time to time with judgments, evaluations, analyses, interpretations" (p. 516). He also says that though the biographer cannot take liberties with his materials, which are "not notably plastic," he must yet give them form; the "shaping spirit of the artist" must inform his work even as the writer of a sonnet, a composer, a sculptor, a portrait painter gives form to his work. When Tolles asks whether the quantity and distribution of the biographer's sources ought determine the shape of his work, he condemns the distortion or grotesqueness which may result; he condones emphasis or distortion which is deliberate, since a change of pace or scale may justly underscore an important incident or period in a life (p. 517).

Tolles's essay is more interesting as a symptom of changing attitudes toward art in the criticism of biography than it is in itself. He seems unaware of what Virginia Woolf thought might or might not be fired out of a life; he stops short of Mumford's concept that the biographer must engage in construction of an archaeological sort; his discussion of form is not so precise or subtle as that of Maurois. The "true inwardness" of a man is, for him, the equivalent of "his qualities as a human being" (p. 519) rather than of the inner life of thought and emotion, and he says nothing about the subjects of interiority or psychology. He does not probe the implications of the biographer's shaping spirit and he says almost nothing about self-expression and undue intrusion or subjectivity. Tolles's essay makes only a small contribution to the scope and depth of the argument for the biographer as artist. Still, his assertion that "whatever else it is, biography is an art" voices a conviction and a confidence which are characteristic of the theory and criticism from the mid-fifties to today.

V

To 1970

Much of the criticism after the mid-fifties assumes that biography is an art, a literary genre which has its own characteristic domain and procedures, a genre which challenges the imagination and creativity of its practitioners. Though it is aware of how and where biography is different from the novel, though it recognizes that readers of a biography are likely to be more interested in its subject than in its author, it recognizes, too, that to select and to order are to interpret, and it is increasingly disposed to focus more closely on the relation of the biographer to his subject. It finds simplistic the notions of the biographer as compiler or even as alembic, and it explores the precise and peculiar nature of the involvement between author and subject. It builds on Maurois's insights about the biographer's point of view and his desire for self-expression, and it examines the conscious or unconscious self-revelation of the author in order to probe his angle of vision. It is concerned, too, with more than lively narration and representation, with more than the means by which bare bones are made to live. It accepts Virginia Woolf's insistence that the inner life is integral and central to a man's being and doing, and it is concerned with the insights which can be intuited or gained through the disciplines which study man's behavior.

LEON EDEL

The most influential study of biography in the post-World War II years is Leon Edel's *Literary Biography* (1957).[1] Edel had read

Nicolson's and Maurois's books when they had appeared in the twenties; they had been written, he says, "under the fertilizing influence of Lytton Strachey" and provided the liveliest discussion of biography in the first half-century (p. 5). His own discussion is equally lively, fertilized as it is not only by the work of Nicolson and Maurois but also by that of Virginia Woolf, Lord David Cecil, and many others who had explored the territory of biography.[2] It reflects also his own special interests and experience in biography and in psychology; he had already finished the first volume of his life of Henry James (1953) and he had recently completed *The Psychological Novel 1900–1950* (1955). Between February 27 and March 3, 1956, he gave the Alexander lectures at the University of Toronto on the subject "literary biography," which he defined as "the writing of the lives of men and women who were themselves writers" (p. 2). Aware though he is that his specialized subject introduces questions of emphasis and shading into his discussion, he yet holds that "all the practices and traditions of biography" apply to it. He prefers to consider biography as a "process" rather than as an art, a science, or a craft, but he thinks that "much more art than science is involved in the process, since biography deals with emotions as well as with the intellect, and literary biography with those emotions which give the impulse to literary creation" (pp. 6–7). His five chapters explore the five crucial steps in the process: the nature of the relation between the biographer and his subject; the biographer's quest for materials; his function as a critic of literature and of evidence; his utilization of modern tools, particularly psychoanalysis, for an understanding of the mind and the human consciousness; and his determination of the scope of his biography and of his narrative techniques, especially as these relate to the question of time.

In his first chapter, Edel builds on Maurois's concept that biography is a means of self-expression for the biographer. He agrees with Maurois that a biographer is usually impelled to write the life of a particular subject by deeply personal reasons, reasons not always conducive to objectivity and to truth, and that there is established from the outset a significant relation between biographer and subject, one which is intimate and subjective (pp. 7–8). The biographer's dilemma is that he must incorporate himself into the experience of his subject and still remain himself. He must project himself empathetically and yet retain his own mind, sense of balance, and appraising eye: "He must be warm, yet aloof, involved, yet uninvolved" (p. 7). It is essential that he try to know himself before he seeks to know the life of his subject, and still "there seems to be considerable evidence that he is seeking to know the life of another in order better to understand himself" (p. 9). He must be careful not to refashion the subject in his own image, but the best he can do is, in Strachey's words, to " 'lay bare the facts of the case, *as he understands them.*' " He absorbs whatever inert materials are available, and his "living, associating, remembering" mind becomes "surrogate for the consciousness that has been extinguished" (pp. 10–11). Since he can set forth his data only in the light of his own understanding, since the extent of his understanding is dependent on his own capacities and resources as well as on his data, he can only produce "*his* vision, *his* arrangement, *his* picture" (p. 10).

Edel shows that Henry James's essay on James Russell Lowell reveals what *he* respected and cherished in Lowell; he shows that Boswell went so far as to create in life incidents, occasions, and encounters for Johnson which he thought would be revealing and interesting in the life he was to write and that there are moments (such as his account of a journey early in 1776) when he so intrudes himself that Johnson is lost sight of (pp. 11–18). Edel's statement that a later biographer "finds that he must ride in the coach not only with the subject but with the former biographer" reinforces his point that biography is interpretative, that it is difficult to divorce biographer and subject. Although he thinks that the greatest biographies have been written by men who knew their subjects in the flesh, he suggests that the biographer who works from documents, including previous lives, has the advantage of objectivity gained from a wider perspective. The inevitability of biography as self-expression is at the root of Edel's exploration of the peculiar relation between any biographer and his subject, but the tenor of his comments is that the biographer analyze himself as well as his subject and that he take care not to reflect his subject in a mirror which is too much himself (p. 20).

Edel prefaces his chapter on the biographer's quest for materials by stating that "readers tend to be more interested in how a piece of fiction or a poem came to be written than in the genesis of a biography"; they are interested not in the writer of a life, but in the life itself. The biographer must, then, reconvert the emotion or passion of his search into "a dispassionate account of the life" (p. 21). The heart of the chapter is a fascinating account of Edel's own quest for Henry James, and since the modern biographer is more likely to have to cope with a superfluity of material than a paucity of it, Edel emphasizes not the discovery of documents but the importance of the biographer's powers of deduction, his imaginative grasp of materials, his capacity for synthesis and ratiocination (p. 37). He shows the difficulty of penetrating the tone of James's letters, of sorting out the exact meaning of his relations with his correspondents (p. 28). He explains that the recognition that James was the subject of a case history in a monograph on angina pectoris is of smaller consequence than recognition of how the episode of his illness is related to his work (pp. 32–34, 37). The tracking down of an early anonymous story by James becomes significant insofar as the story sheds light on the adolescent James's impression of his father (pp. 34–38).

Despite these remarks and despite the analysis of the role of the biographer in his first chapter, Edel does not question the nature of the reader's small interest in the biographer. Indeed, he seems to imply that the biographer as artist is different from the novelist and the poet. He points out that the literary biographer's impulse to write a life stems from his response to a writer's work; like other readers, he is attracted by a writer's voice or style, recognizes that "the voice and what it says are almost inseparable," and asks what sort of man is behind the voice, how and why he came to say what he says (pp. 22–23). No one will contradict Edel's opinion that an artist's voice leads to curiosity about the relation between a man and his work. No one will contradict his statement that readers tend to be more interested in this relation when they read poetry and fiction than when they read biography. But Edel does not tell us whether he thinks the reader's response to a biographer stems from a lack of literary sophistication or whether, though he assumes that "in the study of literature the voice and what it says are almost inseparable," he agrees with readers that the biographer's voice does not possess, as the poet's or novelist's usually does, "highly individual qualities of resonance and depth, or delicate lyricism, or even a certain compelling stridency, with varied shadings of which it alone is capable" (p. 23).

In his chapter called "Criticism," Edel is mainly concerned with the task of the literary biographer to discover the poet behind the poem. Since he is especially interested in the lives of writers, the subject is intrinsic to his discussion in a way it was not to other critics of biography.[3] He complicates the matter of reading the man out of his works by interweaving with it two other aspects of the biographer as critic: his capacity to illuminate the works because he knows the man and his capacity to evaluate evidence. Edel's description of the attempt to recover "the mind and the pulse-beat" of an author is far more subtle and complex than earlier discussions, which were primarily interested in the problems involved in trying to extract literal and specific

autobiographical detail from fiction and drama. He says that after
a biographer has studied a work formalistically and attached it
"to tradition and discipline and influence" he must relate it
"to the consciousness that gave it birth and to the world in
which that consciousness functioned" (p. 41). He looks for a writer's recurrent images, his recurrent modes of thought, "his individual world of words and his peculiar vision of reality," the
characteristic style which is the man. The man is, then, the style,
and this is what the biographer is always trying to show. He grasps
what is characteristic and recurrent in a writer's stories, characters, solutions, ethical views because each work is bound by many
threads to a "fashioning consciousness" and he seeks to discover
"the peculiar mind and body that drove the pen in the creative
act" (pp. 42, 44). Since the act of imaginative writing is as much
an act of expression as it is of communication, since every work
is not only formed in a literary tradition but is also "tissued out"
of a writer's past experience, every work emerges from an artist's
"inner promptings," and it is the biographer's recovery of these
inner promptings which will make it possible for him to learn
"every secret of a writer's soul, every quality of his mind" (p. 43).

The italics are Edel's, and he uses them to underscore those
words of Virginia Woolf which he considers just in a passage he
had quoted in full earlier; he omits her words that a writer's works
record, too, every experience of his life. The reason for his omission
is made clear in his long analysis of the kind of biographical data
which may be gleaned from a careful reading of Gray's "Elegy"
(pp. 51–55). He does not expect to recover actual biographical
detail of a matter-of-fact kind, but he attempts to recover from
the tone and the mood of the poem something of Gray's personal
emotion and the quality of his mind. He is interested in seeing why
it was that Gray chose his subject and what he projected into it,
how a total experience, not a specific and occasional one, sits
behind the poem. He does not expect that every work can be
redissolved into a life, that it will reveal every experience, only
that it can reveal the *"texture"* of a life.[4]

Edel treats less extensively the matters of the application
of biography to a work of art and the biographer's function as a
critic of evidence. In defending the biographical approach to poetry (pp. 49–51), he agrees with T. S. Eliot that the smallest fact
about a piece of art may be useful and that critics who rely on
opinion and fancy may corrupt taste in a way which fact never
does. He holds that the critic who knows nothing about the life
of an artist whose work is surrealist, abstract, dependent on private
symbols, can only project his own feelings upon a work and describe

his own relation to it. The biographer is in a better position to make such a work intelligible because his reasonably clear understanding of the artist and of what his symbols meant to him makes possible the deciphering of the symbolic code. When Edel discusses the necessity of the biographer's working as a judicial critic who must weigh and evaluate evidence in order to impose logic and coherence on a mass of fact, he demonstrates that this process is not only "quasi-legalistic" and "technical" but imaginative (pp. 45–49). The biographer will have to adjudicate, to be sure, between this fact and that. But Edel, like Virginia Woolf, is interested in emotions as well as in facts. He shows very effectively how ingenious a biographer must be to determine where the truth is when he is faced with conflicting testimony (some of it in his subject's own words) about moments of emotion.

For Edel, the newest and most significant of all the biographer's relationships is with pychoanalysis, with "the special techniques developed by Sigmund Freud and elaborated by his successors for the study of the symbols evoked by man which can explain his behaviour" (p. 56). He is fully aware of pitfalls here: the technical skills which the biographer must master, his working with inert data rather than with a living subject, the tendency of diagnosis to reduce the artist to a neurosis, the abuse of concepts, and the use of jargon.[5] His long, complex, and illuminating chapter focuses on Willa Cather and *The Professor's House*: he shows first how a fine critic, E. K. Brown, evokes and illuminates the central symbol of the novel; then, how a psychoanalyst might diagnose the same material; and, finally, how the biographer, "using the material offered by the critic and the psycho-analyst, can more deeply illuminate the work by seeking to determine what the house symbol meant to Miss Cather herself" (p. 61). In one section, he points out that Brown perceives that the professor's depression, as it is expressed in his reactions to the houses in his life, is an unconscious preparation for death, for his last house. In a second, he demonstrates how the psychoanalyst, by singling out the primal elements in the book, finds that "the professor's death-wish, undefined by the author, would appear to be due to lingering infantile needs, so strong that this successful adult teacher and writer, otherwise a figure of dignity and maturity, adheres to a pattern of behaviour which belongs to his childhood. This he masks by rationalization: a love for the past, a dislike of the present" (p. 70).[6] In the third, Edel uses biographical data to show that what motivated Miss Cather's depression in her middle years, when she wrote that "the world broke in two in 1922 or thereabouts," was her changed relation to Isabelle McClung Hambourg; she lost

the security of a fixed abode and of a mother figure, always important to her, and felt she had been rejected. He concludes, therefore,
that "by merging the insights gained from psychology with the
biographical data that give us clues to the workings of the author's imagination, we are able to render a critical evaluation:
we can see the failure of *The Professor's House* as a work of fiction"
(p. 78). The novel is incomplete because Miss Cather's inner problems did not permit her to resolve clearly the motivation of the
professor's state of mind; she so identified with the professor that
she could not supply any " 'rejection motif' " for his depression.
"The truth was that Willa Cather was incapable of admitting to
herself—who can?—that what was troubling her was not the depar-
ture of Isabelle but what it symbolized" (p. 79).

In the last words of this section, Edel says, "By penetrating
more deeply into the life it has been possible to penetrate more
deeply into the work," and he has, in fact, done so. But he has
to some extent misdirected the thrust of his chapter. It was not
the biographer who saw the failure of *The Professor's House* as a
novel; the critic saw that its failure lay in a central character
whose actions and state of mind resisted explanation because what
motivated him was unclear. The special contribution of the biographer was not to point out that the novel was a technical failure;
it was to provide a genetic explanation of *why* the novelist failed.
Edel's emphasis is such that his chapter seems to be a further
justification for a biographical approach to literature, one that
incorporates the psychoanalytical but moves beyond it because it
is more than diagnostic; it can relate the dream to the dreamer;
it knows both the symbols and what they mean to the person who
used them (p. 72). The real contribution of the chapter is that
it demonstrates how psychoanalytical examination of a work led
to the discovery of symbols which revealed a need for security and
a feeling of rejection, furnished clues for the biographer, made him
assess and interpret these with biographical data in mind. Whether
or not the biographical data themselves would have provided
these clues is perhaps open to question, but the penetrating critical and psychoanalytical analysis of the novel here, coupled with
the sensitive application of biographical data (some of it interpreted psychologically), provides wonderful evidence of the way in
which Miss Cather's mind worked and of the emotions which were
at the heart of her being.

The first part of Edel's final chapter is a relatively conventional discussion of the biographer's scope and his techniques
of narration; the second is an acute, perceptive, and detailed
discussion of the biographer's management of time. Edel suggests

that the scope of a biography is in part determined by the quantity and nature of the materials available and in part by the "importance" of a life; it is not clear whether he refers to the importance of the subject in Lee's terms or to "the biographer's own deep interest in the subject" (p. 82). He divides biography according to three main architectural ideas. The "traditional documentary" biography or chronicle is that in which the biographer arranges his material to allow the voice of his subject to be heard constantly, in which he presents documents chronologically and annotates them; it is "arbitrary" insofar as it depends largely on whatever documents have survived; it does not usually attempt to render a life dramatically, but the subject may come alive if the documents are vivid and if the biographer himself has vitality and an informing mind (pp. 82–84). The more circumscribed "portrait" is economical and two-dimensional in its focus on a central figure and pictorial in its attempt to characterize or represent what is vivid and human in a subject; related to it is the critical biography which seeks to convey a picture of the subject's personality and creating mind through a discussion of his works (pp. 84–87). The "narrative-pictorial" or "novelistic" biography, "fashioned increasingly in our time," is that in which the biographer is an omniscient narrator who gives his vision of a subject; he characterizes, comments, analyzes, interprets as only an artist can. He borrows the methods of the novelist without indulging in fiction. He cuts free of documents after he has absorbed them, shows his subject "in immediate action and against changing backgrounds," may violate chronology, disengages scenes and utilizes even trivial incidents which illuminate character (pp. 83–87). Edel differs slightly from Cecil when he calls Strachey the father of this kind of biography "in our time"; he praises Strachey's achievement, and says that biographers can profitably borrow "some" of his theories and methods (pp. 88–89).

Although there is nothing new in Edel's chapter to this point, the rest is provocative because it springs out of Virginia Woolf's *Orlando* rather than out of her critical essays about biography. Edel treats *Orlando* as a fable for biographers, one which speaks for a looser and freer biography. He stresses Mrs. Woolf's appreciation of the "many selves" which are within each person and her awareness that the biography of a person must be recreated out of a total past, not out of a mechanical calendar, but out of the total familial, cultural, and historical inheritance which is important to a person. He agrees with her perception that it is important to record a man's "sense of time, psychological and human, as distinct from clock time" (pp. 94–97). Edel maintains that "biography can violate chronology without doing violence to truth" (p. 99); his example of the significance of Emerson to James proves more than this—that sometimes the only way to get at truth is to violate chronology. He demonstrates that strict chronology is defective in that it cannot suggest the human element of time in a life, the interplay between past and present; he shows that whereas a precisely chronological account of James's occasional encounters with Emerson must be based only on the moments for which records have survived, a composite account can indicate the importance to James of Emerson as a symbol of the tones and values of New England.[7]

JOHN A. GARRATY

In the same year that Edel's book was published, there was also published John A. Garraty's *The Nature of Biography*.[8] Garraty had previously written lives of Silas Wright (1949), Henry Cabot Lodge (1953), and Woodrow Wilson (1956). The Foreword of his book describes his interest in the theory and criticism of biography, and his twenty-eight page "Essay on Sources"[9] is evidence of his familiarity with earlier work. As a historian, he is far more attracted to Tolles than to Lee: his own citation of Lee is almost incidental (p. 5); he clearly approves of Tolles's description of the "new" conception of biography which combines research and scholarly integrity with imaginative, artistic qualities (p. 149). Much more than Tolles, however, he is interested in psychology, and he had studied for a year the technical methods of psychologists whose business was the exploration of personality. He had originally planned his book as a manual which would describe the types of biography, its relation to history, its materials and the problems that arise in using them, and methods of research and writing. The manual became the last half of his book, which contains, too, an introductory essay on the nature of biography and a historical account of its development.

Garraty's preliminary essay focuses on three topics: the interaction between history and biography; the necessity of interpretation, which makes demands on the artistry of the biographer; the merits of personal acquaintance and of historical perspective. For him, biography is related to history in two ways. As the record of a life, it represents "history in microcosm," but it relies on history, too, insofar as it must treat the relation of a man to the social, cultural, and economic forces in his environment. Garraty maintains that the biographer's emphasis on environment reflects his view of the importance of individual intelligence and character in determining the course of events, and indicates whether he thinks the environment produces famous men, whether it is the great man who changes the trend of events, whether luck or chance is a primary determinant. He must make decisions about the relative importance of each view throughout his consideration of a man's career. Garraty's second discussion stems from his belief that the description of personality is of "fundamental importance" to biography (p. 8). Although he does not deny the artistry of many great historians, he holds that the portrayal of personality, as distinct from an understanding of it, is a problem which is chiefly artistic in nature (p. 9). The biographer, unlike the novelist, is bound by fact, but "he can bring great artistry to the selection and interpretation of his evidence" (p. 11). He seeks to represent reality, but since he knows that he cannot attain complete objectivity, he "must interpret, imagine, and select constantly if he is to approach the reality he seeks" (p. 19). In introducing his third subject, Garraty admits that nearly all outstanding biographies were written by men who knew their subjects personally (pp. 24–25). Their merit lies chiefly in the depiction of personality; they are less likely to excel in the evaluation of a subject's career or in assessment of his place in history, for a contemporary biographer lacks both the perspective and the access to records of a later one (pp. 25–27). He holds, then, that though Boswell's *Johnson* may be the world's best biography, it is not a "model" biography: he says that it lacks proportion in describing Johnson's career and that it is pedestrian when Boswell must rely on sources other than his eye and ear. He treats it, then, as a unique personal success, "far superior to the general run of biography," and for this reason he does not feel that it is "profitable" to discuss it or books like Johnson's *Savage* and Carlyle's *Sterling* when he considers the general nature of biography. He says, further, that "if great biography must await the chance congruence of a worthy subject and a talented observer, it has only a limited future, and many important individuals can never hope to be chronicled adequately after they have passed on" (p. 27).

Unlike most critics of fiction and some critics of biography, Garraty is more concerned with quantity than with the towering masterpiece, more interested in promoting adequacy than in describing exceptional excellence. The serious biographer may not be a Boswell, but he may take heart from Garraty's formulation that it is possible to overcome the absence of personal acquaintance by means of sympathy, scholarship, and sensitivity, "whereas perspective (by definition) can come only with time."

Garraty's account of the development of biography is, he says, primarily directed at pointing out the sources from which modern biography "has drawn inspiration and precept" (p. 29). It has its defects. He is aware of the large variety of modern biography, and, though he is more sympathetic to some approaches than to others, his criterion of selection hardly narrows his field; moreover, his analyses of some key figures (for example, Roper, Cavendish, Carlyle, Lockhart, and Froude) are cursory and inadequate. On the other hand, he has a good eye for the illuminating parallel and quotation. For instance, he sees the beginning of debunking biography in the work of Aristoxenus of Tarentum (pp. 39–40). When he considers the vogue at the beginning of this century for biographies which rely on "intuition" or "higher truth" rather than on authenticated fact, he cites the words of Arrian, a second-century historian, about a story of doubtful validity: "If this was really done by Alexander, then I commend him for it; and if it merely seems credible to his biographers that he might have done and said these things, then on this basis too I commend Alexander" (p. 118). He quotes Steele's statement that "the word 'Memoir' is French for a novel" (p. 78) and the Abbé Prévost's words that he wished to make his biographical writing "differ little from the most interesting works of imagination" by reconciling "all the advantages of truth with that agreeable illusion which arises from surprise, from suspense, and [from] impatience" (p. 86). When he refers to Maurois's comments that he wrote a life of Shelley as a way of working out his personal problems, as a means of self-expression (pp. 158–59), he is reminded of other similar statements: Plutarch's, in the life of Timoleon, that he found himself writing not to instruct others, but himself, and that the virtues of great men served as a looking-glass in which he could see how to conduct his own life (p. 44); Freud's perception that some biographers choose their subject "for personal reasons of their own emotional life" and his explanation: that these biographers "enroll the great man among their infantile models, and . . . revive through him . . . their infantile conception of the father" (p. 116); William Bayard Hale's statement in 1920 that every biographer projects "his own prepossessions and desires into his conception of the career of his hero"; and William E. Wilson's in 1951 that he so closely identified with his subjects that he dreaded writing about their illnesses because he acquired their symptoms himself (p. 159).

Garraty's history is best when he describes biography after 1900, and his account of the relation between psychology and biography is better informed and more perceptive than Nicolson's.

He sees that though psychology countered to some degree the emphasis of historians on scientific objectivity and the various kinds of determinism propounded by Hegel, Darwin, and Marx, it, too, was interested in scientific laws and was more concerned with searching for the laws of human behavior than it was in investigating an individual and his uniqueness (pp. 108–10). He approves of Havelock Ellis's attempts to improve biography by stressing the necessity of psychological understanding, but he condemns as oversimplification Ellis's optimism about the value of the application of the rules of psychology (pp. 111–12). Though he confesses in his Foreword that his reading of psychoanalytical biographies did not encourage him to believe that psychoanalysis might be useful for biography and that his study of the utility of psychoanalysis as a tool has left him impressed rather than overwhelmed, his account of Freud's work is altogether fair. The application of psychoanalysis to biography from about the time of World War I is, for him, "the first really important new development in the writing of lives since the eighteenth century" (p. 112). He praises Freud for discriminating between the validity of his method and the validity of the results which may be achieved when there is a paucity of material to be analyzed, and he finds in his concepts a theoretical basis for the importance which small details have in revealing character. He holds that if Freud overemphasized sexuality, he yet forced others to see that it could not be ignored. He says that despite Freud's interest in laws, he used the laws to throw light on an individual, and, moreover, did not insist that the laws determined behavior in every instance but that individuality and accident were also operative. By showing that "man was so complex that no simple determinism could explain him," Freud helped lay to rest the conflict between science and biography (pp. 115–17).

The last section of Garraty's book covers precisely the topics of Edel's as he discusses the subject, the quest for and handling of materials, the problem of personality, and the method of writing. But, whereas Edel focuses within each topic on particular aspects which explore and deepen its implications, Garraty's purpose of providing sound advice for neophytes leads him to try to cover all the aspects in a sensible, relatively conservative way. Thus, "subject," in Edel's hands, emphasizes the peculiar and significant relation between biographer and subject, the biographer's necessary empathy for and projection into his subject, his seeking to express himself as he works with his subject, and, too, his need for self-appraisal and the effort he must make to remain dispassionate and aloof. Garraty quotes Cecil Woodham-Smith on the "strange and mysterious" relation between biographer and subject (p. 155), but he spends no more time on biography as a means of expression than he does on the biography written by relatives, the official life produced to order, and the opportunistic one written because a market exists for it. He advocates that a biographer be "interested" in his subject, but he assumes that the usual biographer will be pragmatic enough to resist the compulsion to undertake some subjects which fascinate him. For him, then, the "importance" of a subject is not determined chiefly by its relevance to the biographer. Although Garraty agrees that " 'an old woman paring her nails may achieve immortality if she chances to be painted by a Rembrandt,' " he says that "unless one is so talented as to be able to produce a work of artistic merit *sui generis*, one ought to steer clear of the *deservedly* forgotten figures of history" (p. 165). One ought, also, not undertake a life unless one is proficient in his subject's field of professional specialization, and one ought to make sure before one starts that one will have access to materials. Garraty grants that an author's "tastes" may determine the *kind* of life he writes, but he advises the writer to determine what sort of life is "needed" at a particular time for a particular subject, and his criteria are utility and lack of duplication (pp. 166–68).

When Garraty discusses the materials of biography, his emphasis, like Edel's, is not on the quest for and discovery of new documents but on the importance of proper assessment and right interpretation. This, the longest chapter of his manual, is full of good advice about the use of personal documents like autobiographies, journals, diaries, and letters, and the uses of reminiscences by relatives and contemporaries, personal interviews, and earlier biographies. Garraty merely mentions the importance to the biographer of his subject's published works (pp. 182–83, 202–4) whereas these were the main object of Edel's attention, and his interest is largely in what information of a personal kind they may contain rather than in what they reveal of the mind of the writer or of the texture of his life. His most interesting chapter, however, is not this one but the next, in which he discusses the problem of personality. He mentions, almost in passing, the traditional methods of getting insight into a subject by making use of autobiographical comment, the opinions of contemporaries, the subject's actions, and the folklore that has persisted about him (pp. 216–17). He does not rule out the use of intuition, so long as intuitive judgments are based on a thorough examination of sources; or of psychoanalysis, so long as it is not abused and its results are explicitly described as speculative (pp. 219–20). His thesis here, however, is that though a biographer would be silly to rely on formulaic assessments of personality, he would be equally silly not to take advantage of those psychological techniques of analysis and evaluation which are objective and which will reveal through the mechanical, statistical study of personal documents those aspects of personality which may otherwise have been missed. He discusses recent experiments in graphology, David P. Boder's studies of the ratios of adjectives to verbs in personal documents for evidence of emotional stability, the methods developed by John Dollard and O. H. Mowrer for measuring emotional tension, Ralph K. White's techniques for measuring values, and Alfred L. Baldwin's approach to personality through "personal structure analysis" (pp. 221–35).[10] Garraty is very much aware that aesthetic and historical considerations complicate the analysis of style; he is aware that there is a large element of subjective choice in setting up systems of classification; he stresses constantly that there is a large difference between the mechanical establishment of significant relationships and the task of understanding and interpreting them. Still, he thinks that the new psychological methods may be useful insofar as they can reduce the biographer's dependence on subjective judgments, help him solve problems caused by conflicting evidence, and confirm his conclusions by keeping them within measurable limits (p. 237).

The bulk of Garraty's chapter on the writing of biography is devoted to a summation of various methods described from the time of James F. Stanfield's *Essay on the Study and Composition of Biography* (1813) to the fine but unworkable "Tentative Set of Rules for the Presentation and Evaluation of Life Histories and Case Studies" of Gordon W. Allport.[11] He advocates the use of a chronological approach, allows for the possibility of alternative arrangements and occasional topical organization, but he says nothing about the complexities of time which Edel considered. The allocation of space in a life should be determined, he says, not by the mere availability of materials but by their importance, their significance in the light of the biographer's interpretation (p. 257). Although he ends by stating that "the significance of every man's deeds changes as time goes by" and that "because the effects of events are unending, no account of events can ever be final" (p. 258), his conclusion is less a rousing defense of the necessity of interpretation than a plea for impartiality, sympathy, and understanding.

When James L. Clifford reviewed Garraty's and Edel's books in 1959,[12] he found it useful to look at them in the old and pertinent framework of biography as art and as craft. He does not explicitly identify Garraty with the theory that biography is a craft and Edel with the theory that biography is an art, but he seems to imply, and rightly so, that Garraty leans in one direction, Edel in the other. Although he states that it is safest to say that the biographer must be both a creative genius who works within definite bounds and a skilled craftsman who has mastered his trade, his own inclination seems on the whole more sympathetic toward the view that biography is an art, particularly since he stresses the number of personal decisions a biographer must make and emphasizes his interpretation as he proceeds with the work of "fashioning his own portrait of another man" (p. 309).

Edel's book is, to be sure, more persuasive than Garraty's in showing the inevitability of the biographer's functioning as an interpretative artist; he is, after all, primarily interested in "literary" biography, which must cope in a peculiarly sensitive way with the quality of a man's mind and his inner life of thought and emotion. But Garraty, too, insists on the biographer's role as interpreter; when, for instance, he speaks of lives written by some eighteenth-century scholars, he says that "they carried objectivity to the point at which they refused to make judgments of any kind, and produced works devoid of interpretation and therefore of meaning" (p. 81). Again, Edel is intensely aware of the relations between biography and fiction, so much so that he moves far beyond the mere techniques of representation which biography may profitably borrow from fiction and incorporates into his view of what biography must strive for even those concepts about human consciousness which Virginia Woolf had incorporated into her novels and into *Orlando*, concepts which she did not herself maximize in her critical writing about biography or in her life of Roger Fry. Garraty stresses the utility of artistic reconstruction based on historical investigation; he is equally interested in personality, in tensions, values, and motivation, but he advocates an approach which is somewhat less imaginative than Edel's, more scientifically controlled. He does so because he feels that only the Shakespeares can master human nature instinctively, that ordinary writers—whom he is mainly concerned with—can benefit from "general and systematic perusal of the human mind" (p. 239).[13]

Garraty, like Edel, is aware that there is likely to be a significant relation between biographer and subject, but he envisions the usual biographer as a competent craftsman rather than as a great artist, and he seems, almost, to prefer things that way. Though the epigraph of his book contains the statement that "the story of illustrious men cannot be too often retold" and the sentiment that "we grasp so much of the spirit as we can comprehend—and as there are infinite gradations of comprehension, so there are infinite varieties of portrayal," he seems to have chosen it because it reflects the historian's notion that every generation must reinterpret the past in the light of new perspectives, with a view toward what is important in the present, not because he has faith in the perpetual value of the insight of the great artist. When, at the end of his section on the development of biography, he says that "perhaps, even now, another Boswell is reaching for his pen" (p. 151), one wonders whether he is very happy that this may be so. He calls Boswell a genius, but one is left to wonder why. For his Boswell is "neither a great stylist nor an intellect of the first rank" and "his book should be called Boswell's Johnson, not Boswell's Life of Johnson" (pp. 94–95). Edel, on the other hand, makes more of the relation between biographer and subject, has a somewhat wider tolerance for biography as a means of self-expression, as an inevitable reflection of the writer's vision. But even he stops short of saying that the value of a life depends mainly on the greatness of the artist who writes it, on the personal vision which comes from a first-rate artist, on his ability to interest the reader in his view of the significance of a subject. For all Edel's emphasis on the voice of the artist, he still advocates some objectivity and dispassionateness for the biographer. He expects the biographer to modulate, regulate, control his voice in a way he would not expect a poet or a novelist to do.

IRIS ORIGO

The influence of Edel's and Garraty's books is apparent in two essays published in 1959. What is most interesting about them is that Mary Purcell's "The Art of Biography"[14] is almost entirely derivative but that in "Biography, True and False"[15] the Marchesa Iris Origo projects an intensely personal voice and point of view at the same time that she implies, without raising her voice, that even the modulated biographical voice advocated by Edel is a little strident. She grants that it is "the writer's implicit view of life that gives style and flavor to his work." She is aware of the curious relation between biographer and subject and of the importance of the biographer's voice: she quotes Virginia Woolf's words when she had finished her life of Fry—"I feel very much in his presence at the moment, as if I were intimately connected with him: as if we together had given birth to this vision of him; a child born of us. Yet he had no power to alter it. And yet for some years it will represent him"—, and she says, too, "Just as we know no other face for Pope Julius II than Raphael's, no other Federico da Montefeltro than Piero della Francesca's, so Strachey's *Queen Victoria* will probably become for many the only Queen Victoria, and it is Boswell's *Johnson* whom most people call Dr. Johnson." The concept of biography as a means of expression, however, so imperils the biographical venture for her that she never explicitly mentions it. The biographer must be "very careful not to drown his subject's voice with his own." His intrusiveness is of various kinds, each of which is likely to cause falsification. The Marchesa uses a small mistake of her own to illustrate how the biographer's lack of familiarity with some times and places may make him misinterpret. His desire to suppress gives her occasion to quote Johnson's sentiment that "if nothing but the bright side of characters should be shown, we should sit in despondency and think it utterly impossible to imitate them in *anything*," and his indulgence in invention calls forth Johnson's stricture, "we don't know *which* half to believe." The biographer's tendency to sit in judgment reminds her of Marc Bloch's words: "To penetrate into the unknown being of a man separated from us by a long stretch of generations, one must almost cast off one's own self. To pull him to pieces, one need only remain oneself. The effort is undeniably less strenuous"; she illustrates the likelihood that his own judgment will change by citing Santayana's answer when she asked him in his old age whether he wished to change much when he was preparing an abridgement of *The Life of Reason*: "I feel I have much the same things to say— but I wish to say them in a different tone of voice."

For the Marchesa, the biographer who wishes to penetrate into a man's character and state of mind, to get "beneath the conscious personality, the purposing man" into his "underworld of discarded characters who have still some life in them," to see "the continuity of emotion" which is important in a life, cannot take refuge in the "short cuts" provided by the mechanical processes which Garraty described; he must rely on his own intelligence and intuition. She does not think of truth as being made of granite, but rather "as resembling a note in music, a note which we instantly recognize as the right one as soon as it is struck."[16] The biographer can hear the right note only "by temporarily casting aside" his own self and his own opinions. She knows that he will have to sift, to select, to draw conclusions, but her emphasis is not on his voice but on his ear and his mind as he *listens* to the note which reveals to him what another man is like.

"Emphasis" is perhaps too strong a word to describe the effect of the Marchesa's essay. Its complete lack of dogmatism is echoed in her suggestion that the biographer can at best faintly apprehend the life of another, that the most he can hope to do (and here she invokes an image of Pasternak's in *Doctor Zhivago*) is "to clear, in the icy crust of each man's incomprehension of other men, a little patch, through which a faint, intermittent light can shine." She draws on E. M. Forster's sentence that "the true history of the human race is the story of human affections" to suggest that it is the biographer's affection and humanity which renews this aspect of history. Her approbation of affection, of empathy, of listening to other voices, does not, however, diminish the effect of her own mellow and cultivated voice, and she leaves us wondering whether she has not undervalued the voice of the biographer.

JAMES L. CLIFFORD

The nature of the biographer's voice is not a primary concern in many of the selections in James L. Clifford's anthology *Biography as an Art: Selected Criticism 1560–1960*,[17] where part of the Marchesa's essay is reprinted, but it is one of Clifford's main concerns. The very publication of the anthology is a manifestation of the tendency to treat biography as a literary genre. In addition, as Clifford points out in his Introduction when he says that almost half of his collection is made up of selections from the last forty years and that though he might have added a mass of interesting material here it would have been difficult to discover other observations of equal importance during the preceding four centuries, the selections are themselves evidence of the increasing tendency since Strachey's achievement to treat biography as an art. Clifford prints excerpts from Roger North's "General Preface" to "Life of the Lord Keeper North" to show that "one practising biographer in the early eighteenth century did think deeply about his craft, and did write a long analysis of the problems involved" (p. xi); but North's manuscript had never before been published. He reprints excerpts from James F. Stanfield's *An Essay on the Study and Composition of Biography*, but he says that the volume, published at Sunderland in 1813, caused little stir. He holds the view, and his selections reinforce it, that during the 1920s and 1930s there was customarily an "implied conviction that art and pure history were irreconcilable" and that during the forties and fifties reconciliation started to take place, slowly, to be sure, as the proponents of history redefined objectivity and recognized what they owed to art, and as the proponents of art saw the dangers of uncontrolled creativity.

In his Introduction, Clifford maintains, too, that there is now widespread acceptance of the fact that "all biographies need not conform to a single set of standards, that quite legitimately there are different kinds of life-writing, each with its own possibilities and rules" (p. xvii). He finds the most significant recent trend to be what he calls "the domestication of psychology"; the modern biographer is expected to know psychiatric theory and to use it without indulging in technical jargon. Within the bounds of his brief introductory remarks, he manages to suggest that "perhaps the most subtle influence of the new psychology appears far below the surface in an increased awareness of the complex relationship of the biographer and his subject" (p. xviii). He thinks that the biographer's awareness that the sources of his dislike for or admiration of his subject "are embedded in his own character and background" makes it more likely that he will study his own motives at the same time as he describes his subject's and less likely that he will take an extreme position toward his subject. The biographer will be less inclined to censor, excuse, or rationalize and more inclined to present evidence so that his reader can judge its significance. He will continue to suggest patterns and unifying themes but will let the reader see what he is doing. For Clifford, the nature of the biographer's involvement with his subject and the effect of this involvement on his interpretation are crucial questions, and he thinks that increasing recognition of the complex psychological factors which form the biographer's own personality and opinions will deepen understanding and appreciation of the biographical process.[18]

ANON., *TLS*

The writer of the front-page review of Clifford's book in the *Times Literary Supplement* for March 2, 1962,[19] does not refer explicitly to Lord David Cecil's Introduction of 1936, much of which Clifford reprinted, but he develops Cecil's view that for all that Boswell achieved in the *Life of Johnson* his primary interest was not in the creation of a work of art and that it was with Strachey that biography emerged as an art consciously practiced. The review is, in fact, a brilliant little essay which moves beyond the views of Saintsbury, Thayer, Maurois, Edel, even of Cecil himself, in its emphasis on the personal vision and interpretative artistry of the biographer; the reviewer calls the advice of the Marchesa Origo that the biographer temporarily cast aside his own self and his own opinions a "dangerous precept." He also stresses, as Clifford himself had done, the nature of the relation or involvement between the biographer and his subject.

The reviewer maintains that the idea of biography as an art is linked with the realization that "a biographer exists in a special relation to his subject, that facts and opinions are filtered into public view through the sieve of an individual mind." It is the biographer who chooses between documents and between interpretations, and the making of such choices is "the act of an artist, not of a chronicler." He says that "with increased understanding of the interplay between the biographer and his subject has come a highly developed scepticism about sources and a tendency to scrutinize the making of a biography much more closely in the light of the biographer's ultimate objective." Since biography and history "rest upon the evidence of fallible human beings," they cannot be "objectively true." The reviewer declares clearly and unequivocally what no one to this point had stated so explicitly: "The truths of biography and history rest in the value of the minds through which they pass."

Since the "completely pure biography," free from "all partiality, all attempt at personal interpretation, all extraneous political and social considerations" cannot exist, the best a biographer can do is to try "to reach his own subjective, yet to him deeply felt and valuable, truth." He will use the traditional tools— a sense of history and an understanding of the world in which his subject lived and of his attitude toward it; scrupulous research and documentation, without invention and with the suppression only of what he thinks irrelevant; a philosophy of life; careful and wary psychological and psychoanalytical investigation. He will not, however, think that he has come to the only conclusion possible about his subject. He can only try to make sure that his portrait "is stamped with his style and personality and that it is the only portrait possible for *him*, the inevitable result of the collision of his own mind and the mind and character of the subject he has lived with over a period of time."

The reviewer insists, then, that "a biography is no more and no less than this, the interpenetration of one mind by another, the attempt to understand and assess the values of one who lived in the past, by one who lives in the present." He holds that since the past can never be recreated as it was, it would be useful to have "a fresh biography written every twenty-five years

of all important and controversial figures in our civilization."
The biographer who has portrayed a subject truly in the light of
his own personality must rest content that his work "aspires to
the condition of art, and that in art there is no final word."

MARK SCHORER

Some two months after the *TLS* review of Clifford's book
appeared, Mark Schorer, whose *Sinclair Lewis* had been published
the autumn before, delivered the Hopwood Lecture at the University of Michigan on the subject "The Burdens of Biography."[20] Schorer admits that in preparation for his lecture he
had read half a dozen books or more on the nature of biography
and he says he learned little from them. The lecture shows, in
fact, the signs of his reading in the books of Maurois and Edel and
in Clifford's anthology, as it ranges over many subjects from the
reliability of witnesses (and the effects on them of human vanity
and the desire for memorialization, of hurt feelings, and of fallible
memory) to the biographer as critic (use of the subject's work as
an index to feelings rather than facts, as "an autobiography of
the spirit") and the use of psychology and psychoanalysis without
their jargon. It shows particularly the influence of Cecil's Introduction and the *TLS* review of Clifford's book in its emphasis on
and development of the concepts of the biographer as artist, the
centrality of his personal vision, and the nature of his involvement with his subject.

Schorer's lecture is artfully discursive and charming in its
recounting of personal experience, but both the discursiveness
and the illustrations of his own involvement with Sinclair Lewis
work most persuasively to underscore the justness of his opinions.
When, for instance, early in the lecture, he makes the conventional enough point that the writer of fiction is free and that
the biographer writes in chains, he disposes quickly of the primary
difference between novelist and biographer, and he can later focus
on their similarities. Even here, however, he vitalizes Maurois's
idea that facts can be more than a burden, that they may have
"an eloquence, even a kind of poetry, that may well go far beyond
the inventions of imagination" (p. 250), by telling the remarkable
and pathetic story of the relations of Lewis with a young actress
who was his mistress and with her mother, and by showing the
lovely coincidence between his recognition that the theme of
Lewis's life was his incapacity to love and his discovery that the
cause of Lewis's death was recorded in a Roman hospital as *paralisi
cardiaca.* He speaks once again of theme when he discusses the biog-

rapher as critic; he discovered that all Lewis's works are built on the idea of a character who tries to escape from restrictions, such as convention, hypocrisy, injustice, institutions, that the restrictions are metaphors for "a restriction that was unutterable for him in his life," and that the second large theme of his life is his own "frenetic and endless and impossible attempt to escape from the restrictions of his self into a freedom that does not exist" (p. 255). When, finally, Schorer speaks of the biographer as artist, of the similarities between biography and fiction, of the role of theme in each, he has deftly prepared his reader for his discussion.

He holds that the biographer must be an artist who can bring shape to the mass of material he has accumulated, who can not only "make his subject live, but also . . . make him live in the reanimated history of his time, make him live in a living world" (p. 255). He holds, too, that "it seems probable that all the principles that pertain to fiction except for one—the free exercise of invention—pertain to proper biography." Like the novelist, the biographer must find the dominant themes in his raw materials, "the strains that seem most persistently to recur," "those tensions or preoccupations or behavioral patterns that occur most frequently in the mass of the life," and these will determine his selection of material. Like the novelist, too, the biographer must unify his themes, must find "an appropriate emphasis, or general meaning." Schorer does not speak explicitly here about the biographer's philosophy or point of view or interpretation, but of his "unifying attitude"; he makes it clear, however, that he is referring to "how the biographer, subjective being, enters the objective facts." When he shows what he intended by the subtitle of his life of Lewis, *An American Life*, he says, "clearly I am talking like a novelist, talking about America as it seems to me, and finding in the objective materials of a single life facts that will support that view." Schorer touches briefly on other topics which the biographer, like the novelist, must handle: the "general shape, or form, or rhythm" of his book, determined by themes and attitude as they emerge from and work on the general chronology of events; the plot, which he defines as "an element of persistent conflict that will animate not only the subject himself but that pattern which his life enacts, over and over in little, and once and once only in the whole that it was"; and the tone, which determines the kind of prose most appropriate to his subject.[21]

Finally, Schorer explores the importance of the relation of the biographer to his subject. He had already, in the context of his discussion of the unreliability of witnesses, drawn an interesting parallel between his own midwestern background and early education and those of Lewis (pp. 250–51). Earlier, too, he had discussed in answering the question, "Who is the best biographer for a given subject?" the disadvantages of personal intimacy, and he had said that "there are deeper forms of intimacy than friendship" (pp. 252–54). Now he shows that he thinks the relation of the biographer to his subject to be largely responsible for the "substance" of a life—not for its facts, themes, and plot, but for its "attitude," its "whole coloration" (p. 257). "Here," he says, "we can differentiate between what goes into fiction (*I*, really), and into history (*they*, really), and into biography (he *and* I)." He uses precisely the words of the *TLS* reviewer when he finds the essential nature of biography in "the interpenetration of one mind by another," and he stresses the subjectivity of the biographer. His account of the "strange affinity" he felt, unconsciously, for Lewis is remarkably like Maurois's analysis of his own identification with and attitude toward Shelley.[22] He comes close to echoing Clifford's words about the centrality of the involvement between the biographer and his subject when he says, "Perhaps this is where the psychoanalyst is really needed—not in the biographer analyzing his subject, but beyond both of them, analyzing their symbiotic relationship" (p. 258).

PAUL MURRAY KENDALL

The nature of this symbiotic relationship becomes, eventually, one of the main concerns of Paul Murray Kendall in his book *The Art of Biography* (1965),[23] but he does not treat the subject in detail until the very end and he arrives at it after various excursions. He broaches the subject even in his Introduction when he says, "On the trail of another man, the biographer must put up with finding himself at every turn: any biography uneasily shelters an autobiography within it" (p. x). He alludes to it in his first chapter, when he explains that biographers have frequently written about men of letters because, "being writers of a kind," they are attracted to other writers "partly, no doubt, in order to seek their own features in a kindred face" (pp. 6–7). At one point he says, "The biographer often finds himself in the grip of an extrarational, even compulsive choice, not unlike that which descends on the novelist or poet. The biographer's subject, it might be said, is a man whom he would have longed to create if he had not existed" (p. 8). At another point, he implies a rather different relation:

> The biographer is forced into a struggle with his subject which
> is, in a way, the opposite of the novelist's struggle. The
> novelist must fight for a detachment from material that is
> a part of him, so that he may see that material in esthetic
> perspective, may ask it the right questions. The biographer
> is already detached from his material, but it is an inert, a
> fortuitous detachment, a detachment that has not been won
> but thrust upon him. Before he can achieve true detach-
> ment, he must first achieve something like the psychic im-
> mersion in his material that the novelist begins with. (P.
> 16)

He refers to the relation between biographer and subject as one of
the two characteristic "tensions" of biography, but his purpose
in his first chapter is to define the nature of biography, especially
in its similarities to and differences from poetry, fiction, and
drama, and to call attention to the other main tension which
challenges the biographer—the problems which arise from the conflict between the implacability or intransigence of facts and the
demands of simulation, which are rooted in art.

For Kendall, biography is a craft in that "it employs techniques which can be learned by anybody"; it can be loosely called
a science, for part of the biographer's job is to collect facts in-
ductively in order to arrive at conclusions; it is an art, "however
lowly, because the biographer is himself interfused into what he
has made, and, like the novelist and the painter, shapes his material in order to create effects" (p. xii). Although Kendall considers history an art (p. 4), he does not consider biography a branch
of history; for him, history is not a mosaic of lives but a generalized
narrative of events, movements, and institutions. He disapproves
the definition of biography as the history or record of a life, for
"record implies documentation, severely factual account, an objective marshaling of evidences, and no biography which hopes to
recapture the sense of life being lived, to suggest the mysteries
of personality, can be any of these things" (p. 14). Biography is,
for him, "a genuine province of literature" (p. 4),[24] and he holds
that if its reliance on fact makes it different from poetry, fiction,
and drama, that difference is not so enormous as it has been made
out to be:

> The writer of fiction, out of the mating of his own experience
> and his imagination, creates a world, to which he attempts
> to give the illusion of reality. The biographer, out of the
> mating of an extrinsic experience, imperfectly recorded, and

his imagination, recreates a world, to which he attempts to give something of the reality of illusion. We demand that a novel, however romantic or "experimental," be in some way *true to life*; we demand of biography that it be *true to a life*. There is a difference in meaning between the phrases; they join, however, in signifying not "factual" but "authentic"—and authenticity lies not only in what we are given but in what we are persuaded to accept. (P. 8)

Kendall maintains that there are times when the biographer's imagination, his vision of character, may serve to correct seeming facts or facts which seem to deny his vision. On the other hand, he maintains that there are times when, unlike other artists, he must resist the enticements of art in order to be true to biographical art: "A literary device, however admirable in itself, which thrusts biographical materials outside the dimension of life-writing, ruptures truth more seriously, because less obviously, than outright error" (p. 9). Biography also differs from poetry, fiction, and drama in that its readers are usually interested in the subject of a life, not its writer. Kendall says that poets, novelists, dramatists "are unmistakably interfused in their work, identified with it," and that "we enjoy linking art with the artist." But, he says, "we do not enjoy being aware of the biographer. Quite the contrary: being aware of the biographer spoils our illusion of sharing in a life." He maintains, then, that "the biographer must have a talent for invisibility" and that "the highest biographical art is the concealment of the biographer" (pp. 12–13). For him, biography is "imagination limited by truth, facts raised to the power of revelation"; like other literary arts, it works "through effects," but it is an art with boundaries. He defines it as "the simulation, in words, of a man's life, from all that is known about that man" (p. 15).

In the second half of his first chapter, Kendall discusses the main problems which factual materials pose to the biographical artist who seeks to simulate a man's life, who hopes to recapture the sense of a life being lived, for he thinks that "the quality of biography is largely determined by the biographer's ability to meet these challenges" (p. 18). Except for the problem of the proper evaluation of the evidence of witnesses, which he discusses very generally, all the problems are concerned in one way or another with aspects of the question of time. He deals, first, with the problem of filling gaps in the available material. Since in a simulated life "the amount of biographical space-time devoted to a moment in the subject's life should approximate the weight of significance of the moment," since the movement of the narrative ought to be determined by the quality of the experience being related rather than by the quantity of material available, the biographer must somehow suggest the life of his subject during the gap (pp. 20–21). He must not leave it empty, must not speculate, invent, pretend to more knowledge than he has, and, still, he must not break the reader's illusion of a life unfolding. From his own experience, Kendall provides an illustration of how this may be done; he gives no rule, but says that the biographer must suggest what he thinks to have been the developing experience of the subject by using what biographical clues he has and what general materials may flesh them out. The second problem involving time Kendall describes as the problem of its management, and he says that the biographer must not manage time as a novelist does. The fictional character is a creature of the novelist's time, and the novelist usually focuses only on a segment of time though he moves forward and backward in order to enrich the segment. The subject of a biography is a creature of actual time, has his own time-dimension, and the biographer must accede to "the grand human chronology of growth, maturity, death" as well as to "lesser patterns of sequential experience." Kendall insists that the biographer must not use his ingenuity to *stage* a life or part of a life; he must *unfold* it, for "biographical time and novelistic time do not mix" (pp. 24–25). He sees, however, that even as the biographer seeks to recreate something of "the noisy cross-currents of man's passage through time," he must sometimes do violence to chronological time, and this raises a third problem. The biographer will have to group some happenings arbitrarily in order to reveal underlying currents of behavior, to elicit the themes of a life, its "patterns of hopes and illusions, preoccupations, fears," its "rhythmic movements of character discernible in the diurnal stream of existence." Kendall maintains that such thematic groupings must not intrude as diagram or as exposition, must not impede the sense of movement which simulates life, and that they must be brought into the narrative at the right place, "when the biographer's ear tells him that the moment has struck" (pp. 25–26). His fourth problem stems from the difference between the time-viewpoint of the subject and that of the biographer, from the fact that "what is the unknown future for the subject is the well-known past for the biographer." Kendall says that the biographer must use the advantage of this difference. He uses it when, in dealing with each critical moment in a life, he selects the crucial psychological and physical happenings leading toward it and those elements which show its effects. His selection, which reflects his vantage point in time, is, in fact, his way of commenting on the life or on part of it even as he seeks to recreate the life. Any comment more overt than this, Kendall holds, mars the simulation of a life because it calls attention to the intrusive voice of the biographer (pp. 27–28).

The three middle chapters of Kendall's book are not so much a history of biography as a chronological reassessment of biographies, autobiographies, and eras. That is why he devotes three pages to the quotation of Suetonius's account of the death of Nero and why he mentions Johnson's *Lives of the Poets* in a line; he wishes to show that Suetonius is "more the essential biographer" than Plutarch (p. 34), and he thinks that Johnson's "services to biography . . . have been too thoroughly and justly elucidated to require comment" (p. 99). So, too, his Chapter III, on the fifteenth century, is twice as long as Chapter II ("Biography in Antiquity and the Middle Ages") and as Chapter IV ("English Biography from the Elizabethan Age to World War I"), for not only does he find "the beginnings of the art of modern life-writing" in the fifteenth century, but he would also show that the achievements of the century were such that they did not reach the fulfillment they portended until the 1920s (pp. 53, 91).

When Kendall deals with the early Middle Ages, he gives attention to the *History of the Franks* by Bishop Gregory of Tours largely because it is "unknown to biographical history" and to Einhard's *Life of Charlemagne* because it is "generally undervalued" (p. 41). His most detailed discussions are reserved for the works he considers most important in his chapter on the fifteenth century: three works which, despite their form and their use of the third person, are essentially autobiographical—*The Book of Margery Kempe*, Jean de Bueil's *Le Jouvencel*, and *The Commentaries* of Aeneas Sylvius Piccolomini (Pope Pius II)—, and three biographies, the *Memoirs* of Philippe de Commynes (which he treats as a biography of King Louis XI), Roper's *Life of More*, and Cavendish's *Life of Wolsey* (the inclusion of both of which is justified because, though written later, they represent "a culmination, not a beginning"; "they spring from the progressive interaction of changing native attitudes and international humanism which developed in the fifteenth century" [p. 77]). Many of Kendall's illustrative passages are chosen because they vividly simulate an encounter or an event; he calls attention to "sustained biographical narrative" (p. 36), the projection of life in "vigorous scenes" (p. 56), "recapturing a life being lived" (p. 59), the appreciation of "those high moments in which character most vividly displays itself" (p. 73), "the evocations of person-

ality shaped into the unfolding of a life" (p. 81). He does discuss
thematic grouping, point of view, and theme, but he does not
often apply systematically or rigorously the stances he took on the
problems he raised in his first chapter. For instance, in defining
the theme of Roper's and Cavendish's books as the relationship
between king and subject, he says, with approbation, "This theme
does not lie implicit in the material but is developed with conscious irony by both biographers as a shaping principle of their
books" (p. 82); he does not raise here the question whether
themes not implicit in the material are elicited or imposed,
whether such themes partake of the kind of overt comment he
deplores.

Especially in his chapter on English biography from Elizabeth to World War I, Kendall's canvas is a broad one, and he tries
to account for the paucity of Elizabethan biography, the flores-
cence of autobiography in the nineteenth century, the poverty
of biography in America, the mediocrity of Victorian biography. He
sets forth the thesis that the quality of biography in any era is
determined by the relation between the psychological awareness
achieved by an age and its "received" or "official" or "established" attitude toward human life. Thus he says that though
the Victorians had a considerably enlarged view of what was known
to be important about a life, that view was smothered by the
received attitude, which inhered in a social image of middle-class
respectability and a psychological image of man as a decorous animal
(pp. 104–6).

In his last chapter, on contemporary biography, Kendall
mentions the inspirational and technical influence of Strachey,
but he emphasizes the change in the biographical atmosphere.
He characterizes the modern age as one intensely conscious of self
and personality and as one which has been offered so many conflicting views of man that there is no single official, socially imposed view. Like Nicolson, he finds in science and in literature
the decisive influences upon modern biography, but he interprets
their effects differently. Science has pushed the biographer toward
higher standards of scholarship, but it has also generally encouraged
the vast collection of data almost as a good in itself. Psychology
and psychoanalysis have provided educated men with new insight
into human nature, but psychoanalysis analyzes, explains, classi-
fies, and it is deficient as an approach to biography because it tells
about a man rather than simulating his life, showing his life being
lived; moreover, reliance on types and profiles reinforces an atmosphere of dehumanization which is antithetical to the biographer's focus on one man. Literature, too, has worked for good

and for bad on biography: the novelist has shown the biographer how to deal with the formal problems of unfolding a life, the techniques of representation and dramatization rather than of exposition, but the biographer, who is confined to truth, must resist both invention and modern novelistic experimentation in the manipulation of time, point of view, and narrative.

All this is prefatory to Kendall's discussion of what he calls the three chief characteristics of modern biography: the decline of autobiography and of biography based on the familiarity of biographer and subject, the wide range of biographical literature, and the development of a mode of writing, not necessarily new, "as a self-conscious practice" (pp. 123–24). About the first of these he says, very briefly, that the formal autobiographer has been inhibited by modern psychology, which has made the self both more exposed and more comprehensible, but also more elusive and less "palatable," and that the autobiographer now prefers memoir-reminiscences to revelation of his personality; both he and the biographer of a friend are aware of the warping effects of retrospect and memory and of the sounder, if perhaps less intimately penetrating, reliance on knowledge gained through research.

In dealing with the second characteristic, Kendall identifies eight types of biography on a scale from "the most literary-least factual" to "the most 'scientific'-least literary": novel-as-biography, fictionized biography, interpretative biography, scholarly biography, research biography, life-and-times biography, works which are essentially compilations of source materials, and—above the center of the scale—what he terms "superbiography" (pp. 126–27). He focuses mainly on the middle of his scale. His discussion of interpretative biography is an attack on the doctrines in Pearson's *Ventilations;* his discussion of "superbiography," which preempts a third of his last chapter, is an even more slashing attack on Edel's theory and practice. He argues that Pearson's notion that the interpretative biographer's invention can reveal an essential truth superior to the truth of facts elevates too much the importance of the biographer and depresses too much his obligation to his subject and to his materials. For all the difficulty involved in determining what facts can be trusted, for all the distortion which the process of selection may introduce, Kendall holds that the biographer must use his imagination and his insight "only so far as his pursuit of the real man and the limits of his sources allow." The primary object of the biographer, he insists, is not merely to present his vision of his subject but "to render his man as honestly as he can," not only to create "a living picture" but one made out of "the materials at hand" which will be a "true likeness." Distortion is different from deliberate falsification, and maimed truth better than outright invention (pp. 128–30).

His attack on "superbiography," the kind which "seeks to be both ultimately literary and ultimately scientific" (p. 127)—and which he says is "eminently represented" by the work of Edel, though he cites no other example—is, like that on interpretative biography, based mainly on its elevation of the biographer to a position which makes him so supremely and objectionably intrusive to Kendall that he must use phrases like "feral whiff of cannibalism" and "self-conscious expertise and Corinthian sophistication" to rise above his customary strain for vigorous and colorful prose (pp. 145–46). Edel, he maintains, is wrong to indulge in the methods and in the omniscient point of view of the novelist: "When the biographer apes the novelist, he loses the sense of life being lived by the subject and produces, as a substitute, the life being lived, as it were, by the biographer" (p. 134). The biographer who has recourse to intrusive analyses, groupings by "synthetic retrospect," the "arbitrary detachment of materials from their time-context" smothers the sense of a life being lived (p. 145). Such a biographer does not "*elicit* the shapes and meanings within his material"; he refashions them, and does not "call into being a world but interposes his prestidigitation between us and the world" (p. 134). Kendall charges that in manipulating time like an omniscient novelist, by shuttling back and forth in time, Edel uses the technique developed by the novelist to give the illusion of the unfolding of life that occurs in the real world, and he maintains that what the novel must create as illusion is inherent in the reality of the materials of biography, that "what the novelist does with time to make an imaginary person seem real may very well tend to make a real person seem imaginary. Put a creature of human time in novelistic time and he is likely to take on novelistic coloring" (p. 136). Although he knows that the sequential experience of real life cannot be imitated, that thematic grouping is necessary, he holds no brief for thematic grouping which abuses the change and development of a subject and which does violence to the particular moment chosen as the nucleus for the grouping (p. 137).

Edel had explained in *Literary Biography* that he had seen fit to group his materials which dealt with James's relation with Emerson—from a letter of 1870 recounting a visit to Emerson at Concord, through his attending Emerson's funeral in 1883, and his essay of 1887 on Emerson occasioned by the publication of Cabot's *Life*—and that, since he thought Emerson was important to James as a symbol of the values of New England, he had introduced his grouping at the time of James's visit to Concord in 1870, "for this is where Emerson belonged and where both can best be placed in their American setting."[25] Kendall does not object to the grouping but to its placement: not only does it falsify James's feeling in 1870 that his visit was of "slender profit" (as opposed to Emerson's view, in a letter to Carlyle shortly after the visit, about the multitude of young men of great promise growing up about him), but it also substitutes Edel's " 'synthetic' memory," his own point of view, his "invented retrospect" for James's point of view (p. 141). Had Edel placed his grouping at the time of James's presence at Emerson's funeral, Kendall says, he might have been able to suggest the play of James's mind backward and forward about the significance of Emerson to him.[26] Kendall insists that it is the subject's consciousness and his sense of time which must be dominant, not the biographer's, and that the biographer who arbitrarily imposes his own sense of time on a life breaks the web of simulation; "In trying to be more of an artist, he becomes less of a biographer" (p. 142).

When Kendall finally treats what he calls the third characteristic of modern biography, a mode which is "new as a self-conscious practice" in "the best biographies of our time,"[27] he finds in these works "the dramatic unfolding of personality-in-action," "the literary projection of experience" which he has advocated, and he says, too, that they are successful simulations of life because the simulation "grows out of a liaison with the subject self-consciously cultivated by the biographer as the *primum mobile* of his enterprise" (pp. 146–48). The steps in this liaison or "simulated life-relationship" Kendall gives in detail. The biographer starts by facing his materials with a detachment which is fortuitous. As he broods over his materials, he becomes deeply attached to his subject and develops feelings about him. Now committed to his subject, he must control and shape his feeling, must struggle for a willed detachment. He does this not to gain a "cold objectivity" but "the kind of love that finds no contradiction between *engagement* and truth," the kind of sympathy that leads to perception (pp. 148–49).[28] Kendall then proceeds to spend as much time on "the importance of *locale*" for the biographer, his becoming through personal experience familiar with the places and settings in which his subject moved, as he had on his explanation of the simulated life-relationship. For him, "the seeking-out of place" operates, like "the force of psychology and the native power of understanding," both on the simulation of the life-relationship and on the simulation of the life itself (pp. 150–52). He concludes by saying that if modern biography has produced no towering masterpieces, if it has no Hemingway or D. H. Lawrence or O'Neill, it has still probably created "the most sustained pitch of biographical excellence that the world has yet enjoyed." But then, he suggests, it is the "appropriate fate" of biography that its greatest masterpiece was written by "the undignified and unedifying Laird of Auchinlech" and, what is more, "biography is *proud* of Boswell."

Kendall would seem to imply, then, what Cecil had stated— that biography is not an important form of literary art. And, for all that he says about the achievement of modern biography, he does not envision biographical works which will exceed the sustained pitch of those he praises. Nor is it difficult to see why. Although he has not, like Garraty, produced a manual for turning out competent biography by the yard, although he casts his argument as a description of the modern biography which he admires, he is still, in his primary emphasis on the simulation of a man's life and in his description of the process of the simulated life-relationship, prescriptive in what ought to be normative in the production of biography by authors who do not have the genius of Shakespeare and Tolstoi and Eliot. By his prescription biography is unlikely to have its Shakespeare, Tolstoi, and Eliot, for, to him, the highest biographical art is the concealment of the biographer, and such men do not have a talent for invisibility.

Kendall's stress on the invisibility of the biographer tends to hide the stress which he also places on the biographer as artist. On the surface, his stress on the concealment of the biographer seems like Sidney Lee's doctrine that the success of the biographer is proportioned to his self-suppression. But Lee was referring to the biographer's need for detachment and right perspective, for the necessity of suppressing his own partialities, and Kendall is far less sanguine about the possibility and desirability of this kind of suppression. He leaves the biographer room for the expression of his artistry and of his point of view. After all, truth in biography is, for him, not "factual" but "authentic," and authenticity lies not only in the facts of a life but also in what the biographer can persuade the reader to accept as ringing true. Kendall does not hold with Lee that the "creation" of the biographer is limited to giving animation to the dead bones, but his primary emphasis on the simulation of a life does echo the importance Lee attached to "the semblance of life and reality." He is even closer to Thayer, who had stated in 1920 that the first aim of biography is to tell a story "as nearly as possible as the actors or hero underwent it" and that the biographer has "to find means through the art of literature to produce an adequate simulation of lifelikeness." Still, though Thayer thought that "fashion in modern biography" did not approve too frequent intrusion by the biographer, though he went so far as to say that "strictly speaking" the biographer ought to intrude his personality as little as possible—and his remarks included prose style as a manifestation of personality—, he admitted that he not only tolerated but enjoyed the intrusion of the biographer so long as it did not harm the truth. Even Lee had not disapproved the place Boswell had given himself in his *Johnson*; it was not, he said, in Boswell's nature to efface himself, but he did not bring himself on the stage at Johnson's expense.

Kendall wants the biographer to remain offstage. So long as he remains in the wings, Kendall does not put limits on the extent to which he may influence the action on the stage. He does not, in fact, restrict the bounds of interpretation—after all, biography inevitably reflects the symbiotic relation between biographer and subject—so long as interpretation does not disturb simulation, the sense of a life being lived. Simulation is, however, the first aim of biography, and it means, among other things, the representation of the subject's attitudes, perspective, comprehension of events and people at moments in his growth and development. The biographer, Kendall would say, may express himself as fully as he wishes if he does so by indirection, if he does not intrude himself to mar the sense of simulation by overt comments, by analysis and exposition, or by literary techniques or expressed points of view which call attention to himself. Kendall agrees with Virginia Woolf's statement (though she limited it to the biographer's desire to expound the private life) that "the biographer's imagination is always being stimulated to use the novelist's art of arrangement, suggestion, dramatic effect," but his view of the danger is different from hers. She had feared that the biographer might be tempted to invent, and she felt that the mixture of the imagined with the real made the real suspect. He thinks that the very introduction of some novelistic techniques, radical shifts in time, in point of view, in narrative mode, so inevitably calls attention to the biographer that it spoils the reality of the illusion he strives for in his simulation of a life being lived.

Kendall would not quarrel with the *TLS* reviewer's emphasis on the personal vision and interpretative artistry of the biographer. He would seem to agree, even, with his statement that the truths of biography rest in the value of the mind through which they pass. But, he would say, the biographer makes himself known quietly, indirectly. Whereas the reviewer says that the biographer tries to make sure that his portrait "is stamped with his style and personality," Kendall would insist that any portrait so distinctly and overtly stamped has been damaged. He is at the other end of the scale from Flexner, who had found merit in the biographer who drew his conclusion overtly for his reader, because the reader could then recognize the biographer's point of view and take it into account whereas he would have to make a new study of the source materials to discover the prejudices of the biographer who kept himself in the background. Kendall calls Strachey a "genius" and he refers to his "genuine accomplishment," but he mentions only "his ironic detachment from his material, his lacquered style, his delicacy of selection and his dramatic touch" (p. 114). He says that Strachey demonstrated that "biography could express the personality of the writer" (p. 114), but he says too, that he was "certainly a minor luminary compared to James Boswell" (p. 102).

Conclusion

The tracing of general discussions of biography makes apparent a substantial movement from a kind of lip-homage paid to the art in biography to a realization that biography is an art. This has come about with the recognition that the biographer is far more than a mere compiler, more than a writer with a flair for dramatic projection and artistic representation. It stems from a growing awareness that biography is essentially dependent upon the sensitiveness of the biographer's response to the personality and actions of his subject, upon the biographer's relation to his subject, upon the vision of the biographer and his skill in projecting his vision. This awareness has been fostered by the examination of what biography has in common with the novel, and by the novelists' exploitation of the inner life of thought and emotion, by their experiments in the manipulation of point of view, distance, and time. It has been fostered, too, by reconsideration of history as an art; by the insights made available in a psychologically oriented climate, one which reduced the question of discretion or candor to the level of libel and raised the genetic study of literature to a sophisticated level; and by increasing attention to the increasingly particularized theoretical and critical discussion of biographical matters.

It is fair to say that biography is now generally thought to be an art, that the work of criticism in its broadest sense has promoted ideas which have created a convention, a convention which has just about won social acceptance. The critical debate has been valuable insofar as its descriptions have heightened the awareness and deepened the perceptions of readers and writers to various aspects of biography. The danger to biography now lies in the possibility that its recognition as an art may lead to attempts to codify it as a literary genre. The best literary theory and criticism from Aristotle on has always been based on a description of what artists have done. The danger lies in treating such theory and criticism prescriptively. Then it makes for a hardening of arteries in critics and readers who find comfort in mechanical measures of excellence and for the flattening out of an art in the work of second-rate artists. Fortunately, the artistic temperament thrives on challenge, is anti-rule and anti-program; for every dogmatic rule there is an artist anxious to show that in breaking it he can increase the delight and instruction of his readers.

In the past, the variety of attitudes toward what biography was—history, literature, didactic aid to religion or morality—made for a fluidity of approach and of form which was inhospitable to genre theory. This was true even in eras when artists and critics were acutely conscious of the demands of genre. For all its utility in providing artists with conventions and challenges, and critics and readers with guideposts for understanding and easy rules for evaluating, genre in its purity was always an ideal construct. Literature has always thrived on the breakdown, diffusion, and intermixture of genre. In a day when drama and fiction and poetry are governed by Proteus, it would be ironic if biography were to submit to Procrustes. It is one thing to realize that the epic has possibilities not inherent in the sonnet, that the biographer's invention is limited in ways which a novelist's is not; it is another to encourage imitations of imitations, to set limits to the personal voice and individual vision of the artist in any genre.

There is some truth in Cecil's statement that it was with Strachey that biography emerged as an art self-consciously practiced. But awareness of biography as an art of a kind goes back in England at least as far as 1640, when Walton cited Plutarch on the first page of his *Life of Donne* at the same time that he professed himself to be artless and said that his lack of art was advantageous to the reader, who would get Donne's picture "in a naturall dresse, which ought to beget faith in what is spoken, for he that wants skill to deceive, may safely be trusted." Walton, however, was no more aware of a genre of biography (the word itself had not yet entered the language) than he was of working within a precise genre or several of them when he wrote *The Compleat Angler*. What made him a man of letters was his ability to project a personal voice and an individual vision; even in writing a kind of fishing manual, he said of himself, "the whole discourse is a kind of picture of my owne disposition." So, too, Johnson, conscious as he was of the decorum of genres, was so quintessentially a man of letters that it is unimportant to ask whether he thought that biography was a kind of art or a precise literary genre. He did not write *Rasselas* and *The Vanity of Human Wishes* with his right hand and the *Lives of the Poets* with his left; all clearly express his own personal voice and individual vision.

There probably was, after Strachey, as Cecil suggests, a shift in the intention of the biographer's principal purpose from giving information and telling the truth to producing an artistic impression through the exercise of his creative powers and the expression of his personal vision. The inferior quality of some of the work of writers who would march with Strachey does not stem from their conception of biography but from their inferiority as artists. An artist does not need to sacrifice life to art any more than he has to sacrifice art to life. The trouble with the works of such biographers lies in their impoverished notion of art, in their reliance on the notion that invention or originality is all, in the insignificance of their individual visions. Their work is inferior not because they adhered to or violated the limits of biography as a genre but because they were insufficient as artists. I know of no such work which I would call a bad biography but a good novel.

Biography is an art, even a genre, different from the novel, with peculiar limitations of its own which are likely to make some artists feel shackled to such an extent that they cannot reveal their voices in all their fullness or cannot reveal them as fully as in another genre. After all, it takes a Milton to project his voice almost as fully in sonnet, in masque, and in classical oration as he did in the epic, and Miltons do not appear very often. The limits of any art can serve to challenge the artistry of a writer. When Virginia Woolf deliberately set out in *Orlando* to flout the limitations of biography, she created a work of art, if not a biography, which revealed her voice as sumptuously as her novels did, a book which will perennially delight and instruct readers. The remembrance of the steady accumulation of volumes of the *DNB* in her father's study and her own theory and criticism of biography made her so much aware of her chains in her *Life of Fry* that she restrained the depth and delicacy of her voice as that voice reflected the depth and delicacy of her mind. In her sketch of Miss Ormerod she had shown that even the scientist who works with the severest of restrictions and limitations may yet expand the universe.[1] She was not willing in her *Life of Fry* to assume that the truths of biography, like the truths of science, rest in the value of the mind through which they pass. Still, her insight into her own life as woman and as writer had led her to envision in some of her criticism and to represent in *Orlando* an expanded universe for biography, for women, for the writing of the lives of women. She saw, with greater understanding and sympathy than Strachey had in his "Florence Nightingale," the availability of what Carolyn G. Heilbrun has recently called "new plots,"[2] especially in the lives of women who sought to break out of old and conventional roles, who searched not just for a room of their own but for an expanded space.

Every life, however prosaic, differs in details; every interesting life has a new plot if the biographer is perceptive enough to find it. A biographer may feel shackled by facts, but he is apt to be more shackled by the limitations of his own vision and insight. Biographers and historians frequently emphasize, and perhaps overemphasize, their reliance on fact and their responsibility to fact; they tend to minimize their dependence on design or pattern or structure. William H. Epstein is right when he says that "with a few notable exceptions" biography has always been an instrument of a particular culture and of that culture's desire to reinforce its own values and structures. To structure is to interpret, and most biographers are bent on *imposing* a structure on a life, one based on their own predilections, biases, and beliefs, which usually reflect the values of their culture. The imposition of a structure or paradigm dictated by and in harmony with the values of a culture bulks so large for Epstein that his notable exceptions seem also to have had patterns imposed on them, patterns opposed to or contrastive with conventional ones: when he mentions Johnson's *Life of Savage*, he treats it as an "anti-model"; when he discusses Nancy Milford's *Zelda* and some other "feminist" biographies, he treats them as an "incipient subgenre," one of a number of "*types*" of life stories which are emerging from "herstory," "the rewriting and rereading of patriarchal history from a feminist perspective."[3] Most biographers, however restrictive they find the facts of a particular life, find it important and necessary to adhere to the facts. Most of them do not have the insight or the penetration to *discover* the significant form that gives coherence to the facts of a life lived with some independence or originality. Nor do they have the rhetorical ability to make new things familiar or familiar things new for readers acculturated to societal norms; they are not able to revivify what is customary or make the unfamiliar obvious enough so that readers acknowledge it to be just.[4] It is difficult for biographers to make fresh and striking what has been seen so often that it is no longer regarded. When their subject is a person of genius, one who lives by his own lights, in accord with his own emotions and intellect, or one who has a new view of man's existential situation and predicament, they must have the empathy and understanding to recognize a pattern that is new and different and the skill to represent that pattern effectively. Their ability must be answerable to that of their subject.

When Johnson wrote his *Life of Savage*, he announced that he was adding another mournful narrative to the volumes already written "to enumerate the Miseries of the Learned, and relate their unhappy Lives, and untimely Deaths."[5] "It has been observed in all Ages," his first sentence says, "that the Advantages of Nature or of Fortune have contributed very little to the Promotion of Happiness." If it is hardly astonishing that the extrinsic advantages of affluence and power raise expectations of felicity which they cannot give, "it seems rational to hope, that intellectual Greatness should produce better Effects"; but, he continues, "this Expectation, however plausible, has been very frequently disappointed" (p. 4). Johnson set out, then, to make the familiar new through his account of the particular misfortunes, the idiosyncratic temperament, and the individual talent of Savage. Boswell called the *Life* "one of the most interesting narratives in the English language," but even if he intended *interesting* to mean *affecting*, his response to the *Life* is much more controlled than the reaction of Sir Joshua Reynolds and the words of the writer of a review in *The Champion*, which he himself recorded.[6] It was the lawyer in Boswell that came through when, after discussing at length "the evidence upon the case" of Savage's parentage, he wrote, "The talents of Savage, and the mingled fire, rudeness, pride, meanness, and ferocity of his character, concur in making it credible that he was fit to plan and carry on an ambitious and daring scheme of imposture" and when he suggested in a footnote that Johnson was deceived by Savage in identifying Savage's pride with his own "noble pride" (pp. 125–27). Boswell knew that Johnson, like Savage, had once been reduced "to the lowest state of wretchedness as a writer for bread"; he knew that "Johnson and Savage were sometimes in such extreme indigence, that they could not pay for a lodging; so that they have wandered together whole nights in the streets"; but he merely found it "melancholy to reflect" on these things (pp. 118–19). Johnson's approach was personal and passionate. Even as he saw and made clear Savage's negligence, irregularity, and want of prudence (p. 140), he thought, too, and demonstrated that Savage's misfortunes "were often the Consequences of the Crimes of others, rather than his own" (p. 4). One cannot imagine Boswell's saying, as Johnson did, "Those are no proper Judges of his Conduct who have slumber'd away their Time on the Down of Plenty, nor will a wise Man easily presume to say, 'Had I been in *Savage's* Condition, I should have lived, or written, better than *Savage*' " (p. 140). Johnson's condition when he wrote the *Life of Savage* was not unlike that of Savage; his understanding of Savage and his compassion for him were such that he did not think "an Apology either necessary or difficult" (p. 139). Still, he was clear-sighted enough to see and reveal the deficiencies in Savage's life and work—his insolence, his resentment, the lack of polish and accuracy in his writing. Although Johnson languished under sufferings similar to Savage's, he had the balance and strength of character not to succumb but to fortify his patience. If he wrote, as Savage had, as a man "oppressed with Want, which he has no Hope of relieving but by a speedy Publication" (p. 140), he wrote, too, with the power and insight that made Savage come to life even as he used the example of Savage to renew an old theme with poignancy and intensity.

Johnson's identification of himself with Savage accounts, at least in part, for the force of his reanimation of Savage. Freud saw, as Maurois did somewhat later, that biographers often chose their heroes "for reasons of their personal emotional life."[7] When he wrote his *Leonardo*, he differentiated himself from such biographers, who, he said, "devote[d] their energies to a task of idealization aimed at enrolling the great man among the class of their infantile models" (p. 80). He would reveal Leonardo's human weakness and imperfection, "bring together the factors which have stamped him with the tragic mark of failure" (p. 81). His shrewd examination of Leonardo led him to three crucial questions: why was Leonardo apparently not interested sexually in women? why did he leave so much of his artistic work unfinished? why did his interest shift from artistic endeavor to scientific investigation? He wished to discover what determined Leonardo's mental (or psychic) and intellectual development.

There is no need at this date to rehearse what Freud did in his analysis of Leonardo's screen memory of the vulture fantasy, how he found answers to his questions in Leonardo's relations with his parents; or to call attention once more either to the way that his use of an inaccurate translation vitiated some of his conclusions or to the way that he extrapolated, selectively and massively, from a paucity of evidence. There is, however, reason to believe that Freud, too, chose his subject for reasons of his own emotional life. He was in his early fifties when he wrote about

Leonardo that "at the summit of his life, when he was in his early fifties—a time . . . when in men the libido not infrequently makes a further energetic advance—a new transformation came over him" (pp. 83–84). At the time Leonardo painted the Mona Lisa, Freud said, "he recovered the stimulus that guided him at the beginning of his artistic endeavours" and conquered the inhibition in his art (p. 84). Freud, it would seem, not only identified with Leonardo but also pitted himself against him. He saw that Leonardo's investigations "extended to practically every branch of natural science, and in every single one he was a discoverer or at least a prophet and pioneer" (p. 26). He followed that observation with one that seems almost adventitious, one that refers to the limits of Leonardo's achievements and measures them by his own: "Yet his urge for knowledge was always directed to the external world; something kept him far away from the investigation of the human mind." It is interesting to glimpse some personal motive behind Freud's *Leonardo*, to add that motive to his explicit interest in originology and screen memory.

What is more relevant, however, to an assessment of the nature of Freud's achievement in the *Leonardo* is that he faulted Leonardo for moving from the "exterior" of a painter's subjects—"animals and plants, and the proportions of the human body"—"to proceed to gain a knowledge of their internal structure and their vital functions, which indeed also find expression in their appearance and have a claim to be depicted in art" (p. 26). Freud thought it was a mistake on Leonardo's part to diminish or minimize the importance of representation, to overrate the value to an artist of the scientific laws on which representation is based. And then, for all the brilliance of his own analysis, for all the elegance of the argument he constructed to get at the root of Leonardo's latent homosexuality, of his inability to finish his work, of his shift (as Freud saw it) from artistic endeavor to scientific investigation, Freud was so driven to investigate Leonardo's internal structure that he neglected to represent vividly and in detail the expression of that structure. His ideas are fascinating, and he presented them lucidly and effectively; his narrative of Leonardo's life is, on the whole, barren and unfeeling.

Erik Erikson has stated that Freud, like Martin Luther, "endeavored to increase the margin of man's inner freedom by introspective means applied to the very center of his conflicts; and this to the end of increased individuality, sanity, and service to men."[8] That is a wise assessment by a man who has himself made a substantial contribution to the expansion of man's space. But Erikson was assessing Freud's general achievement as a pio-

neer in the study of man's inner life as it related to his actions
in society; he was not assessing the *Leonardo*. Ironically, *Leonardo*
opened up inner space for future biographers; but, however admirable was Freud's attempt to show Leonardo as "a human
being to whom we might feel ourselves distantly related" because
of his failings, however much he insisted that his focus on Leonardo's failings does not detract from his greatness and that "we
do homage to him by learning from him,"[9] that focus did little
to expand space for readers who wished to profit in some way from
the example of Leonardo.

Erikson shrewdly saw in his *Young Man Luther* "the degree
to which in the biography of a great man 'objective study' and
'historical accuracy' can be used to support almost any total image
necessitated by the biographer's personality and professed calling"; he saw, too, that "there is always an implicit psychology"
behind the explicit antipsychology of biographers "categorically
opposed to systematic psychological interpretation" (pp. 35–36).
He revealed, candidly, that ideologies pervade psychological theory,
and that his interest in Luther stemmed in part from his finding
in him an example of the identity crisis of late adolescence, one
of his own major modifications of Freudian originology (pp. 14–15,
18–19). He wished to demonstrate that Luther's theological
redefinition of man's condition "has striking configurational par-
allels with inner dynamic shifts like those which clinicians recognize in the recovery of individuals from psychic distress" (p. 206).
Still, he admitted in his Preface his own puzzlement that he
had chosen to write about Luther; his choice of subject forced
him "to deal with problems of faith and problems of Germany,
two enigmas which [he] could have avoided by writing about some
other young great man." Moreover, though he focused on Luther
to his thirtieth year, he carried the life beyond Luther's crisis of
identity; his penultimate chapter took Luther from about 1517,
when he was thirty-four, to about 1527. Early in that chapter he
said "Here, in a way, our story ends," but he saw, too, that "a
completed identity is only one crisis won," and he was interested in the fact that Luther, who had "initiated revolutionary
puritanism—that strange mixture of rebellious individualism,
aesthetic asceticism, and cruel righteousness which came to characterize much of Protestantism," could hardly recognize what
he had generated and was distressed by what he had generated (pp.
233–34).

In his Preface, Erikson provided a brief rationale for his
undertaking in terms of his professional experience even as he
expressed his doubt that "the impetus for writing anything but

a textbook can ever be rationalized." He acknowledged an "emotional" debt in relating an episode from his youth—an overnight
visit in a small village by the Upper Rhine with a friend and the
friend's father, a Protestant pastor who recited at breakfast the
Lord's Prayer in Luther's German; he gave bare mention to a
"traumatic" debt when he said that his memory of the event
"had been utterly covered by the rubble of the cities and by the
bleached bones of men of my kind in Europe." It is not likely that
Erikson moved beyond Luther's crisis of identity merely to summarize his own theory that a series of crises is characteristic of
man's life-cycle or to illustrate sketchily Luther's life in terms
of those crises. Erikson rationalized the attention he gave "Luther" rather than "Martin" by stating that "Martin's"
solution of the identity crisis of his youth "aggravated the crisis
of his manhood," but for some reason he saw fit to explore in
Young Man Luther Luther's crisis of generativity, the crisis that
occurs "when a man looks at what he has generated, or helped
to generate, and finds it good or wanting" (pp. 242–43). He made
much of Luther's deep despair when he recognized what his re-
bellion had done "to the imagination, the sense of reality, and
the conscience of the masses" (p. 242); he indicated his own
distress that Luther's justification by faith, his counterpoising
of praying man to the philosophy and practice of meritorious works,
"was absorbed into the patterns of mercantilism, and eventually
turned into a justification of commercialism by faith" and his
distress, too, that Freud's work was "about to be used in fur-
therance of that which he had warned against: the glorification
of 'adjustment' " (p. 252). It is possible, perhaps even likely,
that *the* impetus for Chapter 7 and *an* impetus for the book as a
whole, which Erikson wrote in his mid-fifties, the age at which Freud
had written his *Leonardo*, was a generativity crisis of his own, an
uneasy feeling that his attempts "to devise, with scientific determinism, a therapy for the few" had led, like those of other
psychoanalysts, to the promotion of "an ethical disease among
the many" (p. 19).

   Erikson's approach was narrative only in part, and even
the narrative of *Young Man Luther* violated chronology; the design
of the book was determined by Erikson's awareness that the key
to Luther's life was his struggle with conscience, that the story
of his inner life was more crucial than the chronological representation of a multiplicity of events. Erikson recognized and delineated the key events in Luther's identity crisis and his break-
through, saw their significance in Luther's own life, and their
importance for Luther's contemporaries and for later genera-

tions. He had the wisdom to perceive the ideological content in both religion and psychoanalysis and the insight to discover in the young Luther a precursor of Freud who had the "grim willingness to do the dirty work" of his age by keeping "human conscience in focus in an era of material and scientific expansion" (p. 9). Even as Erikson's professional knowledge and concern allowed him to grasp what was central in Luther's early life, so his professional and personal concern and his humane outlook allowed him, as he identified with and probed into Luther's crisis of generativity, to write, too, a cautionary tale. His own genius and originality made him see and represent anew the genius and originality in Luther, and he demonstrated the power of biography as a "protestant" art as he re-invented one of the inventors of Protestantism, as he showed that Luther's own way of life was new and different, that Luther created for others a way of life that was new and different, with new rewards and new risks.

Erikson's examination of other biographers' interpretations of Luther led him to point out the dangers in a biographer's reliance on his "professed calling," to show that a biographer's profession may warp his perspective, narrow his outlook, overdetermine an image that he imposes on his subject. The force of his argument is evident even in the briefest of examinations of so accomplished a book as James Thomas Flexner's *Washington: The Indispensable Man* (1974).[10] Flexner's Preface tells of his "determination to describe Washington's indispensable role in the creation of the United States and yet not lose the man in the leader," but his historical bent sometimes influences crucially his design and the image of Washington that emerges. His first chapters effectively overturn the common misconception of Washington as a rich, conservative, British-oriented Virginia aristocrat. Flexner's focus on Washington's national role is, however, so great that he covers Washington's middle years, his "private" years as a Virginia planter, in two of his fifty-two chapters; he treats about a quarter of Washington's life, his life between the ages of twenty-seven and forty-three, in four per cent of his pages. There are some wonderful insights here: Flexner stresses Washington's amiability and gregariousness when he says that the Washingtons entertained two thousand guests in seven years (p. 52); he reveals much about Washington in one sentence when he says that in 1768 Washington went to church on fifteen days, "mostly when away from home," and that he hunted foxes on forty-nine (p. 51); he emphasizes Washington's drive to accumulate land (pp. 54–56). But he makes too little of Washington's many years as a kind of ideal eighteenth-century squire, pragmatic, patrician, fair-minded;

he neglects Washington the planter as he sows the seeds for the Washington who is indispensable. When he says that Washington supervised during these years a "family" of several hundred people, he would point out that, at Mount Vernon, Washington was "an efficient commander in chief" (p. 49); for him, Washington's decision to diversify crops was a "declaration of independence from England" (p. 49); Washington's passion for the accumulation of land was perhaps "motivated (at least in part) by a possessive worship of the continent across which his dreams spread" (p. 54).

I have suggested that Erikson's own professional skill was an important element in what he achieved in *Young Man Luther*. A biographer's "professed calling" may sometimes provide him with the knowledge and understanding necessary to estimate justly his subject's character and accomplishment, but it hardly guarantees success. For instance, in his *Marilyn* (1973), Norman Mailer is contemptuous of biographies of Marilyn Monroe produced by two professional writers: Ben Hecht, he says, "was never a writer to tell the truth when a concoction could put life in his prose," and Maurice Zolotow embellished his facts with "factoids," "creations which are not so much lies as a product to manipulate emotion in the Silent Majority."[11] His own book is almost as full of contraries as the calculation and vulnerability that he finds in Monroe's temperament. If at one place he defines *professionalism* as completing a piece of work "in the allotted time" (and thereby half-apologizes for his rushed performance here—"a formal biography can probably not be written in less than two years") (p. 257), he convincingly demonstrates Monroe's clinging to professionalism despite and because of her disregard of allotted time; and in another place he defines *professionalism* as "the disciplined exercise of one's skill" (p. 20). When he faults Hecht and Zolotow, he does so in a chapter called "A Novel Biography" where he identifies his own life of Monroe as "a *species* of novel ready to play by the rules of biography" (p. 20). But in his species of novel "no items could be made up and evidence would be provided when facts were moot. Speculation *had* to be underlined." Still, he would use the sanction of a novelist "to look into the unspoken impulses of some of his real characters"; he would offer "a literary hypothesis of a *possible* Marilyn Monroe who might actually have lived and fit most of the facts available." His *Life* is full of flaws: despite the short time allotted him, his reliance on secondary sources is unforgivable; if his vulgarity and cheap shots are in harmony with the kind of world he portrays, his indulgence in the claptrap of karma, his constant slurs at Richard Nixon, his generally sour attitude toward Arthur Miller, his Olympian self-intrusiveness mar his book. For all that, his impulse is right: "Set a thief to catch a thief, and put an artist on an artist" (p. 20). For all his self-indulgence, perhaps because of it, he understands and shrewdly illustrates Monroe's mastery of publicity, and his insistence on and demonstration of Monroe's dedication to her craft are insightful, convincing, and moving. He overwrites constantly, but his detailed and understated one-paragraph description of Monroe's apartment in New York (pp. 216–18) injects high voltage into the *de casibus* tradition. Mailer finds a kindred soul in Monroe; he recognizes her problems and her genius, and the design of his work is answerable to Monroe's own originality.

Part of our trouble in assessing the merit of Mailer's book stems from his awareness and appreciation of Monroe's uniqueness and from his unique representation of it. It is hard to know, in light of his own scant spadework, whether he *discovered* what was original in Monroe or whether, out of his own self-centeredness and identification with her, he *imposed* a design on the life. Even if it was the latter, the area of coincidence between her life and his seems to have been large enough so that the design has the freshness and penetration of discovery as Mailer copes with the complexities in Monroe—her drive, her narcissism, her nonconformity, her individuality. Monroe is a phoenix, but so is Mailer, and even the phoenix of poets once predicated the existence of simultaneous phoenixes though he also plaintively assailed his own era as one in which "every man alone thinkes he hath got / To be a Phoenix, and that there can bee / None of that kinde, of which he is, but hee." When, a generation or more after Donne wrote those words, Marvell said that the mind was an ocean "where each kind / Does straight its own resemblance find," he saw that people were disposed to think in terms of types; he assumed that we know the world because of the pre-existence of related forms in our minds. But he thought, too, that the mind could imaginatively create forms that transcended reality, and in "The Garden" he transcended the poetic genre that he used as his base. His own transcendent creation stemmed, however, not only from his fancy but also from his own acute observation of the world and his own reflection on experience. He did not rely on the customary predispositions of man or society; he was insightful enough to see freshly into things.

We have recently witnessed a new direction in biography, one which undermines, I think, the "protestant" quality quintessential to good biography. Shoichi Saeki has said, "I am becoming sceptical about the concept of pure individualism, and about individuality at any cost, or individuality for its own sake. I am not so sure that individuality can be taken as an ultimate value."[12] He thinks that we are, "at least partly, group animals, emotional animals, and are living under the influence of the group ethos—or, if we borrow the Jungian term, the collective unconscious, more than we are aware of" (p. 81); he suggests that modern biographers do not deal sufficiently with a subject's relation to tradition, to man in his relation with society, and that they ought to pay more attention to "the implicit communal ethos, to supra-individualistic values" (p. 82).

In a recent article called "Kipling and Forster," Eloise Knapp Hay uses the subtitle "A Case for Dual Biography."[13] She leans heavily on two new biographies of the men, who never met, to write a kind of Plutarchian comparison, though her purpose is different from Plutarch's. She emphasizes the complementary aspects of her subjects' sexual, political, scientific, and religious views, and projects a work that will allow readers to "see our present world more clearly" (p. 133). Her focus is different from Strachey's playing Newman against Manning and from Flexner's playing Washington against Jefferson and Hamilton; their intent was, in part, to illuminate a past world more clearly; it was mainly to illuminate their subjects by showing the nature of their relations with people they knew whose characters or ideologies were different from theirs. The focus of Strachey and of Flexner may not seem to vary considerably from that of Margot Peters when she defines "group biography" as "the interweaving of a number of lives by one writer to show how they interact with each other"; such lives, she suggests, "may be linked in common by any number of forces: a family, a place, an organization, a movement, a cultural affinity, a point in time," but she says that "implicit in group biography will be the notion that the individual is less than the whole, that the sum is greater than any of its parts."[14] She is herself well aware that such a concept would not have entered Plutarch's mind, though he contrasted Greek and Roman characters, and that Strachey made no attempt to connect his four major eminent Victorians, whatever their lives, and his representation of them, had in common. She finds a parallel, however, in Bernard Shaw's statement to Mrs. Patrick Campbell about changing attitudes toward drama and dramatic production—"The single-star system is dead"—and the radical change in historical, sociological, and psychological assumptions that undermined Carlyle's idea that "the History of the World is but the Biography of great men." For Peters, Carlyle's idea is a manifestation of "Victorian male gigantism," and she says that in the world affected by Darwin, Marx, Freud, and Strachey "we no longer have heroes," that we are inclined to believe that "great men were created by the accidental circumstances of history," that "the course of human events depends less on individualism than upon the endless ramifications of human interaction," that "communalism has replaced individualism," that "political, sociological, and psychological theory has fostered this shift in perspective from individual to group" (pp. 42–46).[15]

Peters differentiates her own group biography, Bernard Shaw and the Actresses (1980) from other group biographies she mentions in that she has a major character in Shaw himself. In writing her biography, she says, she "found" that a pattern and a tempo emerged: Shaw progressed chronologically and steadily, but the women appeared "alternately and often retrospectively and only in their connection with Shaw." And, she says, this pattern started to embody a theme she was not wholly aware of when she began: "the creative life of an actress is a short and ephemeral thing, since she is simply the vehicle for the word; but . . . the life of the artist as the creator of the word is long"; she "found" that her biography was about the old theme that life is short and art is long. When she refers to Arnold Kettle's observation that "good fiction has both life and pattern," she says that the biography of a single subject has "one kind of built-in pattern—the progress of the protagonist from cradle to grave: beginning, middle, end," but she maintains that "if biography has not been taken seriously as literature, it is because it lacks the patterning of theme, symbol, and imagery characteristic of fiction." Here, her generalization does not distinguish between the log of a person's life and a good biography. More perceptive is her statement that since group biography does not necessarily have even the basic life-progress form, "the writer is challenged to impose some kind of pattern upon his or her material" (pp. 49–51).

Peters would stress the "great experimental potential" of group biography in content and pattern; its practice, she thinks, promises to expand the scope of biography considerably (p. 51). But if we are living in a world that takes for granted the primacy of the group rather than of the individual; if we assume that groups are more important now than they were under the city-state, the Roman church of old, the guild system; if corporate endeavor is the ideal, in science and in government, of a computerized age; if writers insist on advocating cultural norms more strenuously; then we must remember that group biography imposes in its fundamental assumption of the importance of a group ethos and that it tends to *impose* cultural patterns instead of *discovering* new ones. We ought to remember, too, that even in a communally oriented world, there are individuals who lead, who revolt, who insist on going their own way. In such a world, there is all the more reason to reassert the importance of biography's focus on the individual, of biography as a protestant art; and to reassert the wisdom of Edel's statement that "every life takes its own form and a biographer must find the ideal and unique literary form that will express it"—to reassert, in other words, the importance of a biographer's insight in discovering what is original in a life and the importance of his skill in representing that originality.

Notes

PREFACE

    1. *Theory of Literature* (New York: Harcourt, [1949]), p. 291.

    2. *Anatomy of Criticism* (Princeton: Princeton University Press, 1957), p. 245.

    3. *Critiques and Essays in Criticism 1920–1948* (New York: Ronald, 1949).

    4. Mark Schorer, Josephine Miles, Gordon McKenzie, eds., *Criticism: The Foundations of Modern Literary Judgment*, rev. ed. (1958; New York: Harcourt, 1948).

    5. *The Present Age in British Literature* (Bloomington: Indiana University Press, 1958), p. 145.

    6. *The Nation*, 73 (December 5, 1901), 431. Unsigned; perhaps by the editor, E. J. Mather, Jr.

    7. Carl Van Doren, "Biography as a Literary Form," *Columbia University Quarterly*, 17 (March 1915), 180–85.

    8. *English Biography* (London: Dent, 1916), p. 197.

    9. Charles K. Trueblood, "Criticism of Biography," *The Dial*, 83 (December 1927), 515.

    10. *Biography: The Literature of Personality* (New York: Century, 1927).

    11. *Literary Biography* (Toronto: University of Toronto Press, 1957), p. xi.

    12. *Biography as an Art* (New York: Oxford University Press, 1962), p. ix.

13. *biography*, 1 (Summer 1978), 83–86.

14. Donald J. Winslow, "Current Bibliography on Life-Writing," *biography*, 1 (Fall 1978), 76–81.

15. Leon Edel, "Biography and the Science of Man," in *New Directions in Biography*, ed. Anthony M. Friedson (Honolulu: University Press of Hawaii, 1981), 1–11.

16. E. L. Doctorow, "False Documents," *American Review*, 26, ed. Theodore Solotaroff (New York: Bantam, 1977), 229, 231.

17. Our worry, it turns out, ought to be about the nature of the documentation for the specific date cited by others. Strachey had read carefully Edmund Sheridan Purcell's examination of the evidence in his *Life of Cardinal Manning* (London: Macmillan, 1895), I, Note A, pp. 693–94.

I. TO 1920

1. "A New 'Biographia Britannica,' " p. 850.

2. "Johnsoniana" in *Studies of a Biographer*, I (London: Duckworth, 1898), 121.

3. Frederick W. Maitland, *The Life and Letters of Leslie Stephen* (London: Duckworth, 1906), p. 367. For Stephen, the value of a history did not inhere in accuracy alone. He admitted that Froude "suffered from constitutional inaccuracy, made strange blunders even in copying a plain document, and often used his authorities in an arbitrary and desultory fashion," but since Froude was a "most skilful historical artist" who wrote a vivid and interesting narrative, Stephen was willing to take his story "not as definitive truth, but as an aspect of the truth seen from a particular point of view." "James Anthony Froude" in *Studies of a Biographer*, III (London: Duckworth, 1902), 222–23.

4. "A Statistical Account" in *DNB*, I (reprint of 1949–50), lxxiv. Maitland, pp. 371–72, estimates that Stephen wrote the lives of more than half the greatest men of letters and much more than half the great speculative thinkers. Among his early contributions were accounts of Addison, Austen, Berkeley, Boswell, the Brontës, Fanny Burney, Burns, Butler, Byron, Carlyle, Coleridge, and Congreve.

5. *A Handbook to the Literature of General Biography* (Ventnor: G. H. Brittain, 1885), p. 24.

6. The same sentiment is voiced by the author of "A New Theory of Biography," *The Dial*, 24 (May 1, 1898), 281–83 (unsigned, but probably by the editor, Francis F. Browne): "a

finer method of analysis than critics have been wont to apply will disclose personal elements in the most impersonal of utterances." The author professes to offer an answer to the argument about Shakespeare, older than that about Wordsworth and Browning, which has raged in the *Saturday Review* and in the *Athenaeum*, but he never defines his "finer method."

7. *Literary World*, 16 (May 16, 1885), p. 171.

8. *The Phillips Exeter Lectures . . . 1885–1886* (Boston: Houghton, 1887), pp. 179–208.

9. *Macmillan's Magazine*, 66 (June 1892), 97–107.

10. I have used Maurice Saillet's edition of *Spicilège* ([Paris]: Mercure de France, 1960); my quotations are from Lorimer Hammond's translation of *Imaginary Lives* (New York: Boni and Liveright, 1924).

11. *Aspects of Biography* (Cambridge: University Press, 1929), pp. 57–60; "The Art of Biography" in *Confessional* (New York: Panurge Press, 1930), pp. 174–76. Harris does not cite his source.

12. Introduction to Sir Sidney Lee, *Elizabethan and Other Essays* (Oxford: Clarendon Press, 1929), pp. xvi–xvii.

13. "A Statistical Account," *DNB*, I (1949–50), lxiii, lxxi, lxxiv.

14. Introduction, *Elizabethan and Other Essays*, pp. xiii–xv, xxi.

15. Printed for presentation to the members of the Second International Library Conference, 1897.

16. Delivered at Cambridge on May 13, 1911, and published there in the same year by the University Press; reprinted in *Elizabethan and Other Essays*, pp. 31–57.

17. This was a presidential address to the English Association delivered on May 10, 1918 (F. S. Boas, ed., *Elizabethan and Other Essays*, p. 58, n. 1). It was published separately in the same year as Pamphlet No. 41 of the English Association, and reprinted, without its occasional first section, in *Elizabethan and Other Essays*, pp. 58–82.

18. Lee says that he became aware of Asquith's essay on "Biography" when it was reprinted in *Occasional Addresses 1893–1916* (London: Macmillan, 1918), pp. 27–56. Originally an address delivered at the Edinburgh Philosophical Institution on November 15, 1901, it was printed in the *National Review*, 38 (December 1901), 526–39, and reprinted in *The Living Age*, 232 (February 8, 1902), 321–31. It is a potpourri of comments on biography and autobiography, which Asquith does not differentiate, interspersed

with stories from the *Autobiography* of Benjamin Robert Haydon and from *The Personal Life of George Grote* by his widow, Harriet. For Asquith, the purposes of biography are boundless: it vivifies history, philosophy, and poetry; "it brings comfort, it enlarges sympathy, it expels selfishness, it quickens aspiration." Still, he thinks it not necessary to the production of "an immortal biography" that either the subject or the writer be a man of genius. The subject need only have "the power of permanently interesting his fellow–men" and the writer need only be able to recall the subject to life by means of "quick observation, a retentive memory, a love of detail, a dash of hero-worship," an appreciation of environment, and, if possible, personal intimacy. Asquith expresses himself strongly on one controversial subject: "to have 'seen Shelley plain' would have been, indeed, a godsend to some of the accomplished gentlemen who have contributed to 'the chatter about Harriet' "; he hedges a little on another: he speaks of the impersonal quality of "most" of Shakespeare's writings, a quality, he says, "which I myself am heretic enough to believe extends to by far the greater part of the Sonnets." His most original suggestion is that the printing of fewer letters by the subject and of more written to him might reveal how the subject's personality affected others. Asquith's words that "it is not the function of a biography to be a magnified epitaph or an extended tract" were quoted and amplified by Edmund Gosse in "The Ethics of Biography," *Cosmopolitan*, 35 (July 1903), 319–20, but his strictures about "filial piety," the biography with a thesis, and edifying biography were not new to Sidney Lee. His emphasis on autobiography, however, may have provoked Lee to express himself on this subject.

19. "At a Journey's End," *Nineteenth Century and After*, 72 (December 1912), 1161, 1164.

20. His remarks here elaborate what he had said in *Principles of Biography* (p. 51) about the necessity for the national biographer "to arrange his bare facts and dates so as to indicate graphically the precise character of the personality and of the achievement with which he is dealing." He had not treated this subject in his lecture on "National Biography," and his consideration of it probably stems from Leslie Stephen's slightly later essay of the same name. Stephen discusses the quandary of the dictionary writer who must give significant facts but who must save space by leaving the discovery of their significance to the reader. The good writer, he says, will arrange his facts "in the order or connection which makes them explain their meaning" (*National Review*, 27 [March 1896], 61; reprinted in *Studies of a Biographer*, I 25).

21. To those enumerated here should be added one which was the subject of two separate essays—the degree to which an author can be discovered through an examination of his work. Lee grants that Cicero and Burke reveal their precise likes and dislikes, convictions and prejudices in their orations, but he insists on the "impersonality" of Shakespeare in his plays (*The Impersonal Aspect of Shakespeare's Art* [English Association Pamphlet No. 13, 1909], reprinted in *Elizabethan and Other Essays*, pp. 85–115) and (albeit indirectly) even in his sonnets ("Ovid and Shakespeare's Sonnets," *Quarterly Review*, 210 [April 1909], 455–76, reprinted in *Elizabethan and Other Essays*, pp. 116–39). The subject is obviously important to Lee; perhaps he felt that it was too specialized to include in his general essays about biography and that he could not present his arguments in shorter space. It is likely, however, that he thought of this subject as primarily a literary matter and therefore rather too belletristic to include in biographical discourse.

22. "The Agony of the Victorian Age" in *Some Diversions of a Man of Letters* (London: Heinemann, 1919), p. 319. Gosse's agreement with Strachey on this point is not typical of his usual attitude toward Strachey or of Strachey's toward him. A few weeks after the publication of *Eminent Victorians*, Gosse protested Strachey's portrait of Sir Evelyn Baring, in a letter to the editor of the *Times Literary Supplement* (June 27, 1918, p. 301), and Strachey defended his view of Baring's character in the next issue. The pervasive, if often polite, antagonism in their relations is made clear by Michael Holroyd in *Lytton Strachey: A Critical Biography* (New York: Holt, 1968), I, 276–77; II, 321–23, 505–8.

23. *Anglo–Saxon Review*, 8 (March 1901), 195–208.

24. Gosse protects his place in the world by saying that he knows of only one instance in modern biography where the influence of the Widow has not been disastrous; he names no names.

25. His preoccupation with this subject is clear in his making it the central concern of a separate article, "The Ethics of Biography," *Cosmopolitan*, 35 (July 1903), 317–23.

26. Gosse uses "pure" to delimit a particular biographic domain which has not been invaded by other disciplines. His usage differs, of course, from that of Saintsbury, to whom "pure" connoted the biographer's imaginative absorption of source materials and "applied" a mixture of directly quoted materials and connective narration.

27. William Roscoe Thayer, "Biography," *North American Review*, 180 (February 1905), 261–78.

28. *The Art of Biography* (New York: Scribners, 1920). The last lecture, "Biography in the Nineteenth Century" had been

separately published in two parts in the *North American Review*, 211 (May, June 1920), 632–40, 826–33. The text in the magazine and in the book is essentially the same; the magazine lacks the sentence about Morley's *Walpole* on p. 124 of the book and Furness's reaction to Carlyle and the paragraph which follows on pp. 136–37.

29. *National Review*, 63 (April 1914), 266–84; reprinted in Cook's *Literary Recreations* (London: Macmillan, 1918).

30. Waldo H. Dunn, *English Biography* (London: Dent, 1916).

31. Both Charles Richard Sanders, in *Lytton Strachey: His Mind and Art* (New Haven: Yale University Press, 1957), pp. 208–9, and Michael Holroyd, in *Lytton Strachey*, II, 262, 404, recognize the importance of the review.

32. Holroyd, *Lytton Strachey*, II, 448–49.

II. THE TWENTIES

1. "Lee and Psychography," pp. 269–83 of *Lee the American* (Boston: Houghton, 1912). The chapters of the book had been published independently in various magazines, and this appendix first appeared in the *South Atlantic Quarterly*, 11 (January 1912), 63–74. There, it has an introductory paragraph which starts, "In my series of articles on Lee, I have not attempted to write a biography."

2. Bradford says that S. R. Gardiner, "for all his fairness, obviously praises the Puritans because they were Puritans, the Cavaliers although they were Cavaliers." His ideal is impartiality, but he suggests that "it is not impossible that the open, avowed, and evident partisanship of Clarendon . . . makes safer reading than the disguised, insinuating partisanship of Gardiner" (p. 270). He does not develop the idea or exploit its implications.

3. Letter of April 21, 1921, to Prof. Ambrose W. Vernon in *The Letters of Gamaliel Bradford, 1918–1931*, ed. Van Wyck Brooks (Boston: Houghton, 1934), p. 64.

4. *A Naturalist of Souls* (New York: Dodd, 1917), pp. 3–24. "Psychography" is dated 1915; the other essays are printed in chronological order (1892 to 1913), and Bradford suggests that the earliest two demonstrate the beginnings of his psychographical interest and method and that the last two are "elaborate specimens" of "finished" psychographs (pp. 23–24).

5. The *OED* cites Saintsbury's use in a review of a volume of poetry in *The Academy*, 23 (January 20, 1883), 36, where it means "the imaginative power which reproduces and dramatises

a certain mood of mind." It cites, too, William Archer, in 1895: "a sort of spiritual biography . . . what has recently been called a psychography."

6. *Saturday Review of Literature*, 1 (May 23, 1925), 769–70.

7. Quoted in the Preface of *The Journal of Gamaliel Bradford, 1883–1932* (Boston: Houghton, 1933), p. x, by the editor, Van Wyck Brooks.

8. In "Psychography," he admits that psychography is interpretative, subjective, undefinitive, and that "the generalisation of actions is always imperfect." *A Naturalist of Souls*, p. 10.

9. See *Journal*, p. 467; Bradford feels, however, that "development in the sense of any fundamental or vital change rarely occurs."

10. "Spiritual Autopsies," *The Literary Review of the New York Evening Post*, April 8, 1922, p. 562.

11. *The Letters of Gamaliel Bradford*, p. 105.

12. *Journal*, pp. 329–30.

13. *The Doctor Looks at Biography* (New York: Doran, 1925).

14. Collins has no use for Freudian biographers. Harvey O'Higgins, he says, "is attempting to do for biographies what Dr. George M. Gould did a few years ago in his biographical clinics. Only he substituted the Oedipus–complex for Eye Strain" (p. 31).

15. "There has never been a great biographer who was not a great artist" (p. 44).

16. "Biography is the story of a life, told by the man who lived it or by the student of it" (p. 15).

17. *Portrait of the Artist as a Young Man*, Dorothy Richardson's *Pointed Roofs*, *À la Recherche du Temps Perdu*.

18. "The Significance of Biography" in *Biography: The Literature of Personality* (New York: Century, 1927), pp. xv–xxi.

19. He is interested in what he calls "neglected" aspects (pp. 109–34). The nature, not the amount, of the biographic material available, he says, ought to determine the kind of life which is written, and a biographer ought to decide on the extent of a life before he writes. Chronology is not sacred to biography; a variety of orders is possible, and he praises Bradford's "keynote" method. He discusses the dangers inherent in the use of letters.

20. "Incidents that indicate temperament, opinions, personal habits, oddities, and prejudices, to whatever extent they affect character, must be noted; but they are not ends in themselves and should be dwelt upon only in so far as they are distinctively characteristic. Overemphasis, however, of even the unique

and personal will produce a distorted picture, perhaps quite unlike the real individual" (p. 229).

21. The whole of Chapter IV develops this idea. Johnston dismisses both the reader's desire for raw revelation and the wishes of the family of the subject for suppression. He attacks a double standard for biography and autobiography: if Carlyle's candor in the *Reminiscences* is admirable, Froude's equal candor in his *Life of Carlyle* is equally admirable.

22. *The Dial*, 83 (August 1927), 128–36.

23. The word makes some sense here, but I think it may be a misprint. Trueblood probably wrote "conscious."

24. Trueblood pursues the idea that biography is a serious sort of prose fiction in "Criticism of Biography," *The Dial*, 83 (December 1927), 515–18. "The biographer as much as a dramatist or novelist, has the right so far as the facts permit, to consider himself the historian of thought and feeling in its conflicts, its life and death; and of individual character, not alone in its out-lines, but in its causes, its growth, its battles, its decay. The facts of biography are given, like the mytho–historic frame of an Attic tragedy and it is for the biographer to infer and image forth the spirit." Trueblood calls fictionalized biography a "stultified hy-brid," but he says that biography can learn from fiction "lessons in story-structure, time-scheme, the management of subordinate incident and character"; "modes of personal atmosphere and mental background, in the setting particularly, and personal *locale* of the subject"; and the management of narrative that is eco-nomical, precise, colorful, and lively.

25. See my pp. xi–xii.

26. "Criticism of Biography," p. 518.

27. *Biography*, Oxford Reading Courses (New York: Oxford University Press, 1927).

28. For instance, Valentine says that biography is more popular than ever before "partly perhaps because in this material age most of us demand concrete and certified truths rather than imaginative expressions, and also because in the narrowness of our lives many of us seek to escape into the lives of more free and interesting souls" (p. 8). Trueblood would emphasize a more radi-cal motive, a deep curiosity about particulars which reveal modes of life ("Criticism of Biography," p. 516).

29. *The Development of English Biography* (London: Hogarth, 1927), pp. 145–46.

30. Five years after its publication, Dunn's book seems not to have come to the attention of the distinguished scholar and biographer, Wilbur Cross. "Someone, perhaps will some day

write a little treatise and call it 'The Development of Biography,'" he wrote, in "From Plutarch to Strachey," *Yale Review*, 11 (October 1921), 140.

    31. *TLS*, July 7, 1927, p. 468.

    32. "The New Biography," *New York Herald Tribune Books*, October 30, 1927, pp. 1, 6.

    33. He calls it "a masterpiece" and a book which "won a signal victory for intellectual liberty." *The Development of English Biography*, p.145.

    34. The fact is that Nicolson conceives of Boswell and of the ideal English biographer as John Bull. "The Anglo-Saxon mind is at its best when proceeding inductively, building up the facts of life slowly, humourously, patiently; interpreting these jumbled facts not by any consecutive process of reason, but by the sweeping lighthouse flashes of intuition and imagination. This, our national habit of guess-work, while it creates 'actuality,' has its disadvantages; but at least it is our own; and when we depart from it and endeavour to copy our Latin neighbors, endeavour to be clear and earnest and logical—at such moments our happy April humour is taken from us, and the English genius, through a mist of sobriety, shines as a pompous winter sun" (pp. 109–10).

    In his next paragraph, Nicolson insists that "it cannot be sufficiently emphasised that the art of biography is intellectual and not emotional. So long as the intellect is undisturbed by emotion you have good biography." He seems to feel, then, that what he calls "sweeping lighthouse flashes of intuition and imagination" are the product of intellect rather than of emotion. His next sentence reads, "The moment, however, that any emotion (such as reverence, affection, ethical desires, religious belief) intrudes upon the composition of a biography, that biography is doomed." It is clear that Nicolson uses "intellectual" and "emotional" in a very special way. Not only does he assume that intuition and imagination are intellectual, but he also assumes that reverence, affection, ethical desires, and religious belief are emotional.

    35. *The Nation and Athenaeum*, March 17, 1928, p. 908.

    36. Reprinted in *Granite and Rainbow* (London: Hogarth, 1958), pp. 149–55.

    37. Aileen Pippett, *The Moth and the Star* (Boston: Little, Brown, 1955), pp. 242–43.

    38. *A Writer's Diary: Being Extracts from the Diary of Virginia Woolf*, ed. Leonard Woolf (London: Hogarth, 1953), p. 105; Pippett, p. 243.

    39. *A Writer's Diary*, p. 108; Pippett, p. 248.

40. See, for example, *A Writer's Diary*, pp. 109–13, and Pippett, pp. 245, 248–50, 252–53.

41. *Virginia Woolf and Lytton Strachey: Letters*, ed. Leonard Woolf and James Strachey (London: Hogarth, 1956), p. 115.

42. Pippett, p. 254.

43. *New York Herald Tribune Books*, October 16, 1927, pp. 1, 5–6. Published also, with the omission of some material about Sir Walter Scott, as "The Art of Fiction" in *The Nation and Athenaeum*, November 12, 1927, pp. 247–48; reprinted in *The Moment and Other Essays* (London: Hogarth, 1947), pp. 89–93.

44. E. M. Forster, *Aspects of the Novel* (London: Arnold, 1927), pp. 32–33.

45. Mrs. Woolf's point of view was, of course, not unlike that of other experimental novelists. In his essay, "Experiment in the Novel," printed in *Tradition and Experiment in Present-day Literature* (London: Oxford University Press, 1929), J. D. Beresford says that Dorothy Richardson maintained that the more marked incidents of human life, such as love and marriage, what she referred to as the "high spots," were only so because of the emphasis laid upon them by novelists, and that "in the adventure of the personality, which should be the true subject for the novelist, the 'high spots' are of an entirely different order." Beresford thinks that she is therefore led to record a movement in space and in time different from the conventional, for she would show that the consciousness is not always attentive to its present circumstances (pp. 44–45).

46. She uses the words about Forster on November 20, 1927, when she interrupts the routine business of the day to make an entry in her diary (*A Writer's Diary*, p. 117).

47. It is plain that Virginia Woolf was educated in her father's house. These ideas she had clung to for almost two decades. In reviewing Wilbur Cross's *The Life and Times of Laurence Sterne* for the *TLS* on August 12, 1909, p. 289, she had written that "no one takes a character in fiction quite seriously" because "the aesthetic effect of truth is only to be equalled by the imagination of genius": "There are a thousand incidents in a second-rate novel which might have happened in a dozen different ways, and the least consciousness of indecision blurs the effect; but the bare statement of facts has an indisputable power, if we have reason to think them true. The knowledge that they are true, it may be, leads us to connect them with other ideas; but if we know that they never happened at all, and doubt that they could have happened in this way, they suggest nothing distinct, because they

are not distinct themselves." Reprinted in *Granite and Rainbow*, p. 168.

48. Though Virginia Woolf called *Orlando* (London: Hogarth, 1928) "A Biography," she avoided the risks and dangers by creating a work which was so flagrantly inventive and fantastic that its biographical intent was not easy to discover. She wildly manipulated a substratum of fact in order to provide access to the inner life of thought and emotion of the subject, who is, on occasion, Victoria Sackville-West, and, on occasion, Virginia Woolf herself. Nicolson's example in *Some People* led her to a method which moved her farther from him than he had moved from Strachey; it furnished the clue which allowed Mrs. Woolf to write about what she, not Forster, called "life," about "Vita" (as Victoria Sackville-West was known), in a way which would be "truthful but fantastic" (*A Writer's Diary*, p. 114). *Orlando* is a fourfold fiction, intellectualized in its concentration on the problems of personality and time, sometimes novelistic in its treatment of character in society, sometimes mythic in its handling of sex (as well as place and time), and confessional in its use of stream of consciousness and in its female vision. The conventional, plodding biographer is ridiculed as Mrs. Woolf exploits some of the perhaps 2,052 selves which lodge in a single human spirit; as she considers some of the perhaps "seventy–six different times all ticking in the mind at once" (p. 277), or the hour which "may be stretched to fifty or a hundred times its clock length" or "may be accurately represented on the timepiece of the mind by one second" (p. 91); as she imaginatively demonstrates the force of genealogy, of culture, of tradition; as she destroys the stereotypes about women in a multiplicity of artful ways. Truth as it is found in the British Museum is not to be found in *Orlando*, though, with lovely irony, Mrs. Woolf gives prefatory thanks to the British Museum and to the Record Office "for their wonted courtesy"; but *Orlando* is an extraordinary *tour de force* whose truths rock the foundations of biography and make the ordinary biographer despair.

49. *Conseils à un jeune Français partant pour l'Angleterre* (Paris: Les Amis d'Edouard, 1927), pp. 11–12, quoted in Georges Lemaitre, *André Maurois* (Stanford University Press, 1939), p. 30.

50. Maurois lectured in English but recast the lectures in French, and *Aspects de la Biographie* appeared in 1928 (Paris: Au Sans Pareil). There are small changes in each of the two later French editions, that published by Bernard Grasset in Paris (1930) and that in vol. 6 of *Oeuvres Complètes* (Paris: Fayard, 1950). S.

C. Roberts translated the recast lectures into English, and these were published by the University Press, Cambridge, and D. Appleton & Co., New York. My page numbers refer to the Cambridge volume.

51. He blames the Reformation theory of predestination and seventeenth–century classical psychology for minimizing change and complexity of character. The awareness of Montaigne and Shakespeare did not re-emerge, he says, until Dostoevski and Proust (pp. 27–29).

52. "Think of your own life," he says, echoing Virginia Woolf's appeal at the end of her essay. " 'But that is not myself,' you would say, 'those things were of no interest except to my doctor' " (p. 91).

53. Maurois's consideration of "the scientific study of man" (p. 90) has its main focus in physico–chemical and biological points of view. He never overtly challenges Nicolson's view that psychology is a science with high standards which impose their own discipline and sanctions, either because he does not believe it or because he feels the necessary evidence must remain inaccessible for the subject of a biography.

54. Almost certainly, Maurois has taken over Trueblood's conclusion that nothing is more characteristic of personality than the persistence and continuity of "its feeling-life, its temperament" and that the biographer must by a kind of poetic divination give a lifelike sense of his subject's temperament as the "timbre" of his feelings, thoughts, and acts.

55. He raises more questions than he answers when he admits that his first attempt to deliver himself from his Shelley–like concerns was not successful; he says only that *Ni Ange, ni Bête* was not a good novel (p. 108).

56. "In the first place," Maurois says, "the hero is always greater than the biographer; secondly, a biographer never discovers the whole of his own character in a historical character. It is merely one aspect of his character that he discovers, and often a very fleeting, a very limited aspect" (p. 111). Both his statements need modification, of course. Johnson was immeasurably greater than most of his subjects; a biographer of limited capacities and interests, like Walton, may discover the totality of his character in one aspect of his historical subject.

57. The concept of self-expression does not, for Maurois, depend on perfect congruence of an extensive sort. "It is not necessary," he says, "to have experienced an emotion for a long time in order to be aware of it" (pp. 111–12). Nor does it depend on congruence of attitude. Maurois explains that he wrote *Ariel*

because he wanted to kill the romantic in himself: "in order to do it, I scoffed at it in Shelley, but I loved it while I scoffed" (p. 108). He says, too, that desire for self-expression can stem from antipathy to a character ("as in Mr Strachey") as well as from sympathy (p. 116).

58. Maurois quotes with approval Forster's distinction between a character in fiction and a character in biography:

> If a character in a novel is exactly like Queen Victoria— not rather like but exactly like—then it actually is Queen Victoria, and the novel, or all of it that the character touches, becomes a memoir. A memoir is history, it is based on evidence. A novel is based on evidence + or − x, the unknown quantity being the temperament of the novelist, and the unknown quantity always modifies the effect of the evidence, and sometimes transforms it entirely.
>
> The historian deals with actions, and with the characters of men only so far as he can deduce them from actions. He is quite as much concerned with character as the novelist, but he can only know of its existence when it shows on the surface.

It is the function of the novelist, Forster said, "to reveal the hidden life at its source: to tell us more about Queen Victoria than could be known, and thus to produce a character who is not the Queen Victoria of history" (*Aspects of the Novel*, pp. 65–66). Maurois's comment reflects his belief that the truth of fiction is superior to the truth of history; he says, "May I add 'who is not the Queen Victoria of history, but is more like Queen Victoria than the Queen Victoria of history' " (pp. 169–70).

59. Cf. Emil Ludwig's statement about the bad historical novelist: "To take the liberty of fabrication under the aegis of history does not merely entail a transgression against one's subject; also, it is a deliberate choice of inferior materials, since God is expert, is more imaginative than the poet, and has always imbued the course of His creatures' lives with a deeper logic than even the most skilled constructor can invent" (*Genius and Character*, trans. Kenneth Burke [New York: Harcourt, 1927], p. 5).

III. THE THIRTIES

1. It was one of five pairs of addresses, delivered at the City Literary Institute in London during Lent term in 1929 on

the novel, poetry, drama, biography, and criticism, and published in *Tradition and Experiment in Present-day Literature* (London: Oxford University Press, 1929), pp. 161–78.

2. Despite the grounds on which he praised Pepys, Burdett says that Maurois's neglect of Shelley's poetry proves that his purpose "was romantic to the verge of fiction" (p. 173).

3. In an address on "Experiment in Criticism," delivered under the same auspices as Burdett's, T. S. Eliot was equally sensitive to contemporary interest in psychology and even more adamant about its ancillary role. Writing after the publication of I. A. Richards's *Principles of Literary Criticism* (1924) and *Practical Criticism* (1929), he says that the contemporary literary critic is expected to be familiar with various branches of science, "especially of course psychology, particularly analytical psychology." But, he continues, "As the number of sciences multiply, of sciences that is which have a bearing upon criticism, so we ask ourselves first whether there is still any justification for literary criticism at all, or whether we should not merely allow the subject to be absorbed gently into exacter sciences which will each annex some side of criticism. Just as in the history of philosophy, we find many subjects surrendered from time to time by philosophy, now to mathematics and physics, now to biology and psychology; until there seems to be almost nothing left to philosophize about. I think that the answer is clear: that so long as literature is literature, so long will there be a place for criticism of it, for criticism, that is, on the same basis as that on which the literature itself is made" (*Tradition and Experiment in Present-day Literature*, pp. 206, 213). That basis Eliot defines as the ability "to give a peculiar kind of pleasure which has something constant in it thoughout the ages, however difficult and various our explanations of that pleasure may be."

4. Philadelphia: Lippincott.

5. *Hesketh Pearson by Himself* (New York: Harper, [1965]), p. 219.

6. Pearson was not, of course, alone in his advocacy of intuition and invention to supplement and improve on the facts for the purpose of arriving at "essential truth," at a truth of impression more quintessentially representative and revealing than the literal truth that could be extracted from available fact. S. Stephenson Smith, in a chapter on "intimate biography" in his book *The Craft of the Critic* (New York: Crowell, 1931), calls Elinor Wylie's *Orphan Angel* a fanciful romance (Shelley is resurrected from the Bay of Leghorn and goes to America), but he also calls it "a truer portrait than *Ariel*." Though he says

that there is not a fact in it, he holds that "the lies are framed in the best fashion": they are true to Shelley's character and "the story is true to his temperament" (p. 97). Smith praises "the new biographers who have applied the technique of the art novel" for their concentration, proportion, and artful arrangement, but he finally admits that he does not like "the fictional habit of mind" they have acquired with the novelists' method (p. 102).

Orlo Williams, in "The Subject of Biography," *National Review*, 100 (May 1933), 693–702, says that the very question of the "subject" of biography "illustrates in extreme form the elusiveness of truth about human identity once you start refining upon the apprehensions of sense or looking for it behind first appearances." He holds that *biographie romancée* may contribute something to our knowledge of a subject that is beyond the power of an orthodox biographer, that the "artistic recreator" of a subject may attain truth "by proceeding beyond analysis to a dramatic synthesis." He goes so far as to say that Shakespeare is "the proper subject of biography, the model of all subjects." With a subject like Shakespeare, a biographer can write about "a man about whom very little is known but what he put into his plays, without being bothered to reconcile what he says with inconvenient events from which more than one deduction is possible" and "every biographer is free to create him anew, on Pirandellian, Proustian, Frank Harrisian or any other lines he pleases."

7. Jones spoke on December 31, 1929; his paper was published as "Methods in Contemporary Biography" in the *English Journal*, 21 (January and February 1932), 43–51, 113–22.

8. In the course of his article, Jones makes two favorable references to Maurois's *Aspects* (pp. 43, 115), but it is likely that his omission of Maurois from this list reflects his disapproval of Maurois's main doctrines.

9. *Current History*, 31 (November 1929), 257–64, reprinted in Adams's *The Tempo of Modern Life* (New York: Boni, 1931), pp. 171–86. Jones referred to his article, and its effect on him is clear.

10. Oddly enough, Adams adopts "the current and convenient Freudian jargon" to describe these biographers as men whose work derives from "superiority complexes"; in like fashion, the work of the debunkers derives from "inferiority complexes."

11. *The Tempo of Modern Art*, pp. 187–99.

12. In another essay, he attacks Bradford's essay on Henry Adams (pp. 214–15).

13. *London Mercury*, 30 (July 1934), 236–43.

14. The first volume of Bryant's reassessment of Pepys had appeared in 1933.

15. *Harper's Magazine*, 166 (January 1933), 181–92.

16. *English Journal*, 23 (January 1934), 1–9.

17. Although Mumford does not refer specifically to De Voto's "The Skeptical Biographer," he devotes a paragraph of praise to Van Wyck Brooks's psychological analysis of the inhibitions and terrors of Mark Twain's boyhood in *The Ordeal of Mark Twain*, which he obviously prefers to De Voto's attempt to explain Twain in terms of the frontier environment.

18. *An Anthology of Modern Biography* (London: Thomas Nelson and Sons, 1936).

19. *One Mighty Torrent: the Drama of Biography* (New York: Stackpole, 1937), pp. 578–81.

20. In the same year in which Cecil's anthology was published, there appeared in the United States another anthology with a similar purpose. Marston Balch's *Modern Short Biographies* (New York: Harcourt, 1936) is, however, a collection of short lives, for he wishes to present this form "for perhaps the first time as a literary *genre*" (p. vii). Like Cecil, Balch thinks that biography was "scarcely an acknowledged art" before Strachey (p. 14), and he finds "the art of biography an established fact" after Strachey (p. 16). His Introduction contains some of the ideas set forth so succinctly by Cecil; his Preface makes the interesting statement that "as biography has gained importance its authors have taken precedence over their subjects, so that we hear less about a new life of Byron or Wellington, more about a new book by M. Maurois or Mr. Guedella."

21. *Contemporary Biography* (Philadelphia: University of Pennsylvania Press, 1934).

22. Though he considers Strachey's *Elizabeth and Essex* not biographical "in the strictest sense," he considers it "a searching interpretation" just as good as or better than what biography can achieve (pp. 58–59), and he says that regardless of the fact that many of the passages of Hendrik Van Loon's *R. v. R.* are "obviously fictional," they "only serve to heighten the vividness and accuracy of those parts of the interpretation of personality which are biographical" (pp. 232–33).

23. *The Enjoyment of Literature* (New York: Norton, 1935), pp. 78–108.

24. *Atlantic Monthly*, 163 (April 1939), 506–10; reprinted in *Death of the Moth and Other Essays* (London: Hogarth, 1942), pp. 119–126.

25. *A Writer's Diary*, pp. 257, 288, 309. She completed her first draft on March 10, 1939 (p. 311).

26. *Convention and Revolt in Poetry* (Boston: Houghton, 1919), p. 95; see pp. 93–133 on "Originality and the Moulding of Conventions."

27. Her meaning is clear enough, though her choice of a character from one of Shakespeare's histories raises complications which she does not discuss. Her next sentence is "Micawber and Miss Bates we may be certain will survive Lockhart's Sir Walter Scott and Lytton Strachey's Queen Victoria."

28. See my pp. 176–77 (n. 47).

29. *La Machine à Lire les Pensées* (Paris: Nouvelle Revue Française, 1937); translated by James Whitall as *The Thought-Reading Machine* (New York: Harper, 1938).

30. "Gordon W. Allport" in Vol. V of *A History of Psychology in Autobiography*, ed. Edwin G. Boring and Gardner Lindzey (New York: Appleton, 1967), pp. 9, 11.

31. Gordon W. Allport, "Personality: A Problem for Science or a Problem for Art?" *Revista de Psihologie* (Cluj), 1 (October-December 1938), 491. (These words, and those by Murray in the next quotation, are cited in John A. Garraty's *The Nature of Biography* [New York: Knopf, 1957], pp. 9–10.)

Allport places biography with fiction and drama when he speaks of "the literature of character," and he considers the biographer an artist who differs from other artists in so far as he must contend with certain requirements for external validation (pp. 494–95). He thinks that the psychologist interested in personality can learn much from studying "literary biography," and he holds psychology largely responsible for an increasing rigor, objectivity, and heartlessness in biography which makes it resemble scientific autopsy (p. 499). Still, he says that if the psychologist will learn from literature lessons about the dominant disposition of a character which leads him to respond in particular ways to particular stimulations or situations, about the self-consistency of character, and about sustained interest in and focus on an individual, he may eventually be able to write "more revealing and accurate biographies than most of those that literature has produced" because his discipline as a scientist makes for "reliability, verifiability, lessened bias and relative freedom from self-projection into the products of his work" (pp. 493–99, 501).

32. *Explorations in Personality* (New York: Oxford University Press, 1938), pp. 608–9.

Allport and Murray contributed autobiographical accounts

to the fifth volume of A *History of Psychology in Autobiography* (1967). Allport says that long before he wrote his account, he used the problem of the psychological life history as the basis for a seminar; he says, too, that he does not know how such a life should be written and that he must "bumble along" as best he can (pp. 3–4). Murray uses a bouncily eccentric style and strives for impressionism through literary virtuosity.

33. Published in the *Journal of the Royal Society of Arts*, 87 (July 21, 1939), 925–35.

34. The rest of Guedella's lecture is devoted, first, to a slight consideration of the history of biography, interesting mainly for his attempt to show, in a modification of Nicolson's story, that the brevity, irony, and brilliance credited to Strachey are part of a tradition of "informal biography" which stems from Macaulay (who was indebted to Voltaire). Then, he suggests how the biographer may set about his task, and he comments briefly on the subjects of right perspective; discretion (his criterion for revealing personal life is "relevance"); sympathy for the subject, and its proper control; the dangers of the biographer's intrusion— a refutation of Maurois's thesis that biography is disguised autobiography; and the necessity of a chronological approach which assumes "the principle of growth and change in human beings."

IV. TO THE MID-FIFTIES

1. This is true also of three lectures delivered at meetings of the English Institute at Columbia University in September, 1942, on the subject, "Interpretation in Biography." André Maurois's "The Ethics of Biography," Newman I. White's "The Development, Use and Abuse of Interpretation in Biography," and Arthur M. Wilson's "The Humanistic Bases of Biographical Interpretation" were printed in *English Institute Annual, 1942* (New York: Columbia University Press, 1943), pp. 6–73, with a foreward by Donald A. Stauffer. Maurois starts by comparing the obligations of the portrait painter and of the historian to truth and to beauty, and he associates the biographer with the historian. He maintains that the painter's primary duty is to produce an artistic work, for without beauty his likeness is less good than a photograph. The historian and the biographer may achieve useful work by stressing truth rather than beauty, but only a book written by an artist in history or in biography can lead to the deeper understanding missing in a collection of facts (pp. 6–8). Maurois's assumptions here do not differ from those in *Aspects of Biography*, though here he does not probe the relations of biography and

fiction nor does he argue so overtly for the place of self-expression in biography. White finds fault with Maurois's stress of "pattern" in *Aspects,* warns of the dangers in the biographer's determining patterns prematurely, and is so wary of possible intrusion by the biographer that he says, "he should fine down his very style until it casts the faintest possible shadow of his own personality over the personality it is his whole duty to illuminate" (pp. 47–49, 55). Wilson distinguishes "historical biography," which seeks to understand a man's career because it assumes that a man's significance can be revealed by describing his accomplishments, from "humanistic biography," which focuses not on a man's career but on understanding what is timeless, universal, and significant in a man himself (pp. 60–65). He compares merely "qualified practitioners" of biography to run-of-the-mill physicians; they have "no feeling for the artistic overtones of their activity" and do not do the job of making their subjects come alive (p. 73). All three men assume the importance of interiority in biography. Maurois refers to the "interior view of the mind" which the biographer must analyze and describe (p. 21). For White, who insists that interpretation has been important to biography from Plutarch's time, "the single great modern innovation in biography" is "the interpretation of character from within" (pp. 29–32). Wilson holds that "we really come to know a man, whether in life or in research, by seeking out the origin and development and conflict of his loyalties and attachments," by studying "interior facts" as well as the "concretized facts" memorialized in encyclopedias (pp. 63, 69). On the relations of psychology to the inner life, White and Wilson say nothing; Maurois approves Longaker's statement that "every good biographer is a good psychoanalyst, but every good psychoanalyst is not necessarily a good potential biographer" (p. 23).

2. *Humanistic Studies in Honor of John Calvin Metcalf,* University of Virginia Studies, I (Charlottesville: University of Virginia, 1941), pp. 247–67.

3. It is listed, with a misprint in the author's name, on p. 262 of the "Essay on Sources" in John A. Garraty's *The Nature of Biography* (1957), a miscellany of footnotes and bibliography which is not indexed; it is cited on p. 246 of the bibliographical appendix in James Clifford's *Biography as an Art* (1962).

4. Weedon is well aware that what he calls "experimental or romantic" science operates in a different way, that it works much in the same way as he will describe biography as working, in that "the universal element (pattern) is emergent from the dialectic of descriptive designation" (p. 259).

5. Weedon maintains that this does not mean it is necessary for a biographer to represent all the facts. He should choose on the principle of "redundancy": "no piece of fact which does not in some sense increase our knowledge of the activity is worthy of inclusion or representation" (p. 265).

6. *Saturday Review of Literature*, 26 (October 9, 1943), 3–4, 19.

7. Thirty years after he wrote these words, Flexner put them into practice in his *Washington: The Indispensable Man* (Boston: Little, Brown, 1974). His approach is chronological, but he describes Washington's life as a civilian at Mount Vernon in two chapters, "A Virginia Businessman" and "Washington in His Landscapes," each of which covers the years from 1759 to 1775. His penultimate chapter, "Washington and Slavery (1732–1799)," focuses entirely on Washington's attitudes toward slavery and his policies as an owner of slaves.

8. *Cornhill Magazine*, 166 (Summer 1953), 471–80; reprinted in *American Scholar*, 23 (Spring 1954), 151–61.

9. He cites Sir Sidney Lee's reference to King Edward VII's tendency to "pounce and gobble at dishes placed before him" in the sentence, "He had a splendid appetite at all times, and never toyed with his food." Though he thinks Lee's method extreme, he seems to approve his "delicacy" and "ingenuity."

10. *Yale Review*, 44 (Autumn 1954), 33–40.

11. He is here indebted to Bryant, who had contrasted the dry bones available to the biographer to the materials which are for him "*terra incognita*" and put him in "the position of the early cartographers, who in the midst of vast and unexplored continents were driven to hide their ignorance by the phrase: 'Here be elephants'" ("The Art of Biography," p. 237). Lewis says that even Boswell, for all his access to Johnson, does not tell us why Johnson had to touch lampposts and count his steps. About such matters "we can guess, but we cannot know."

12. The Tredegar Memorial Lecture, read on April 21, 1955; published in *Essays by Divers Hands* (Transactions of the Royal Society of Literature), NS29 (1958), 55–72.

13. Humphry House, *All in Due Time* (London: Rupert Hart-Davis), pp. 258–68; originally presented on the BBC Third Programme on July 13, 1948.

14. Guedella had stressed the work of Gosse and of Lord Rosebery. House refers to Carlyle's *Sterling*, several famous series of biographies (including *English Men of Letters*), Mark Pattison's *Milton*, J. A. Symond's *Shelley*, and some of the longer articles in the *DNB*.

15. Only Thayer, in 1920, and White, in 1942, had raised the question of the real importance of style on biography before this time. Thayer had praised the "transparency" of Boswell's style and had speculated about the impression of Johnson which would have emerged had his life been written by Walter Pater.

16. House intrudes this interesting stipulation into his discussion abruptly and without apology or explanation. He does so, I suppose, because it maximizes his argument about the dangers of the "artistic" convention.

17. House says that academic biographies, for all their learning, fail because they, too, are so thoroughly impregnated with their authors' personalities. He defines the scholar's personality as one "obsessed with the evaluation of evidence, with cruces, with doubts, with anxiety to fill in gaps and to prove points" and he says that such a personality usually expresses itself in a style which is "heavy, hesitant, circumlocutionary." The scholar, he says, is interested in a series of problems, and he misses "the multiform vitality" of a life, "the startling inter-relevance of detail" (p. 268).

18. *The Craft of Letters in England*, ed. John Lehmann (London: Cresset Press), pp. 6–25.

19. The other also cites someone else's view of the art of biography (p. 12).

20. *The Craft of Letters in England*, pp. 183–204.

21. Frederick B. Tolles, "The Biographer's Craft," *South Atlantic Quarterly*, 53 (October 1954), pp. 508–20.

22. "Biographer's Creed," *William and Mary Quarterly*, 10 (April 1953), 190.

V. TO 1970

1. *Literary Biography* (Toronto: University of Toronto Press, 1957).

2. Edel refers in his Notes (p. 105), for instance, to Donald A. Stauffer's "two valuable books" on early English biography, *English Biography before 1700* (Cambridge, Mass.: Harvard University Press, 1930) and *The Art of Biography in Eighteenth-Century England* (Princeton: Princeton University Press, 1941), though he mentions Stauffer in his text only to say (in a parenthesis) that he does not speak of Stauffer's "more specialized" works because even Nicolson's *The Development of English Biography* and Maurois's *Aspects of Biography* tend to be neglected (p. 5).

3. See, however, my pp. 3, 58–59, 168–69 (n. 6), 170 (n. 18), and 170–71 (n. 21).

Though the problem of the relation of an author and his work had merely been touched on in the articles and books with a broad concern for biography, it had concerned some literary critics ever since Strabo had said that it is impossible for one to become a good poet unless he has previously become a good man, and it was, of course, central to the New Criticism's attack on the biographical heresy or fallacy. Among the more important studies relevant to the debate at mid-century are John Livingston Lowes, *The Road to Xanadu* (Boston: Houghton, 1927); Chauncey Brewster Tinker, "Assault upon the Poets: The Biographical Approach to Poetry," pp. 3–33 in *The Good Estate of Poetry* (Boston: Little, Brown, 1929); Edmund Wilson, *Axel's Castle* (New York: Scribners, [1931]) and *The Wound and the Bow* (New York: Oxford University Press, 1947); E. M. W. Tillyard and C. S. Lewis, *The Personal Heresy* (London: Oxford University Press, 1939); "The Critical Significance of Biographical Evidence," pp. 5–101 in *English Institute Essays, 1946* (New York: Columbia University Press, 1947)—cited by Edel, p. 108; W. K. Wimsatt, Jr., and M. C. Beardsley, "The Intentional Fallacy," *Sewanee Review*, 54 (1946), 468–88; M. H. Abrams, "Literature as a Revelation of Personality," pp. 226–62 of *The Mirror and the Lamp* (New York: Oxford University Press, 1953); Robert Gittings, *John Keats: the Living Year* (London: Heinemann, 1954). See, too, for the relation between a philosopher's work and his life, Alexander Knox White, "The Philosophical Significance of Biography," *Journal of Philosophical Studies*, 1 (1926), 481–96.

4. Edel's major addition to *Literary Biography* when it was published as a paperback (Garden City: Doubleday, 1959) is a demonstration of how much of an author's inner life is discoverable in his work when no biography of him exists. He focuses on aspects of T. S. Eliot's poetry from *Prufrock* to the *Four Quartets* and treats Eliot's work as the objective correlative of his "wholly personal inner experience." He maintains that the emotional continuum which he exposes is far more important to literary biography than any mass of external fact or any accumulation of sources and influences derived from knowledge of Eliot's education and reading (pp. 70–88).

5. In the 1959 edition, Edel calls Ernest Jones's *Life and Work of Sigmund Freud* "an archetypal study," not only because it brilliantly illustrates the relation of psychoanalysis to biography but also because Jones failed to translate technical concepts into the language of everyday life (pp. 95–97).

6. Edel points out that this and other psychoanalytic diagnoses of characters in novels offer only "a virtually mean-

ingless diagram, highly speculative": "We juggle, so to speak, with the obvious when we invoke such universal symbols." He points out, too, that a purely psychoanalytic approach leaves out all the fine social criticism in the novel and provides no help in assessing it as a work of art. Although he has called the biographer's relation with psychoanalysis "most significant," he contends that "the method used in this approach leads us to a 'diagnosis' which can have little meaning unless it is translated into different terms." That translation, he holds, must be made by the biographer, who is aware of what particular symbols mean to the person using them (pp. 71–72).

7. In a section added in 1959, Edel says that by integrating materials the "scenic method" gives a life a dramatic quality it would not otherwise have and that it aids in conveying a sense of continuum, a time–atmosphere like that which a novelist creates. He also builds on Maurois's suggestion that the biographer can learn from the novelist's techniques and encourages experiments with multiple points of view in order to deepen biographical portraiture (pp. 150–52).

8. *The Nature of Biography* (New York: Knopf, 1957).

9. Despite its form and its occasional inaccuracies, the "Essay" is very useful; it lists more titles than any other printed bibliography on the subject.

10. He discusses, too, the utility of applying to individuals the findings of social psychologists and anthropologists (pp. 237–39).

11. Garraty published the "Rules" in *biography*, 4 (Fall 1981), 283–91.

12. "Biography: Craft or Art?" *University of Toronto Quarterly*, 28 (April 1959), 301–9.

13. I do not mean to minimize the differences in Garraty's and Edel's attitudes toward psychoanalysis. Edel is, of course, more sanguine than Garraty about its utility for biography. Clifford sees some possibilities in the experimental techniques for the measurement of personality described by Garraty, once they have been perfected by psychologists (p. 305). On the other hand, he thinks that the biographer who does not avail himself of the aid of psychoanalysis shirks his duty though "the chances for individual error are increased thousandfold" (pp. 308–9).

14. *Studies, An Irish Quarterly*, 48 (Autumn 1959), 305–17. Indebtedness to Edel and Garraty is apparent in all but two or three paragraphs. Miss Purcell makes no comment on Edel's view of the relation between biographer and subject or on his views about criticism and psychoanalysis; she shows her disapproval of

his remarks about time only by indirection. Unlike Garraty, she thinks it is not essential for the biographer to "study the technical and theoretical aspects of psychology," and she maintains that "observation and discernment" are more helpful than the intensive study of a period in providing authentic historical background (pp. 315–16).

15. *Atlantic Monthly*, 203 (February 1959), 37–42. The essay was drawn from the Ann Radcliffe lecture delivered at Radcliffe College in the fall of 1958; it was also published, with additions, in the *Cornhill Magazine*, 171 (Autumn 1960), 379–94.

16. She cites Virginia Woolf and Proust here, but she would also seem to have in mind Maurois's ideas that the truth about a life is "a confused medley of actions, thoughts, and feelings, often contradictory, yet possessing a certain unity which is, as it were, a sort of musical tone" and that the biographer must reproduce "the sound of that individual and authentic note."

17. *Biography as an Art* (New York: Oxford University Press, 1962).

18. Clifford treats the subject of "The Biographer's Involvement" in a chapter of his book, *From Puzzles to Portraits: Problems of a Literary Biographer* (Chapel Hill: University of North Carolina Press, 1970), pp. 99–112. His account of the views of several biographers on the question would seem to indicate that most of them, including Nicolson and Cecil, though aware of their emotional involvement with a subject, had not thought deeply about the effect of this on their writing. On the other hand, recognition of the centrality of the question made Edgar Johnson define biography as "a psychological intersection between the personality of the biographer and that of his subject" (p. 112).

19. "Portraits in Prose," *T L S* (March 2, 1962), pp. 129–30.

20. Schorer spoke on May 23, 1962 (I am indebted to Professor James Gindin for this information); his lecture was printed in the *Michigan Quarterly Review*, 1 (Autumn 1962), 249–58.

21. "For the life of Sinclair Lewis, I decided, lived with so little dignity and so much fret and fury, and, on the literary side, producing so much loose and garrulous bulk, the tone must be casual—never exalted, seldom formal, but rather conversational, perhaps rambling a bit, frequently ironical, now and then a little snide" (p. 257).

22. "In my relationship with Lewis . . . there were both love and hate, and there were also pity, shame, much impatience. There were also self-love and self-hate and self-pity, and the shame and the impatience were as much for myself as for him." Schorer

feels he was challenged by the fact that his mature literary tastes had moved as far away from Lewis's as is possible. He mentions the affinities of their beginnings, and many more: "all the careless writing, all the ill-conceived ambitions, all the bad manners, all the irrational fits of temper, all the excesses of conduct, all the immature, lifelong frivolities and regrettable follies." He says, too, "And those of my critics who have complained of an imputed lack of sympathy with my subject might have said with equal accuracy and greater justice, with sharper perception certainly, and probably with more kindness, that I had refused to be self-indulgent" (pp. 257–58).

23. *The Art of Biography* (New York: Norton, 1965; Toronto: George J. McLeod; London: George Allen & Unwin).

24. He says that "the notion is accepted by default rather than by debate" and that it is "a province which that kingdom has generally tended to ignore" (p. 4).

25. *Literary Biography*, pp. 99–102.

26. Kendall does not explore the implications of a grouping placed at the time of a funeral, the immediate effects of the death of a man upon others' estimates of him; he assumes, too, that James's impressions of Emerson in 1883 remained essentially the same in the next four years.

27. He lists the following: Churchill's *Marlborough*, C. V. Wedgwood's *Strafford*, Cecil's *Melbourne*, Rupert Hart-Davis's *Hugh Walpole*, Sir John Neale's *Queen Elizabeth*, Nicolson's *George V*, Schorer's *Sinclair Lewis*, Andrew Turnbull's *Scott Fitzgerald*, Catherine Drinker Bowen's *The Lion and the Throne*, Samuel E. Morison's *Admiral of the Ocean Sea*, Garrett Mattingly's *Catherine of Aragon*, Clifford's *Young Sam Johnson*, Douglas S. Freeman's *Lee*, and Herschel Baker's *William Hazlitt* (pp. 146–47). On his scale of kinds, these fall in the middle range— interpretative, scholarly, and research biography.

28. Kendall quotes Schorer's term, "symbiotic relationship" (p. 148). He does not indicate when he says that "Schorer has briefly revealed the process at work as he undertook the life of Sinclair Lewis" that his description of the process differs from Schorer's. Schorer says that it was only after he was well into his book that he began to wonder about his relation to Lewis and the effect it was having on his book. He did not "self-consciously" cultivate a relation with Lewis; he believes he was challenged to write the life because of what he unconsciously felt to be a strange affinity with Lewis.

Kendall's phrase, "a simulated life-relationship," clearly depresses the urgency of the involvement of some biographers with their subjects, though it perhaps reflects accurately his own ex-perience in working with figures remote in time and in activity from himself—Richard III, Warwick the Kingmaker, and Louis XI of France. Some biographers do not have to strive self-consciously to accept commitment to their subjects; they feel unconsciously impelled toward them. They do not work to establish a symbiotic relation; it may be overwhelming from the start.

CONCLUSION

1. First published in *The Dial*, 77 (December 1924), 466–74.

2. "Discovering the Lost Lives of Women," *New York Times Book Review*, June 24, 1984, p. 26.

3. "Milford's *Zelda* and the Poetics of the New Feminist Biography," *Georgia Review*, 36 (Summer 1982), 335–50.

4. I rely here, of course, on Johnson's dicta in the *Life of Pope*, the *Life of Cowley*, and elsewhere.

5. Samuel Johnson, *Life of Savage*, ed. Clarence Tracy (Oxford: Clarendon Press, 1971), p. 4.

6. James Boswell, *Life of Johnson*, ed. R. W. Chapman, cor-rected by J. D. Fleeman (London: Oxford University Press, 1970), pp. 121–23.

7. Sigmund Freud, *Leonardo da Vinci and a Memory of His Childhood*, trans. Alan Tyson (New York: Norton, 1964), p. 80.

8. Erik H. Erikson, *Young Man Luther*: A *Study in Psycho-analysis and History* (New York: Norton, 1958), p. 252.

9. Freud, *Leonardo*, pp. 80–81.

10. James Thomas Flexner, *Washington: The Indispensable Man* (Boston: Little, Brown, 1974).

11. Norman Mailer, *Marilyn: A Biography* (New York: Gros-set & Dunlap, [1973]), p. 18.

12. "The Curious Relationship between Biography and Autobiography in Japan" in *New Directions in Biography*, ed. An-thony M. Friedson (Honolulu: University Press of Hawaii, 1981), p. 82.

13. Eloise Knapp Hay, "Kipling and Forster," *biography*, 7 (Spring 1984), 123–33.

14. Margot Peters, "Group Biography: Challenges and Methods," in *New Directions in Biography*, ed. Anthony M. Fried-son (Honolulu: University Press of Honolulu, 1981), p. 41. Peters refers to Norman and Jeanne MacKenzie's *The Fabians* (New York: Simon and Schuster, [1977]), Leon Edel's *Bloomsbury: A House of Lions* (Philadelphia: Lippincott, [1979]), and Stanley

Weintraub's *Private Shaw and Public Shaw: A Dual Portrait of Lawrence of Arabia and G. B. S.* (London: Cape, 1963), *Four Rosettis: A Victorian Biography* (New York: Weybright and Talley, [1977]), and *The London Yankees: Portraits of American Writers and Artists in England* (New York: Harcourt, 1979). Her definition and examples leave room for the consideration of many books, from Roger North's eighteenth-century memoirs to the proliferating corporate and family biography in such recent works as John H. Dessauer's *My Years with Xerox* (Garden City: Doubleday, 1971), Peter Collier and David Horowitz's *The Rockefellers: An American Dynasty* (New York: Holt, [1976]), James Thomas Flexner's *An American Saga: The Story of Helen Thomas and Simon Flexner* (Boston: Little, Brown, 1984), and John H. Davis's *The Kennedys: Dynasty and Disaster, 1848–1983* (New York: McGraw–Hill, 1984).

15. Peters's latest book, of 534 pages, is *Mrs Pat: The Life of Mrs Patrick Campbell* (London: Bodley Head, 1984).

Index